James,
1 & 2 Peter,
and Jude

TEACH THE TEXT COMMENTARY

John H. Walton
Old Testament General Editor

Mark L. Strauss
New Testament General Editor

Volumes now available:

Old Testament Volumes

New Testament Volumes

Visit the series website at www.teachthetextseries.com.

TEACH the TEXT
COMMENTARY SERIES

James, 1 & 2 Peter, *and* Jude

Jim Samra

Mark L. Strauss and John H. Walton
GENERAL EDITORS

ILLUSTRATING THE TEXT

Kevin and Sherry Harney
ASSOCIATE EDITORS

Adam Barr
CONTRIBUTING WRITER

BakerBooks
a division of Baker Publishing Group
Grand Rapids, Michigan

Published by Baker Books
a division of Baker Publishing Group
P.O. Box 6287, Grand Rapids, MI 49516-6287
www.bakerbooks.com

Printed and bound by CPI Group (UK) Ltd, Croydon, CR0 4YY

Library of Congress Cataloging-in-Publication Data
Names: Samra, James George, 1972– author.
Title: James, 1 & 2 Peter, and Jude / Jim Samra ; illustrating the text Kevin and Sherry Harney ; Mark L. Strauss and John H. Walton, general editors.
Other titles: James, one and two Peter, and Jude | James, first and second Peter, and Jude
Description: Grand Rapids, MI : Baker Publishing Group, 2016. | Series: Teach the text commentary | Includes bibliographical references and index.
Identifiers: LCCN 2016018845 | ISBN 9780801092404 (pbk.)
Subjects: LCSH: Bible. James—Commentaries. | Bible. Peter—Commentaries. | Bible. Jude—Commentaries. | Bible. James—Sermons. | Bible. Peter—Sermons. | Bible. Jude—Sermons.
Classification: LCC BS2785.53 .S26 2016 | DDC 227/.907—dc23
LC record available at https://lccn.loc.gov/2016018845

16 17 18 19 20 21 22   7 6 5 4 3 2 1

Contents

Welcome to the Teach the Text Commentary Series

Why another commentary series? That was the question the general editors posed when Baker Books asked us to produce this series. Is there something that we can offer to pastors and teachers that is not currently being offered by other commentary series, or that can be offered in a more helpful way? After carefully researching the needs of pastors who teach the text on a weekly basis, we concluded that yes, more can be done; the Teach the Text Commentary Series (TTCS) is carefully designed to fill an important gap.

The technicality of modern commentaries often overwhelms readers with details that are tangential to the main purpose of the text. Discussions of source and redaction criticism, as well as detailed surveys of secondary literature, seem far removed from preaching and teaching the Word. Rather than wade through technical discussions, pastors often turn to devotional commentaries, which may contain exegetical weaknesses, misuse the Greek and Hebrew languages, and lack hermeneutical sophistication. There is a need for a commentary that utilizes the best of biblical scholarship but also presents the material in a clear, concise, attractive, and user-friendly format.

This commentary is designed for that purpose—to provide a ready reference for the exposition of the biblical text, giving easy access to information that a pastor needs to communicate the text effectively. To that end, the commentary is divided into carefully selected preaching units (with carefully regulated word counts both in the passage as a whole and in each subsection). Pastors and teachers engaged in weekly preparation thus know that they will be reading approximately the same amount of material on a week-by-week basis.

Each passage begins with a concise summary of the central message, or "Big Idea," of the passage and a list of its main themes. This is followed by a more detailed interpretation of the text, including the literary context of the passage, historical background material, and interpretive insights. While drawing on the best of biblical scholarship, this material is clear, concise, and to the point. Technical material is kept to a minimum, with endnotes pointing the reader to more detailed discussion and additional resources.

A second major focus of this commentary is on the preaching and teaching process itself. Few commentaries today help the pastor/teacher move from the meaning of the text to its effective communication. Our goal is to bridge this gap. In addition to interpreting the text in the "Understanding the Text" section, each unit contains a "Teaching the Text" section and an "Illustrating the Text" section. The teaching section points to the key theological themes of the passage and ways to communicate these themes to today's audiences. The illustration section provides ideas and examples for retaining the interest of hearers and connecting the message to daily life.

The creative format of this commentary arises from our belief that the Bible is not just a record of God's dealings in the past but is the living Word of God, "alive and active" and "sharper than any double-edged sword" (Heb. 4:12). Our prayer is that this commentary will help to unleash that transforming power for the glory of God.

The General Editors

Introduction to the Teach the Text Commentary Series

This series is designed to provide a ready reference for teaching the biblical text, giving easy access to information that is needed to communicate a passage effectively. To that end, the commentary is carefully divided into units that are faithful to the biblical authors' ideas and of an appropriate length for teaching or preaching.

The following standard sections are offered in each unit.

1. *Big Idea*. For each unit the commentary identifies the primary theme, or "Big Idea," that drives both the passage and the commentary.
2. *Key Themes*. Together with the Big Idea, the commentary addresses in bullet-point fashion the key ideas presented in the passage.
3. *Understanding the Text*. This section focuses on the exegesis of the text and includes several sections.
   a. The Text in Context. Here the author gives a brief explanation of how the unit fits into the flow of the text around it, including reference to the rhetorical strategy of the book and the unit's contribution to the purpose of the book.
   b. Outline/Structure. For some literary genres (e.g., epistles), a brief exegetical outline may be provided to guide the reader through the structure and flow of the passage.

c. Historical and Cultural Background. This section addresses historical and cultural background information that may illuminate a verse or passage.
   d. Interpretive Insights. This section provides information needed for a clear understanding of the passage. The intention of the author is to be highly selective and concise rather than exhaustive and expansive.
   e. Theological Insights. In this very brief section the commentary identifies a few carefully selected theological insights about the passage.
4. *Teaching the Text*. Under this second main heading the commentary offers guidance for teaching the text. In this section the author lays out the main themes and applications of the passage. These are linked carefully to the Big Idea and are represented in the Key Themes.
5. *Illustrating the Text*. At this point in the commentary the writers partner with a team of pastor/teachers to provide suggestions for relevant and contemporary illustrations from current culture, entertainment, history, the Bible, news, literature, ethics, biography, daily life, medicine, and over forty other categories. They are designed to spark creative thinking for preachers and teachers and to help them design illustrations that bring alive the passage's key themes and message.

Abbreviations

Old Testament

Gen.	Genesis	2 Chron.	2 Chronicles	Dan.	Daniel
Exod.	Exodus	Ezra	Ezra	Hosea	Hosea
Lev.	Leviticus	Neh.	Nehemiah	Joel	Joel
Num.	Numbers	Esther	Esther	Amos	Amos
Deut.	Deuteronomy	Job	Job	Obad.	Obadiah
Josh.	Joshua	Ps(s).	Psalm(s)	Jon.	Jonah
Judg.	Judges	Prov.	Proverbs	Mic.	Micah
Ruth	Ruth	Eccles.	Ecclesiastes	Nah.	Nahum
1 Sam.	1 Samuel	Song	Song of Songs	Hab.	Habakkuk
2 Sam.	2 Samuel	Isa.	Isaiah	Zeph.	Zephaniah
1 Kings	1 Kings	Jer.	Jeremiah	Hag.	Haggai
2 Kings	2 Kings	Lam.	Lamentations	Zech.	Zechariah
1 Chron.	1 Chronicles	Ezek.	Ezekiel	Mal.	Malachi

New Testament

Matt.	Matthew	Eph.	Ephesians	Heb.	Hebrews
Mark	Mark	Phil.	Philippians	James	James
Luke	Luke	Col.	Colossians	1 Pet.	1 Peter
John	John	1 Thess.	1 Thessalonians	2 Pet.	2 Peter
Acts	Acts	2 Thess.	2 Thessalonians	1 John	1 John
Rom.	Romans	1 Tim.	1 Timothy	2 John	2 John
1 Cor.	1 Corinthians	2 Tim.	2 Timothy	3 John	3 John
2 Cor.	2 Corinthians	Titus	Titus	Jude	Jude
Gal.	Galatians	Philem.	Philemon	Rev.	Revelation

General

AD	*anno Domini*, in the year of our Lord	etc.	*et cetera*, and others
BC	before Christ	ibid.	*ibidem*, there the same
cf.	*confer*, compare	i.e.	*id est*, that is
chap(s).	chapter(s)	pl.	plural
e.g.	*exempli gratia*, for example	sg.	singular
esp.	especially	v(v).	verse(s)
		//	parallel passages

Ancient Versions

LXX   Septuagint

Modern English Versions

ESV	English Standard Version	NASB	New American Standard Bible
GNT	Good News Translation	NEB	The New English Bible
GW	GOD'S WORD Translation	NET	The NET Bible (New English
HCSB	Holman Christian Standard Bible		Translation)
		NIV	New International Version
KJV	King James Version	NLT	New Living Translation

Modern Reference Works

BDAG   Frederick W. Danker, Walter Bauer, William F. Arndt, and F. Wilbur Gingrich. *A Greek-English Lexicon of the New Testament and Other Early Christian Literature.* 3rd ed. Chicago: University of Chicago Press, 2000

TDOT   G. J. Botterweck, H. Ringgren, and H.-J. Fabry, eds. *Theological Dictionary of the Old Testament.* 15 vols. Grand Rapids: Eerdmans, 1974–2006

TWOT   R. L. Harris, G. L. Archer, and B. K. Waltke, eds. *Theological Wordbook of the Old Testament.* 2 vols. Chicago: Moody, 1980

Introduction to James

The Epistle of James presents a multifaceted picture of what it means to be a mature Christian, a doer of the Word and not a hearer only—one who demonstrates their faith through actions.

Importance of James

James is widely prized and taught because its theology is so practical. While definitely a letter, James has some affinities to Wisdom literature in the Old Testament, like Proverbs. The subjects that James covers and the way that he covers them have made James a beloved and important book. Topics such as trials, money, words, favoritism, fighting, pride, planning, and prayer fill this epistle with useful instruction. For the individual believer and for communities of faith, James does what the epistle says ought to happen in Scripture in general: it provides a mirror by which Christians can take a long, hard look at themselves and then go away and make changes.

In practical matters, James has rightly exerted incredible influence. The statements about caring for widows and orphans as the essence of religion (1:27) have inspired many Christians to help the poor and oppressed. If a church has elders pray for the sick, it is because of 5:13–16. Most who experience spiritual warfare find James's injunction to submit to God and resist the devil as essential to the battle (4:7). The phrase "Lord willing" and the idea of holding future plans loosely come from 4:15. Many Christian employers pay appropriate wages to their employees because of 5:1–6. Christians who seek wisdom from God to deal with the trials of life find explicit urging to do so in 1:5. And these are just a few examples of James's influence.

Despite the emphasis on practical matters (or maybe because of it), James makes significant theological contributions to the doctrines of faith and works, sin and temptation, God's Word and the understanding of the law, and the purity and goodness of God.

In so many areas of theology and life, James provides a unique and useful perspective within the New Testament.

Author, Setting, and Date

The author of James is traditionally believed to be James the Just, Jesus's half brother (Matt. 13:55).[1] He was not one of the twelve apostles (this James is not James son of Zebedee or James son of Alphaeus). James was not a believer during Jesus's public ministry (John 7:5) but became a highly influential leader in the early church in Jerusalem after coming to faith (Acts 12:17; 15:13; 21:18; Gal. 2:9, 12), presumably when Jesus appeared to him after his resurrection (1 Cor. 15:7). His brother Jude was likely the author of Jude (Jude 1).

James is writing to the "twelve tribes scattered among the nations" (1:1). Though many see this as a literal reference to Jewish Christians, it is probably better to take it as a metaphorical reference to Jewish and gentile Christians living in a world that is not their home. It would be highly unlikely that the leader of the Jerusalem Council in Acts 15 would single out Jewish Christians from gentile ones with this letter (see the comments on James 1:1). So while James is writing out of a Jewish background, he is addressing all believers.

As for the date of James, nothing in the epistle allows for any way to date it with any certainty.[2] What we know of James the Just requires only that, if he was the author, it was written before his death sometime in the 60s. Therefore a date in the 50s seems as reasonable as any.

James's purpose is for believers to live out their faith in concrete ways and to demonstrate the maturity that true faith brings.

Theological Themes and Suggestions for Teaching

James is noteworthy because of the absence of any explicit theological emphases related to Jesus or the Holy Spirit. Jesus is directly mentioned in 1:1; 2:1; and 5:7–8. The Holy Spirit is not mentioned at all (see the comments on James 4:5). However, the ethical undertone of James's epistle resonates with Jesus's teaching in such a way that it is fair to say that an important theological theme of James is the ethics of Jesus.

Central to James's Epistle is the relationship of faith and works. Genuine faith demonstrates itself in good deeds. All of James's ethical admonitions are grounded in this theological understanding. The person who believes that God will respond to prayers for wisdom cannot waver back and forth on whether or not God will do so (1:5–8). Genuine believers in Jesus must not show favoritism (2:1), and they must do concrete caring actions for those who are in need (2:15). If someone believes that humans are created in the image of God, then they must not speak evil of others (3:9–10). If someone believes that God answers prayer, then they should go to the elders for prayer when they are sick (5:13–15).

Tied to this concept is a robust theology of God's Word, meaning the Scriptures. To simply hear the Word and not do it is to not truly believe that it is the "word of truth" (1:18) that can save you (1:21). The Word of God brings freedom and blessing (1:25). God's Word reveals the royal law of loving one's neighbor (and loving God) and expresses the will of God.

Mercy is another important theme for James. Care for the poor and oppressed, treating all without favoritism, paying workers proper wages, refraining from cursing or speaking evil of others, and endeavoring to turn sinners from the errors of their ways all point to the mercy of God and his people.

Paradoxically, given the theme of mercy in James, it is worth noting that James can be a difficult book to teach and preach because of its seemingly harsh tone, which is so foreign to many modern readers. However, in this seemingly harsh language there are also great words of encouragement for those whom James is looking out for. Orphans, widows, the poor, oppressed workers, those being slandered, and others are encouraged as they hear James's blunt language used to protect and serve them. Those who are suffering will be encouraged to know that God is working through them to accomplish good and that those in need of miraculous help from God have it available to them through prayer. Teachers can and should go out of their way to show the kindness and mercy of God expressed in part through the denunciation of oppression and apathy.

Most important, to do James justice, the teacher must constantly think how to help people to be doers of the Word and not merely hearers.

The Trials of Life

Big Idea

By having the proper attitude and asking God for wisdom, we are able to endure the trials of life, which are designed to bring us to maturity.

Key Themes

- Enduring trials and tribulations brings blessings now and in the future.
- Trials and tribulations are necessary for Christian maturity.
- Believers are to ask God for wisdom to enable us to endure trials and tribulations.
- Not having abundant financial resources or not being able to use financial resources to avoid trouble in life can actually be a blessing.

Understanding the Text

The Text in Context

Given that James's goal is to help his readers to be mature in their Christian faith, it is not surprising that he begins by discussing enduring trials and tribulations in life. The idea of becoming more mature through suffering is a common theme in the New Testament (e.g., Rom. 5:3–4; 8:17–18; 2 Cor. 4:7–18; Phil. 3:7–11; Heb. 2:10; 1 Pet. 1:3–9). James not only explores the theme of trials and tribulations but also introduces other topics to which he will return later, such as true faith (chap. 2), wisdom (chap. 3), and poverty and wealth (chap. 5).

While 1:13 carries on the discussion, James shifts the focus of the Greek word *peirasmos* from "trial" to "temptation," and therefore 1:12 provides a helpful point at which to end this section. The next section addresses the question of whether God tempts believers to sin.

Structure

One way of approaching the text is to follow James's thematic development. After the greeting, the passage can be broken down into five sections. There are two statements about blessings of trials (1:2 and 1:12), which serve as an introduction and conclusion to this theme. In between James addresses three themes commonly associated with trials: enduring suffering as the road to maturity (1:3–4), needing wisdom from God to endure suffering (1:5–8), and the relationship of trials to poverty and riches (1:9–11).

Another helpful way of viewing this section is through the lens of the five major imperatives (in Greek) that James uses in this section: (1) *consider* it pure joy when you face trials (1:2); (2) *let* perseverance *finish* its work (1:4); (3) *ask* God for wisdom (1:5–6); (4) *do not expect* to receive if you doubt (1:7); and (5) *take pride* in your high position (1:10).

Interpretive Insights

1:1 *James, a servant of God.* On James, see the introduction to James.

To the twelve tribes scattered among the nations. This is a reference to both Jewish and gentile Christians. The language of exile ("scattered") is an acknowledgment that this world's governments, systems, and values are not those of believers (cf. 4:4). The members of James's Christian audience are the spiritual heirs of those Old Testament saints who wandered the world (cf. Heb. 11:13–16) and of truly believing Jews forced to live outside the promised land because of the sin and disbelief of others.[1]

1:2 *Consider it pure joy.* The word "consider" has the notion of making a deliberate, conscious, and rational choice (see 2 Cor. 9:5; Phil. 2:6; 3:7–8; Heb. 11:26). The Greek word order emphasizes the words "joy" and "trials." It is not intuitive that trials should cause joy, so James asks his readers to make a deliberate effort to set aside their natural inclinations of fear, discouragement, and anger and choose to be joyful in the midst of trials.

whenever you face trials of many kinds. The word for "trial" (*peirasmos*) can mean either "trial, tribulation, trouble" (see 1:2) or "temptation to sin" (see 1:13). The key to distinguishing meanings is the origin of the trial or temptation. In 1:2 it is trials "you face," meaning that they originate outside of us and happen to us. Likewise, the parallel phrase "testing of your faith" in 1:3 implies something being done to us from the outside. On the other hand, in 1:13–16 James is speaking of the temptations to sin that come from within us.

Trials that originate outside of us could include being dragged into court (2:6), lacking material resources (2:15), verbal abuse (3:9–10; 4:11), being the victims of divisiveness and quarreling (4:1), structural economic injustices (5:4–6), sicknesses (5:14), and any general kind of "trouble" (5:13).

1:3 *the testing of your faith produces perseverance.* We should be joyful in the midst of trials because enduring trials is producing something— perseverance—of inestimable value *right now.* The focus shifts from the present to the future benefits of trials in 1:12.

1:4 *so that you may be mature and complete.* The word for "mature" (*teleios*) can also be translated "without defect, perfect." However, the sense here is being mature in this life, not a state of sinless perfection possible only when Christ returns. One can be mature and still need to grow, as Paul says of himself in Philippians 3:13–15 (using *teleios*).

1:5 *If any of you lacks wisdom, you should ask God.* The word "lacks" picks up the mention of "lacking" in 1:4, and so in this context 1:5 instructs the reader to ask God for wisdom for dealing with trials of life, something that even the most mature still need.

What kind of wisdom does James have in mind? James is writing to "the twelve tribes" (1:1) and has peppered his letter with examples of Old Testament people (Rahab, Abraham, Job, Elijah), so the first place to look for examples of God's wisdom for the trials of life is the narrative portions of the Old Testament. Many Old Testament characters inquire of God seeking guidance from the Lord, something to make sense of what is happening to them or how to best respond. Rebekah asking God why her pregnancy is so difficult (Gen. 25:22), David wanting to know what is causing the famine in Israel (2 Sam. 21:1), and Jeroboam needing wisdom about whether or not his son will live (1 Kings 14:2–3) are a few of the many examples. In addition, perhaps James is thinking of Jesus asking the Father for guidance in Gethsemane (Matt. 26:36–46) as to whether there is another way other than the cross, or his own situation from Acts 15 where the early church needed counsel from God to help settle the dispute regarding gentile inclusion.[2]

who gives generously to all without finding fault. James is anticipating the two most likely objections to the idea of asking for wisdom from God. The first objection is that God gives wisdom only to people like Rebekah, David, or James—those who seem special or important in salvation history. But James says, God "gives *generously to all*." This is reinforced in chapter 5 when James insists that Elijah is no different than we are—his prayers were answered, and ours will be answered too (5:17–18). The second objection is that God will be angry, annoyed, or disappointed with believers who seek wisdom in the midst of trials. James wants to reassure his readers that this could not possibly be the case (see also Matt. 7:9–11).

1:6 *believe and not doubt.* Or, "Ask in faith, doubting nothing." Doubt is often portrayed as the antithesis of believing (Matt. 21:21; Mark 11:23; John 20:27; Rom. 4:20; 14:23). Just as in Romans 4:20, "not doubting" is being "fully persuaded" that God will do what he has promised, even with seeming evidence to the contrary. So readers must be fully persuaded that God will answer every request for wisdom. But more is in mind here.

In James 2, true faith demonstrates itself in good works and obedience to the law of God. Asking in faith, then, probably includes the idea of asking from a place of obedience to God. In Ezekiel 20 God will not allow the leaders of Israel to ask him for wisdom because of their rebellious ways. So too, asking God for wisdom in a trial of life while refusing to obey God's commands for sexual purity, for example, is not asking "in faith." Furthermore, in 5:15, James speaks of the prayer offered "in faith," which will make the sick person well. Praying in faith means that we are not demanding healing from God but submitting our requests to God with the acknowledgment that he knows better than we do whether healing is the best path. So too, to ask God for wisdom "in faith" means approaching God with the attitude of allowing him to provide whatever kind of wisdom in whatever way he wants and believing this wisdom to be the best possible advice for the given situation.

1:9 *Believers in humble circumstances ought to take pride in their high positions.* The same counterintuitive logic that allowed his readers to rejoice in their many trials appears in 1:9–11. Believers in humble circumstances should "take pride in" their "high positions." If more trials bring more maturity, then the poor should consider their poverty as an asset rather than a liability, since poverty brings with it a whole host of trials that the rich never experience. "To take pride in" doesn't mean to be arrogant (Gal. 6:4). This means not arrogantly bragging to others but thinking about and drawing encouragement from God's work through these humble circumstances. Other positive examples of pride include 1 Corinthians 1:31; 2 Corinthians 10:17; 12:9; and Galatians 6:14.

1:10 *the rich should take pride in their humiliation.* Wealthy Christians should rejoice when they experience being brought low, that is, when they experience suffering through trials. This includes not only a reversal of fortune where the rich become poor but also the humbling that can take place through sickness, betrayal in personal relationships, or persecution for being a believer—in other words, any trial from which their financial resources cannot rescue them.

1:11 *its beauty is destroyed.* The image of grass and flowers standing for the fragility of human life draws on Isaiah 40:6–8 and Psalm 103:15. The words "its beauty" are a translation of a phrase that reads in Greek, "the appearance of its face." The thought is similar to 2 Corinthians 4:16–18, where Paul concludes his discussion of suffering in this life by talking about outwardly wasting away while inwardly being transformed because what is seen is temporal, while what is unseen is eternal. Wealth is like a flower—it is "seen" and therefore temporal. Trials produce maturity, which, though unseen, is eternal and far more valuable.

1:12 *crown of life.* In Greco-Roman culture one who successfully won a race was given a crown to signify their victory (see 1 Cor. 9:25; 2 Tim. 2:5). The crown is "life," meaning the fullness of an eternal life that has been refined through suffering. The idea is not a distinct crown earned for every trial successfully endured. Compare Jesus's similar statement in Matthew 5:11–12.

Theological Insights

The problem of suffering is one of the central themes of life and consequently of the Bible. While other passages of Scripture deal with various causes for suffering (e.g., Job 1–2; Luke 13:1–5; John 9:1–3; Heb. 12:4–11; 1 Pet. 4:14–15), James focuses on the goal no matter what the cause: Christian maturity. Likewise, the Bible has much to say about how one becomes more mature as a Christian, and James reminds us that enduring suffering is a key aspect of the theology of sanctification.

In addition to the theology of suffering and maturity, 1:5–8 plays an important part of a larger discussion about prayer and seeking guidance from God. Some today view God "deistically"—that is, unconnected and uninvolved with the decisions and workings of daily life. But the Bible presents a different picture, a God who is ready, willing, and able to provide guidance and direction for all aspects of life. James 1:5–8 explicitly urges Christians to engage with God in a more personal way, inquiring of him and seeking guidance from him in all the circumstances of life, since he is our Father (c.f., e.g., Josh. 9:14; Ps. 73:24; Isa. 8:19; 30:1–2; John 10:4).[3]

Teaching the Text

Two very helpful ways of approaching this passage were laid out in the "Structure" section above. One approach is to orient the teaching around the five imperatives in this passage. There is very little that we can do about the trials of life that happen to us, but we can and should do five things. First, we choose to rejoice when we are going through trials. In order for true rejoicing to take place, people must understand the truth that enduring suffering brings maturity. Second, we must choose not to interrupt the trial, instead waiting for God to complete in us what he is doing in forming our character through this trial. Too often we look for ways to escape trials and tribulations rather than looking for God-given ways to stand up under them, as urged in 1 Corinthians 10:13. Third, we ought to ask God for wisdom in the midst of trials: "How am I to endure?" "What purpose does this trial have in my life and your greater purposes?" "What is the cause of this trial in my life?" "Where is your grace evident in the midst of what I am going through?" Fourth, we must not think that we will receive wisdom from God, unless we ask properly, that is, "in faith." Fifth, we should pride ourselves in our socioeconomic struggles, recognizing these as divinely permitted trials producing perseverance and maturity. Those who are wealthy should value the times when God shapes their character through sufferings that monetary resources are powerless to alleviate.

Of these five imperatives, it is interesting to note that the only one that gives any real "action" to take is the second: ask God for wisdom. Most of the emphasis in this passage is on having the right attitude and proper perspective on trials. We are quick to want to do something when trouble hits. This passage teaches that it is more important *to think correctly* and *pray correctly* than to take specific action.

A second way to approach this text is thematically. Verses 2 and 12 are parallel, with both emphasizing the blessed nature of enduring trials, focusing on the present and future benefits, respectively. Between these two bookends of blessing, James addresses three topics: how enduring trouble leads to maturity, receiving wisdom from God in the midst of trials, and the role of socioeconomic troubles. In order for people to truly be able to rejoice in the midst of difficult times, these are the relevant topics to cover.

Finally, when teaching about asking God for wisdom, the teacher should realize that this passage is not promoting a general request for wisdom from God like Solomon's in 1 Kings 3. Given the context, James is talking about wisdom from God for specific situations. A teaching on the need for general wisdom from God is better reserved for James 3, which focuses more broadly on wisdom from God as opposed to the wisdom of the world.

Illustrating the Text

Trials bring maturity.

Human Experience: Consider how many times we are tempted to take the easy way out of a difficult situation. A romantic relationship hits rough waters, so we withdraw. Our boss is giving us a hard time at work, so we look for a new job. We don't get along well with our neighbors, so we start praying that they would move. Our extended family gets on our nerves on vacation, so we rent our own room to get away from them. We're feeling depressed, so we turn to food to ignore our problems. In the very big trials and the daily small trials, we can be tempted to insulate ourselves or escape from the struggles. We might relieve some of the pain, but we certainly will not learn to persevere. Trials alone do not bring maturity. It is only as we persevere through struggles that we grow. If we seek to insulate ourselves from any difficult circumstances, we'll never experience the growth God wants us to have.

In the midst of trials, we should ask God for wisdom.

Human Metaphor: Passenger jet pilots are incredibly capable people. They are people who bear a serious responsibility, tasked to carry hundreds of people through the air from one place to another. They have vast amounts of experience before they ever pilot their first commercial flight. In short, they are experts at what they do. Yet even the most gifted pilot must seek the wisdom and guidance of the control tower when they approach for landing.

If they attempted to land the flight without listening to the tower, the results would be catastrophic. How often do we try to navigate our way through life without seeking divine wisdom?

When we pray, we need to exercise faith.

Scenario: How do you approach God in prayer? Do you see God like a loving father who wants to make sure you have everything you need? Or do you see him more like a loan shark who is willing to give you what you need at 50 percent interest? Or as a boss who is pleased with you only if you do your assignments well? Or as a judge to whom we have to prove our innocence in order to receive a favorable response? What we believe about God will have a profound impact on how we approach him in prayer. If we believe he's not only able to help but also more than willing, we will come in faith.

The Goodness of God

Big Idea

God would never tempt believers to sin, because God never deviates from his singular purpose of creating believers with character of the highest quality.

Key Themes

- Temptation leads to sin, and sin leads to death.
- God's pure character and purposes prevent him from even considering the idea of tempting us to sin.
- God's Word gives birth to believers.

Understanding the Text

The Text in Context

The connection to the previous section might be missed in English since the same word is being translated "tempted" (*peirasmos*) as was translated "trial" in 1:2 and 1:12. While the meaning has switched from "trial" to "temptation," these topics are related. Because God uses trials to cause us to grow, one might assume that God also tempts us to sin because trials can bring with them temptations to sin (e.g., a terminal illness is an opportunity to become bitter toward God) or because temptations to sin are trials in and of themselves (e.g., fighting against proud thoughts is a real struggle). Because of this close connection between trials and temptations, James now addresses the question, does God tempt us to sin?

The answer is a resounding no! Why would God want us to sin, when his unchangeable goal for us is that we might be mature and complete, having character of the highest quality? While God often tests our faith, our maturity is God's goal, and he would never work at cross-purposes with himself by encouraging us to sin. A house divided cannot stand. A God who tempts believers to sin cannot achieve his goal of mature believers.

At the end of this section, James introduces the idea that God has given birth to believers through "the word of truth" (1:18), an idea James will carry into 1:19–27 as he discusses the importance of "doing the word" and not just hearing it.

James will revisit the ideas of temptation and sin in 3:1–4:10, adding this world and Satan as sources of temptation. Establishing God's absolute goodness in this section will allow James to speak about hating favoritism (2:1–13), speaking well of others (3:1–12), imitating God's mercy toward oppressed workers (5:1–6), and being patient in suffering (5:7–12). Another prominent idea in this section—that sin leads to death—will be picked up in the very last section of this letter (5:19–20).

Structure

1. The true cause of sinful behavior: ourselves, not God (1:13–15)
2. The unchangeable purpose of God: to give good gifts to us so that we might become mature (1:16–18)

Interpretive Insights

1:13 *For God cannot be tempted by evil.* How does God not being able to be tempted contribute logically to the argument that God doesn't tempt us? Not only can God not tempt us, but he cannot even be tempted to consider the idea of tempting us. The idea of tempting us to sin is absolutely repulsive to him and totally contrary to his nature. He can't even entertain the thought. James here opens the way for 1:17, where he tells us that God is pure goodness and the source of all goodness (see 1 John 1:5).

1:14–15 *dragged away . . . enticed . . . has conceived.* The first two verbs, "dragged away" and "enticed," are technical terms for fishing[1] and give the idea of being "baited" and "reeled in." James envisions evil desires as master fishermen, selecting just the right bait and, once it is taken, reeling us in. The word translated "has conceived" in 1:15 is also used in Luke 5:9 of fish being "caught," so it is possible that James continues his fishing language, saying that we are not only "baited" and "reeled in" but also "caught." However, most translations take "has conceived" with the next set of terms, which are words from the realm of human development.

gives birth to . . . when it is full-grown, gives birth to. While James does use fishing terminology, the more dominant terminology in this section is that of human development. This is not surprising since James's main theme is spiritual maturity, which fits naturally with the language of human development. Here, however, James is talking not about the growth of the Christian but of desire conceiving and giving birth to sin and sin growing into death.

The key idea in both human development and fishing language is the seemingly inescapable progression: normally when a fish takes the bait, it is then reeled in and caught. Though these are three stages, each succeeding stage follows upon the one before it. Even more inevitable, when a baby is conceived,

James 1:13–18

it will be born, and once it is born, it will grow. James knows that when a believer yields to temptation, it will result in sin, and that sin will lead to death. By death, James means separation from the life that God provides. Because he is talking about believers, James is not referring to eternal separation from God in hell here. But when believers sin, we cut off our access to God and receive discipline from God. This can result in physical death (e.g., Acts 5:1–11); separation from fellowship and being given into Satan's power (e.g., 1 Cor. 5:1–13); sorrow (e.g., 2 Cor. 7:8–10); reenslavement to sin and powerlessness in the Christian life (e.g., Rom. 6–7); sickness (e.g., 1 Cor. 11:30); shame, spiritual blindness, and rebuke (e.g., Rev. 3:18–19); loss of strength, groaning, and wasting away (e.g., Ps. 32:3–4); and more.

1:16 *Don't be deceived.* This same phrase appears three other times in the New Testament: 1 Corinthians 6:9; 15:33; and Galatians 6:7. In all three cases a crucial piece of information is unknown or forgotten. Without that knowledge, the reader is in real danger of being deceived. In all three cases that crucial piece of information follows the phrase "Don't be deceived." So it is here. The crucial piece of information in the battle to understand and avoid temptation is the truth of 1:17–18: God is the source of good and will never deviate from his stated purpose of bringing us to maturity. If James's reader grasps this truth, then great progress can be made in understanding and avoiding temptation. After all, the very first deception in human history was Satan's attempt to get Adam and Eve to doubt the goodness of God (Gen. 3:1).

1:17 *Every good and perfect gift.* What the NIV has rendered with one idea in English is represented by two slightly different phrases in Greek and could be translated as "every good giving and every perfect gift." While many commentators agree with the NIV that these two phrases are synonymous, it may be that James intends slightly different nuances. The word "giving" (*dosis*) focuses on the action of giving (as in Phil. 4:15), while "gift" (*dōrēma*) focuses on the gift given. The complete goodness of God is seen in the fact that he is the source of every good act of giving as well as every good thing given.

the Father of the heavenly lights, who does not change like shifting shadows. Admittedly, the phraseology is tricky, but the idea is the constancy of God. Although the language James uses ("change," "shifting shadows," and "Father of the heavenly lights") is often found in the world of astronomy, the background is more Jewish theology than Greco-Roman philosophy. Because shadows were associated with changes that came from the fading of daylight (e.g., Jer. 6:4), they often represented instability and impermanence in Hebrew thought (1 Chron. 29:15; Job 8:9; 14:2; 17:7; Pss. 109:23; 144:4; cf. Col. 2:17; Heb. 8:5; 10:1). Often such instability and impermanence in humans was contrasted with the permanence of God and his constancy in fulfilling his purposes and plans.

James may be alluding to Psalm 102 here, a psalm that contrasts human impermanence with God's permanence. The same themes that James is talking about—God as Creator ("Father of . . . lights"), who does not fade or change like shadows and who purposes to produce a people for himself—are present in Psalm 102.

The immutability of God is less a Greek philosophical point and more an affirmation of this theology: while we are often confused and uncertain during the trials and temptations we suffer, God is absolutely unwavering in his singular pursuit to create a new people who will praise his name. The focus on the new birth of this new people is where James will now head in verse 18.

1:18 *He chose to give us birth.* James returns again to the imagery of human development. There is a strong parallel to 1:15, in which sin "gives birth" (same word as here) to death. God would never tempt us to sin, because sin gives birth to death, and God gave birth to us so that we might have life.

through the word of truth. There are connections here to the Genesis account where God uses the spoken word to bring creation into existence. Here God creates new life in believers through the "word of truth." These two creative acts of God are also paralleled in 2 Corinthians 4:6 (on "word of truth," see the sidebar).

The Word

The "word of truth" (1:18), the "word planted in you" (1:21), and "listen to the word" (1:22–23) most likely all refer to the same thing, but what does James have in mind? One option is that "word" refers to the gospel, since God gave birth to us through the "word of truth" (1:18). But James doesn't use the word "gospel," and central aspects of the gospel—namely, the death and resurrection of Jesus—are not mentioned in James. A second option is that the "word" refers to God's law, since "listen to the word" is parallel to "looks intently into the perfect law that gives freedom" (1:25). (On James's view of the law, see "Theological Insights" in the unit on James 2:1–13.) However, since having God's law on our hearts (Jer. 31:31–35) is the result of the new birth in Christ and not the cause, it is hard to see how God's law is what God uses to give us new birth, as in 1:18.

The third option, which is best, encompasses both of the first two. "Word" refers to the broader revelation of God to humanity, whether in the gospel or in God's law. This revelation of God to humanity is recorded in the Scriptures. After all, James thinks that the royal law is found in the Scriptures (2:8), and the Scriptures are where the gospel is recorded in written form. But could James be referring to the New Testament, since most of the New Testament had not been written by the time James composed this letter? He seems to think that his own letter is part of the "Word" that listeners are to listen to and do, extending the category of "Scriptures" beyond just the Old Testament (see the comments on 2 Peter 3:16).

a kind of firstfruits. In the Old Testament, "firstfruits" often refers to the portion of the agricultural crop that is harvested first in time. But it could also indicate the portion that is best (e.g., Exod. 23:19; Num. 18:12). That is the idea here. God gave us new birth so that as he causes us to grow and mature, we might be the best part of his creation.

Theological Insights

This passage makes an important contribution to the teaching that the Bible presents on sin. First, James helps us to see that temptation itself is not sin. This is useful to keep in mind in thinking through issues such as human sexuality: desire for illicit sexual activity is not the same thing as engaging in illicit sexual activity. However, having said that, we should note, secondly, that James is presenting sin as the seemingly inevitable next step in the process that begins with temptation and ends with death. This three-step process, desire-sin-death, has parallels in Jesus's teaching in John 8:21–47, which closely connects lies, sin, and death, and Paul's teaching in Romans 6–8, which closely connects the law, sin, and death.

In addition to the theology of sin, this passage forces the Christian interpreter to answer the question, What about passages such as 1 Samuel 16:14–15; 2 Samuel 24:1–17; and 1 Kings 22:19–23, in which it seems that God does tempt people to sin? More detailed answers can be found in the relevant commentaries, but in general it appears that in these passages God is allowing humans to be tempted or tormented by forces of evil (as with Job or Peter) as opposed to God being the agent of temptation, actively enticing humans to fall into sin. Jesus's approach to the situation with Peter in Luke 22:31–32 is a beautiful picture of God allowing temptation while earnestly desiring for us to escape successfully.

Teaching the Text

If we are going to teach this text in a way that is consistent with what James wants to accomplish, two major points should be taught: (1) how we end up experiencing temptation, which leads to sin and death; and (2) that God is for us and earnestly desires that we avoid temptation.

With regard to the first point, it is important to catch James's insistence on the nearly unavoidable advance from desire to sin, which leads to death. Many Christians feel that they can allow evil desires and cravings to fester, thinking that they can divorce their thought life from the actions they engage in.[2] This text says otherwise. Both the fishing language and the human development metaphors provide nice windows into discussing the domino effect of desire-sin-death. This text also provides an opportunity to talk about the fact that desires for sin come from within us. Whether those longings for sin come through genetic predisposition (nature) or social encoding (nurture) is immaterial.[3] The teacher should be concerned not with how the temptations got there but with the fact that these temptations come from within us.

With regard to the second point, the emphatic comment "Don't be deceived" should highlight the fact that doubting the goodness of God and his unchanging purpose of wanting us to become mature is easy to do. We often think of God as being neutral, sitting back judgmentally and waiting to see whether we pass or fail the temptation. When God tests our faith through trials, it is only because he longs for us to succeed and works toward that end by giving us good gifts in the midst of the temptations we are going through. This text provides a great opportunity to teach the pure goodness of God. One of the prime deceptions that Satan uses with believers is to get them to doubt the goodness of God. In order to help listeners "resist the devil" (4:7), the teacher must shine the light on God's goodness and not assume that everyone understands this. Emphasizing this point will pay dividends later when James discusses subjects that presuppose what he has said in this section—subjects like favoritism, mercy for the poor, and speaking evil, when we have been created in God's image. Along these same lines, using the logic that Jesus used, that a house divided against itself cannot stand, can be effective. What benefit would God get out of tempting us to sin? How would God abandoning us in the middle of our temptations help him accomplish his purpose of creating a mature and holy people?

Illustrating the Text

Satan deceives us, tempting us to doubt God's goodness.

Nature: The cobra lily is a pitcher plant, a kind of plant that lures an unsuspecting insect down into the plant until it falls into a pool of digestive juices. However, the cobra lily is unique. It has a set of leaves that are semitransparent. When an insect wanders in, it is dazzled by the light show it finds inside. Eventually, it is totally disoriented and slowly crawls forward, down a path with thousands of fine hairs, all pointed toward the "stomach" of the lily. When the insect tries to turn back, it quickly discovers it's too late. Similarly, Satan masquerades as something he is not, a trustworthy broker of truth. He attempts to undermine our trust in God. If he can get us to give up on that, then our battle is lost. We are lost!

God is the great gift giver, especially during trials and temptations.

Human Experience: Giving and receiving gifts is a tricky proposition. Bad gift givers tend not to give gifts or to not put much time or effort into giving a gift.

On the other hand, good gift givers usually think long and hard about what to give. They often find you something that you don't think you will need and you end up loving it. God is the perfect gift giver. He loves giving gifts all the time, and he relishes giving us just what we need. In the middle of trials and situations, he gives us not what we want but something far better, like his presence and power, friends to walk with us on the journey, and spiritual maturity to handle what we are going through.

Whether or not we seek it, sin inevitably gives birth to death.

Personal Testimony: For the birth of our fourth child, my wife and I had become somewhat lax in rushing to the hospital. Three times prior we had arrived in plenty of time, but this fourth child came more quickly. By the time we arrived at the hospital, he had already begun to make his entry into this world. We skipped the prep room and rushed right into delivery. It was a great reminder that the result of conception is birth—a birth that we cannot control. So too, when sin is conceived, it gives birth to death. And we cannot control its coming.

God's Word is the seed that births new believers.

Props: Hold up a packet of tomato seeds and explain what you have. Ask the question, "Now, can I plant these seeds and expect to get bell peppers? Lettuce? Carrots?" Then answer, "Of course not! If I want tomatoes, I have to plant tomato seeds. And if I plant tomato seeds, I expect they are going to produce tomatoes." New believers are birthed only through an encounter with God's living Word, and when we implant God's living Word in people's souls, we can expect a harvest of new believers.

Doers of the Word

Big Idea

Become doers of the Word so that you can experience the blessings of God in your life.

Key Themes

- God's Word can rescue us from the power of sin.
- We must become doers of the Word and not hearers only.
- Controlling the tongue, caring for widows and orphans, and avoiding corruption by the world are key characteristics of the mature Christian.

Understanding the Text

The Text in Context

The first chapter of James deals with the theology of maturity. To this point James has presented one of the major means by which Christians become more mature, enduring suffering (1:2–12), and one of the great hindrances to maturity, the problem of sin (1:13–18). Now James is ready to discuss the second major means by which Christians become more mature: hearing and doing the Word of God. For James this is the means by which we experience the blessings of God in our lives. After this section James transitions from the theology of maturity in general to how Christian maturity works itself out in relation to specific issues.

To prepare us for this transition, we are introduced to three major issues in 1:26–27 that will reappear throughout the letter: controlling the tongue (3:1–12; 4:11–12), caring for the less fortunate (2:1–26; 5:1–6), and avoiding friendship with the world (4:1–10). These three themes are the main evidence of maturity in the life of a believer.

Structure

1. Becoming mature by keeping away from sin, putting off the old nature, and receiving the implanted word (1:19–21)
2. Being doers of the implanted word and not just hearers (1:22–25)

3. Examples of maturity: controlling the tongue, caring for widows and orphans, and avoiding corruption by the world (1:26–27)

Note that verses 19–21 are the transition from verses 13–18 and could have been included with that section.

Interpretive Insights

1:19 *slow to speak and slow to become angry.* Because 1:20 drops "listening" and "speaking" and focuses only on anger, we know that when James says "slow to speak," he is referring not to the general wisdom that less talk is better than more (e.g., Prov. 10:19; 13:3; 17:28; 29:20) but to speaking out in anger or in a way that creates anger in others (e.g., Prov. 15:1; 17:27). Ephesians 4:25–31 also closely intermingles speech with anger (see the sidebar).

1:20 *human anger does not produce the righteousness that God desires.* Notice the contrast between the anger of humans and the righteousness of God, that is, anger that boils up from our humanity versus righteousness that is produced in us by God. Because of this contrast, "human anger" does not include righteous indignation, which ultimately comes from God (see "Theological Insights" below). "Righteousness" refers not to God's declarative righteousness (as is often the case in Paul) but to our righteous activity (so 2:14–26). God declares us righteous so that we might become more and more righteous in our actions by his power. Anger is not how someone becomes more righteous, nor is it characteristic of a righteous or mature person.

James 1 and Ephesians 4

James 1:19–21 has at least seven things in common with Ephesians 4:17–31: (1) believers as God's new creation (*ktisma/ktizō*: James 1:18; Eph. 4:24); (2) to "put off" or "get rid of" (*apotithēmi*) old behaviors (James 1:21; Eph. 4:22); (3) "anger" (*orgē*) as a primary example of the kind of behavior to be put off (James 1:20; Eph. 4:31); (4) to get rid of the "evil" (*kakia*) (James 1:21; Eph. 4:31); (5) the synonymous issues of "moral filth" and "impurity" (James 1:21; Eph. 4:19); (6) the corrupting influence of "desire" (*epithymia*) (James 1:14–15; Eph. 4:22); and (7) beginning with "take note of this" / "so I tell you this" (James 1:19; Eph. 4:17), a common practice for this type of moral encouragement literature.

Why are these two passages so similar? Probably not because James has read Ephesians or Paul has read James. However, as in James 2 and Romans 4, there may be a common Old Testament text in the background, possibly Zechariah 3. Most likely the commonalities are due to the fact that both are talking about the same thing: getting rid of the old life and growing to maturity. Because of the similarity, Ephesians 4 provides some help in our interpretation of James 1.

1:21 *the word planted in you, which can save you.* "Save you" refers not to the initial gift of salvation but to the working out of the salvation process. This verse is about not conversion but maturity, just as in Ephesians 4:17–31 (see the sidebar). "Save" is used this way in 5:20, where James has in mind rescuing a person who is already a Christian from the death that comes with wandering into sin. James has just finished telling us that sin leads to death (1:15), but God has given us new life through the "Word" (1:18). Now James is following up on that point by claiming that the same "Word" that God used to give us new life has been implanted in us and can continue to save us from the power of sin in our lives as we live in accordance with the truth we first began to learn at our conversion. Admittedly, James's use of "word" is difficult, but as was argued in the previous section at 1:18, if *logos* ("word") is going to have the same referent in 1:18, 21, 22, and 23 it has to be the broader referent, which is that of the written revelation of God in the Scriptures.

1:22 *Do not merely listen to the word, and so deceive yourselves. Do what it says.* I prefer to translate this verse: "Become doers of the Word and not hearers only and so deceive yourselves." James uses the present-tense imperative of "become" (*ginomai*). This word and its tense reflect the process of becoming something as opposed to a one-time action. Each time we do what God says to us through his Word, we become more and more a doer of the Word. James also uses two nouns ("doers" and "hearers"), not two verbs ("do" and "listen"). This reflects a contrast between two types of people rather than simply two different kinds of actions. Become a doer, not a hearer only.

1:23 *who looks at his face in a mirror.* Luke Timothy Johnson observes that in the ancient world the mirror was used metaphorically as a tool of moral self-improvement. As a result, "the mirror can be regarded as an instrument for improvement in another way, which brings us closer to the use in James 1:22–25. In this case, the mirror does not give an accurate image, but an *ideal* one. In the mirror, one can see a model for proper behavior."[1] The Bible doesn't just show us who we are; it shows us who we are supposed to be.

1:25 *perfect law.* This is the third time James has used the word "mature/perfect" (*teleios*) in this chapter: in 1:4 it is used for humans becoming *mature*, and in 1:17 it refers to the *perfect* gifts God gives. Here "mature/perfect" draws on both prior referents: the law is perfect (because it comes from God), and it brings maturity to those who hear it and obey. Psalm 19:7 is a beautiful parallel: "The law of the Lord *is perfect*, refreshing the soul. The statutes of the Lord are trustworthy, *making wise the simple* [i.e., maturing them]." What we see in God's Word is the perfection that transforms us to be mature.

will be blessed in what they do. Notice the connection to 1:22: those who "do" the Word will be blessed in what they "do."

1:26–27 *Religion.* This word refers to outward acts of religious piety, here referring to Christian good deeds. Controlling the tongue, looking after orphans and widows, and remaining unstained by the world are the outward signs of maturity.

Theological Insights

Sometimes the Bible presents anger positively or at least neutrally (e.g., Exod. 34:6; Mark 3:1–6; 1 Cor. 13:5; Eph. 4:26–27). When James speaks of being slow to anger in 1:19, he is speaking about the attitude of anger that fits in this tradition. The Bible also presents anger negatively (e.g., Eccles. 7:9; Matt. 5:22; Eph. 4:31). This is where 1:20 fits. There are two differences between these kinds of anger: (1) Righteous anger is anger patterned after God's anger toward sin, but God is slow to anger, and those who are angry in this way should be slow to anger. (2) The anger that the Bible says to get rid of is anger associated with angry outbursts, cursing speech, and violent rage. Notice in Matthew 5:22 that being angry with your brother or sister is paralleled with calling them a fool.

Teaching the Text

The central idea of this passage is being doers of the Word. If you are a doer of the Word, this will save you from sins like anger or from the hypocrisy of claiming to be a believer and yet not controlling your tongue, not taking care of the less fortunate, and not remaining free from the world's corruption. Therefore, the most important aspect of teaching this text is to help people become doers of the Word and not hearers only. This is the key to experiencing God's blessing in our lives, as 1:25 makes clear.

How does one teach others to be doers of the Word? Kirkegaard's urging that while reading God's Word you must "remember to say to yourself: It is I to whom it is speaking; it is I about whom it is speaking"[2] is still useful for us today. Given the influence of modern secular scholarship, there can often be a tendency in Christian circles to emphasize the human author of Scripture over the divine Author. This tendency can cause Christians to view the Bible as something that was written by people long ago for people long ago, with the danger that the Bible becomes only a historical book to be studied rather than a word from the Lord to be obeyed. Help people recapture the sense that while the book of James was written by James the Just to a first-century audience, it is also written by God to us today. One way to do this is to show how James uses other Scriptures in his book. James 4:6 uses the present-tense verb "says," not the past tense "said," to refer to Proverbs 3:34. The person who is speaking in James 2:8–11 through the law is God. And to sit in judgment over the law in 4:11–12 is to sit in judgment on God.

Another way I have found very helpful in moving people toward being doers of the Word is talk to them about "performing the Scriptures." That is, instead of just looking at the Scriptures as a source of timeless principles that need to be applied to our lives, it is helpful to encourage them to see the Bible as a living script in which we are all acting out our parts. In this way, when I come to the Scriptures I find myself in the story, or as teachers we help people find their place in the story. If I am a "doer of the Word," it means that in reading the story of David fighting Goliath (1 Sam. 17) I not only look for timeless principles to apply to my life but I also view 1 Samuel 17 as the script of the story in which I find myself. What is happening today in my life or in our church may be a re-presentation of that same story, and we are being called to play the role of David.[3] One example of a New Testament person doing this with an Old Testament story is Mary with the story of Hannah. Mary is in many ways playing the role of Hannah so that while her circumstances are similar but different, Mary exemplifies the spirit of Hannah.

Illustrating the Text

Anger is characteristically immature; caring for widows and orphans is characteristically mature.

Literature: *Les Misérables*, by Victor Hugo. In this story, the character of Jean Valjean represents both the anger denounced in James 1:20, before his conversion, and the care for widows and the poor encouraged in 1:26–27, after his conversion. At the beginning of the story, Jean Valjean is characterized by angry outbursts. When he is saved, he is given a new identity and dressed in new clothes. While there were some glimpses of concern for the poor before he went to prison (since he went to prison for stealing bread for his sister's kids), after his conversion his new life is overwhelmingly characterized by concern for the less fortunate, including widows, orphans, and the mentally ill. Moving from anger to empathy for widows and orphans is a movement from immaturity to maturity.

Be a doer of Scripture.

Quote: *The Treasury of David*, by Charles Spurgeon. Spurgeon gives this example of his "reliving" Psalm 91:

> In the year 1854, when I had scarcely been in London twelve months, the neighborhood in which I labored was visited by Asiatic cholera, and my congregation suffered from its inroads. Family after family summoned me to the bedside of

the smitten, and almost every day I was called to visit the grave. I gave myself up with youthful ardor to the visitation of the sick, and was sent for from all corners of the district by persons of all ranks and religions. I became weary in body and sick at heart. My friends seemed to be falling one by one, and I felt or fancied that I was sickening like those around me. A little more work and weeping would have laid me low among the rest; I felt that my burden was heavier than I could bear, and I was ready to sink under it. As God would have it, I was returning mournfully home from a funeral, when my curiosity led me to read a paper which was wafered up in a shoemaker's window in the Dover Road. It did not look like a trade announcement, nor was it, for it bore in a good bold handwriting these words: 'Because thou hast made the Lord, which is my refuge, even the Most High, thy habitation; there shall no evil befall thee, neither shall any plague come nigh thy dwelling.' The effect upon my heart was immediate. Faith appropriated the passage as her own. I felt secure, refreshed, girt with immortality. I went on with my visitation of the dying in a calm and peaceful spirit; I felt no fear of evil, and I suffered no harm. The providence which moved the tradesman to place those verses in his window I gratefully acknowledge, and in the remembrance of its marvelous power I adore the Lord my God.[4]

The Word does us no good if we don't respond.

Object Lesson: Using a handheld mirror, make the point that it does us good only if we actually look into it and make appropriate adjustments in response to what we see.

Do Not Show Favoritism

Big Idea
Favoritism by Christians toward the rich is foolish, unlawful, and unkind.

Key Themes
- Do not show favoritism in the church.
- God has given the blessing of strong faith to many who are monetarily poor.
- It is necessary to obey God's law in all areas of life.
- Those in need require mercy, not judgment.

Understanding the Text

The Text in Context

Having completed a more general discussion of the theology of maturity in his first chapter, James launches into a series of case studies of maturity (or immaturity). He begins in 2:1–13 with the issue of economic favoritism. A person's or community's approach to money is a window into their spirituality, something Jesus also taught (e.g., Matt. 6:24; Mark 10:17–31; 12:41–44; Luke 12:13–34).

Concern for the less fortunate (widows and orphans) is a hallmark of true Christian religion (1:27). Now James elaborates on this point by addressing giving preferential treatment to the rich over the poor. The next section, 2:14–26, will expand this case study from money to the more general idea of faith showing itself in action, using care for the less fortunate as an example (2:15–16). The issue of money and possessions already appeared in 1:9–11 and will resurface in 5:1–6. The topic of the law will come up again in 4:11–12.

Structure

1. The command not to show favoritism (2:1)
2. A hypothetical example of favoring the wealthy (2:2–4)
3. The first reason why favoring the rich is a bad idea: it's foolish (2:5–7)
4. The second reason: it's unlawful (2:8–11)
5. The third reason: it's unmerciful (2:12–13)

Interpretive Insights

2:1 *must not show favoritism.* Every other time this word "favoritism" is used in the New Testament, it is used to say that God does not play favorites (Rom. 2:11; Eph. 6:9; Col. 3:25). Christians must not show favoritism, because God does not.

2:2 *a man . . . wearing a gold ring and fine clothes, and a poor man in filthy old clothes.* Both persons' outward appearance is emphasized, setting up not only the contrast between one being rich and the other poor but the problem of judging based on outward appearance. Even in 2:3 the rich man continues to be identified by the clothes he is wearing. This focus on outward appearance sets up the irony in 2:5, where those who look poor "in the eyes of the world" are actually rich in faith. Focusing on outward appearance leads to an error in judgment: the richly dressed man is poor in Christian maturity, while the poorly dressed man is rich in Christian maturity.

2:3 *If you show special attention.* Although God does not play favorites, there are times in which he is said to "show special attention" (e.g., Luke 1:48; cf. 1 Sam. 1:11; 9:16). Therefore, James is not saying that everyone in the church must be treated identically and equally. There is still a place for honoring a person who has served faithfully or providing more attention and help to a person with special needs. The difference between James 2:3 and Luke 1:48 is that God shows special attention to Mary because of her low social status (Luke 1:52) as well as the character of her heart (Luke 1:50). In the hypothetical situation James proposes, special attention is given on the basis of outward appearance, which is exactly the opposite of how God pays special attention (cf. 1 Sam. 16:7, where "do not consider" is translated in the LXX with the same word as "show special attention").

2:4 *evil thoughts.* The word "thoughts" could also be translated "reasoning." The idea of paying special attention to the rich person is not just a thought that suddenly pops into one's mind. Instead it is a rational, reasoned decision consistent with one's approach to life. Such a person has a warped worldview that James is trying to remake.

2:5 *rich in faith and to inherit the kingdom.* To inherit the kingdom of God is a promise of future blessings in the age to come, while being "rich in faith" focuses on the present blessings God gives to righteous but materially poor believers. "Faith" here refers not to conversion faith but to faith present in our daily living, as in 1:6 ("when you ask, you must believe," i.e., ask "in faith"). While not all poor Christians are strong in their faith, all things being equal a poor Christian will have stronger faith because they will have struggled through more adversity than a rich person (1:9–11). Faith is like a muscle; the more you exercise it, the stronger it gets. Financially poor believers have more opportunities to trust God for food, work, housing, and so on, and as a result they will have stronger faith than rich Christians. Anyone who has interacted with Christians from poorer nations can testify that often their faith in God puts many rich Christians in the West to shame. This is a shameful irony: believers with such strong faith should be honored, but by playing favorites "you have dishonored the poor" (2:6).

2:6 *Is it not the rich who are exploiting you?* The word for "exploiting" (*katadynasteuō*) is used for demonic oppression in Acts 10:38 and for Egypt "tyrannizing" and "repressing" Israel in slavery (Exod. 6:7 LXX; cf. Exod. 1:13). In Amos 8:4 the verb is used for Israelites trampling down the poor, impoverishing them through fraudulent business, and then buying them as slaves. The *Epistle of Diognetus*, an early Christian text, provides an interesting parallel: "for happiness is not a matter of lording it over [*katadynasteuō*] one's neighbors, or desiring to have more than weaker men, or possessing wealth and using force against one's inferiors" (10.5).[1] The word *katadynasteuō* indicates acting in an oppressive way, using wealth to exercise power and influence over others for selfish ends. Whether Christian or non-Christian, those who are wealthy are more likely to act in this oppressive and exploitative manner.

Are they not the ones who are dragging you into court? One of the ways the rich oppressed the poor was through the court system, where the rich exercised the most influence and power, using the courts to gain advantage over the poor and those in the middle class.

2:7 *blaspheming the noble name.* The three things James mentions— exploiting, dragging into court, and blaspheming the noble name of God— are not three separate, unrelated charges. More likely the general charge is exploiting, which is evidenced by their propensity to drag Christians into court, which, as 2:7 tells us, results in blaspheming God's name. How?

In Isaiah 52:4–5 Israel is being "oppressed." As a result God's name is being blasphemed among the nations because the gentiles have concluded that belief in God is useless and that God is unable to protect and defend his people. The blaspheming referred to in James 2 is not the rich cursing God directly. Rather, dragging poorer Christians into court and oppressing them causes onlookers to think God isn't strong enough to protect his people and that their belief in God is useless. This is compounded if it is a rich Christian taking another Christian to court (cf. Rom. 2:24; 1 Cor. 6:1–6).

2:8 *keep the royal law.* "Keep" (*teleō*) here has the sense of "complete" or "fulfill." In 2:10 James uses a different word for "keep" (*tēreō*), and there the emphasis is on obeying. This word "keep" (*teleō*) is related to the adjective "perfect" (*teleios*), which modifies "law" in 1:25. Putting 1:25; 2:8; and 2:10 together we see that the law is "perfect," and those who "obey" its commands "fulfill" the law of loving one's neighbor and are therefore perfect/mature. On the law, see "Theological Insights" below.

2:10 *whoever keeps the whole law and yet stumbles at just one point is guilty of breaking all of it.* To break one law is to break all of them, because to disobey the law on one point is to disobey the God who spoke the law (cf. 2:11).[2]

2:11 *he who said, "You shall not commit adultery," also said, "You shall not murder."* Why these two commandments? The following are some possible reasons: (1) These are the first two commandments on the second tablet of the Ten Commandments, the tablet that focuses on loving others. (If this is the reason, it is strange that James lists #7 [adultery] before #6 [murder].) (2) Just as murder kills life and adultery kills marriage, favoritism kills identity. Those who constantly experience discrimination for not being rich can lose any sense of who they really are as children of God. (3) James 4:4 calls friendship with the world "adultery," and favoritism toward the rich is friendship with the world's values about money; 5:6 says mistreating the poor is "murder." (4) It may be that favoritism encompasses the remaining three commandments of the ten: favoritism steals from someone the position or honor they are entitled to as children of God; favoritism lies to someone about their real value to God; and favoritism comes from coveting influence or power from those who are rich.

2:13 *judgment without mercy will be shown to anyone who has not been merciful.* This is probably an allusion to the teaching of Matthew 18:23–35, especially given the language of "dragging into court" from James 2:6. The violent nature of "dragging into court" in James 2:6 resonates with the physical violence in Matthew 18:28 and the "violent" use of the legal system in 18:30 that results in the man who begged for mercy being "thrown into prison." Because of God's great compassion, he has cancelled believers' debts, because we are too poor ever to pay. Now Christians must show this same kind of mercy to others.

Theological Insights

The role of the law. James 2:8 mentions the "royal law," which corresponds to the "perfect law that gives freedom" (1:25) and the "law that gives freedom" (2:12). But James is not referring to the Mosaic law, per se. Nowhere in this letter does he mention Sabbath or circumcision, two central aspects of the Mosaic law. Furthermore, in Acts 15:13–21 James concludes with the early church that the Mosaic law is not to be imposed on believers. "Law," then, refers not to the Mosaic law but to the new-covenant law written on the heart (Jer. 31:31–35). This is what James alludes to with the phrase "the word planted in you" (1:21). This new-covenant law is best summarized by Jesus in Matthew 22:37–40 with the command to love God and others and in the "new commandment" of John 13:34–35 (cf. 1 John 2:3–11). Paul affirms this summarization (Rom. 13:8–10; Gal. 5:14), referring to the new-covenant law of loving God and others as "God's law" and "Christ's law" (1 Cor. 9:21; cf. Gal. 6:2).

What, then, of the Mosaic law? For us today, the Mosaic law continues to be a useful example of one way to love God and others in a particular context, but it is not binding on a Christian in the same way it was for an Old Testament Israelite, since we do not live under the old covenant. For those who live under the new covenant, the law of loving God and loving others finds its ultimate expression in the person, work, and teaching of Jesus as revealed and explained in the New Testament.

Teaching the Text

To combat the subtle and pervasive favoritism present in all our churches, it is important to teach all three reasons given in 2:1–13 for avoiding favoritism.

First, it is foolish (2:5–7). The world says that favoring the rich will get you influence, power, and access to great resources. James counters that the supposed influence, power, and resources come with a steep price: exploitation and oppression. Many rich Christians give generously with no strings attached, but in general those who are rich like to use their money to control things—including the church. Besides the steep price of catering to those who are rich, James says that it is foolish to favor the rich, because they are not the ones with the real resources. Yes, they have more money. But it is the poor whom God has chosen to be strong in faith. And since faith is the means by which we access the power and resources of God, it is foolish to shame the poor at the expense of the rich.

Second, favoritism is sin (2:8–11). James's emphasis that there are no small "sins" in God's economy is worth noting. Because favoritism is so subtle and so ingrained in how we think, those hearing this text may have a hard time emotionally feeling the weight of the sin of favoritism as opposed to murder or adultery. To teach this point requires emphasizing that God hates favoritism; it is just as much a violation of who he is as are murder and adultery.

Third, favoritism is unmerciful (2:12–13). To choose the rich over the poor is cruel and uncompassionate. Everything in this world is set up to favor the rich. People fawn all over them wherever they go. The poor person, who is equally created in the image of God and loved by God, is usually ignored and rejected. Must it be that way for them in the church as well? Is there not one place that a poor person can go in this world and not feel like a second-class citizen? While the first reason appeals to the mind and the second reason to the conscience, this third reason appeals to the heart and to the power of mercy.

Standing in the background of everything that James is saying is the person and character of God. To teach this passage may require discussing the fact that God does not play favorites. Instead, God shows mercy to the poor and needy without any thought of being repaid.

There are a myriad of modern opportunities for applications of 2:1–13: churches that favor choosing the rich and powerful to be elders and deacons; pastors who are willing to do a funeral for a wealthy person's family member, but not a poor person's; and leaders who allow those giving substantial financial gifts to the church to direct where their money goes but deny the same right to the person who gives just a few dollars. And these are just examples of favoritism with money. The principle of favoritism can apply to anything that the world values: beauty, power, social refinement, popularity, certain ethnicities, and so on.

Illustrating the Text

The poor can be rich in faith.

Bible: **Acts 3:1–10.** Tell the story of Peter, John, and the lame man from Acts 3. The man asks for money, but what he gets from Peter and John is a miracle of healing, far beyond what money could have ever bought him.

Financial riches almost always hinder riches in faith.

Church History: It is said that Thomas Aquinas, who was highly esteemed by Pope Innocent IV, one day went into the pope's chamber. There, they were reckoning large sums of money. The pope is reported to have said to Aquinas: "You see that the Church is no longer in an age in which she can say, Silver and gold have I none." "It is true, holy father," replied Aquinas, "nor can she now say to the lame man, Rise up and walk!"

Blessed are those who embrace the monetarily poor.

Bible: **Mark 12:41–44.** Retell the story of the widow and her two mites. When Jesus says that the widow put in "more," he means she put in something more valuable because it was given in faith. Churches that overlook the offering of the widow in order to run after the million-dollar donors are missing the opportunity to receive faith-empowered blessings from God.

Scenario: Imagine you are on the welcome committee at a church that has been experiencing an ongoing budget shortfall. It is Sunday morning. During the sermon, you look to your left and notice someone who must have slipped in after the service started. He is well dressed in a hand-tailored suit, early fifties, with CEO hair. After a moment, you remember he's the owner of several large car dealerships in your area. You glance around once again. On the opposite side, in the back, you notice another new person. He is wearing ragged clothing. It is clear that he did not shower or shave for this day in church. His eyes are bloodshot, and it looks like he had trouble rolling out of bed this morning. He too looks familiar. Where have you seen him before? Oh, yeah! He was the guy who recently changed your oil at the Quickie Oil Change. No one is sitting close to him either.

The service ends. Both men are leaving the church. No one is talking to them. Worse, they are headed out doors at opposite sides of the church. You will only be able to catch up to one of them. Imagine that whichever one you actually talk to will come back again next week and even start attending the church. Who do you run after?

Faith and Works

Big Idea

Good works signify the presence of true faith, and therefore claiming to have faith in the absence of works is invalid.

Key Themes

- Words without the complementary actions are of no value.
- Works are the evidence for faith and the validation of claims of faith.

Understanding the Text

The Text in Context

Avoiding discrimination against the poor (2:1–13) expands in 2:14–26 to the larger theme of someone who claims to be a Christian but is not acting in accordance with their faith. Given James's theme of maturity, this is a natural question for him to answer: If someone claims to be a believer but is not maturing in such a way that their life is bearing fruit, is such a person truly a believer?

James 2:14–26 picks up the ideas from 1:19–27 in the dichotomy between doers and hearers only. Here the dichotomy is between those who claim to have faith and also have the deeds to back up that claim and those who only claim to have faith.

Structure

1. The uselessness of claiming to have faith but having no deeds, since words without actions are useless (2:14–17)
2. The powerlessness of intellectual assent as a proof of faith, since works are necessary to show others our faith (2:18–19)
3. Evidence that works communicate the presence of true faith from the examples of Abraham and Rahab (2:20–25)
4. Summary statement (2:26)

2:14 *claims to have faith.* James does not begin with "if someone has faith." Instead he writes, "if someone *claims* to have faith." James is framing his discussion of faith and works in regard to a person's claim to have faith and how such claims are validated. This is the idea that runs through this entire section. Immediately James drops the longer phrase "claims to have faith" and writes a shortened version of it with "such faith" in 2:14 and "faith by itself" in 2:17. In both verses, the word "faith" has the article, tying it back to its first usage, which is "claims to have faith," so that we could read "such faith" as "claimed faith."

2:15–16 *Suppose a brother or a sister . . . If one of you says . . . but does nothing.* Verses 15–16 are tied to verse 14. The word "says" in verse 16 is the same word as "claims" in verse 14, and the phrase that opens verse 14, "what good is it," is the same phrase that closes verse 16. It is also important to note that the hypothetical example in verses 15–16 is *not* an example of faith without works. Seeing a brother or sister without food and clothes is not faith, nor is it a claim to faith. James is not yet ready to provide examples of faith and deeds. That will come beginning in verse 20. His goal here is broader and more fundamental. Saying or claiming something without the corresponding action is of no value. A person cannot be warmed or fed with affirming words about being warm and being fed. Words alone are useless. Just as in chapter 1, hearing alone is useless unless it results in action. Affirming that words without actions are useless paves the way to apply this general principle to the more specific issue of claiming to have faith but without the accompanying works.

2:17 *In the same way, faith by itself, if it is not accompanied by action, is dead.* James begins this verse with "in the same way," which shows he is applying the more general principle from 2:15–16, that words without actions are useless, to the narrower category of claiming to have faith without good deeds, in order to answer the question he raised in 2:14. So we can understand this phrase as saying, "In the same way, claiming to have faith by itself is 'dead on arrival' if such a claim is not accompanied by action." The two phrases "by itself" and "not accompanied by action" are almost redundant, and by using both James highlights that he is talking about faith that has no works whatsoever to go with it.

2:18 *But someone will say, "You have faith; I have deeds."* James here introduces an imaginary discussion partner, a common technique (e.g., Luke 3:8; Rom. 3:7; 9:19; 11:19; 1 Cor. 15:35). The problem is trying to figure out exactly how much the discussion partner is saying, since James did not use punctuation when he was writing. Many different solutions have been proposed,[1] but none is completely satisfying. One possibility worth considering is that the closing quotation mark should come after "faith," not after "deeds," where the NIV puts it.[2] In such a reading the text would in essence be saying: "Someone will say to me, 'But, James, you claim to have faith,' to which I would reply, 'Yes, and I have deeds to substantiate that claim. Prove to me that you have faith without works, and I will prove to you that I have faith by my works.'" This makes more sense than to have the imaginary discussion partner claim to have deeds, which clearly works against James's argument.

2:19 *You believe that there is one God.* This is a reference to Deuteronomy 6:4, a central confession said aloud by many Jews at the time James was writing and still today. James's point is that when you say aloud that there is one God and you mentally assent to this truth, this is not enough to provide evidence of saving faith. After all, even the demons mentally assent to the truth that there is one God, but clearly this does not signify the presence of saving faith. It should be noted that believing there is one God is not enough to save someone anyway. At the time of James, non-Christian Jews and some pagan philosophers were monotheists but not believers. Likewise today, Muslims and Jews believe that there is one God but are not necessarily saved.

Even the demons believe . . . and shudder. There may also be a more subtle point James is making: even the demons' "faith" results in some outward response—they shudder. The point would be that people who simply voice the words "there is one God" with no fear or reverence for God are put to shame by demons, who at least shudder at the thought of God.

2:21 *considered righteous.* The verb translated "considered righteous" (*dikaioō*) can also be translated "vindicated" or "shown to be righteous." It is used this way in places such as Matthew 11:19; Luke 10:29; 16:15; and Romans 3:4. "Shown to be righteous" is a different nuance from "declared righteous," which is how Paul often—though not exclusively—uses the word (e.g., Rom. 3:20; 1 Cor. 4:4; Gal. 2:16; Titus 3:7). James is not saying that when Abraham offered Isaac as a sacrifice he "was declared to be righteous," as if this were the moment he exercised saving faith. Instead, when Abraham offered Isaac, this was the moment that he showed himself to be righteous. In other words, what happened in Genesis 22 is the "work" that demonstrated his faith.

2:22 *was made complete.* This is the verb form of the word "mature, perfect, complete" that James uses in 1:4, 17, 25 and is related to the verb in 2:8. Complete and mature Christians have complete and mature faith, which is faith showing itself in actions. This ties this section back to the first. Abraham suffered through the trial of having to offer his son. In this trial his faith became stronger and was shown to be genuine.

2:23 *And the scripture was fulfilled.* This phrase is usually used in connection with the fulfillment of prophecy. Here it signals the proper understanding of the relationship between Genesis 15 and Genesis 22. In the life of Abraham, Genesis 15 is the moment that he is said to have "believed God, and it was credited to him as righteousness." Paul focuses on this moment in Genesis 15 when he argues in Romans 4 that someone is justified by faith alone. James, however, is focusing on Genesis 22, which is not the moment that Abraham is declared righteous but the moment in which he most profoundly demonstrates his righteousness. Therefore, when God declares Abraham to be righteous in Genesis 15, it is also a promise that God will grow Abraham into a man who will demonstrate his righteousness in outward actions. This promise is fulfilled in part in Genesis 22.

2:26 *As the body without the spirit is dead, so faith without deeds is dead.* How do you tell the difference between someone who is sleeping and someone who is dead? One is breathing; the other is not. "Breath," which is another way to translate "spirit," is an evidence of life. So too, works are the evidence of faith. Again, remember that the whole passage is framed by the question of a person claiming to have faith and the validity of that claim—not before God, but before humans. Here we are not talking about how a doctor knows that a patient in the hospital who is hooked up to heart and brain monitors has died. Like God, the doctor has access to a way of knowing whether life is present in ways inaccessible to the average person. James is talking about how the average person would know another is dead—there is no breathing.

Theological Insights

Assurance of salvation. Assurance of salvation is often confused with eternal security, but they are separate issues. Eternal security has to do with whether a genuine Christian can lose their salvation. Assurance of salvation has to do with how someone (or others) can know if they are genuinely a Christian. James is dealing with assurance of salvation here in 2:14–26, and his argument should be taken alongside other Scripture passages dealing with this subject, such as Matthew 25; Romans 8; 2 Corinthians 13; Galatians 5; 2 Peter 1; and the entire Epistle of 1 John.

How does one know if they are a Christian, or if another person is? The answer is if that person has the Spirit. And the Spirit manifests his presence in a person's life in three general categories: (1) correct beliefs (e.g., 1 Cor. 12:3); (2) spiritual actions/fruit, including persevering in faith (e.g., Gal. 5:16–26; James 2:14–26; 1 John 2:19); (3) spiritual experiences, including the inner testimony of the Spirit (Rom. 8:16), experiencing conviction from the Spirit (1 Thess. 1:5), being guided by the Spirit into truth (John 16:12–15), praying in the Spirit (Eph. 6:18), giving and receiving "manifestations of the Spirit" (1 Cor. 12:7–11), and God working miracles by the Spirit (Gal. 3:5).

Teaching the Text

When one is teaching this text, the most important thing to recognize is that James is dealing with the issue of faith and works in relation to other humans, not in relation to God. In other words, James is not trying to address the issue of how someone becomes a Christian. Rather, he is addressing how someone can know that another person (or oneself) is actually a Christian. This is important because it distinguishes James's intentions from what Paul is doing in Romans 4 and other places. Paul is talking about how we become right with God. James is talking about how we can know that we or others are right with God. How we become right with God is by faith alone. How we can know if we or others are right with God is by the works that our faith produces. To teach this text requires great clarity on this point.

James uses multiple rhetorical devices: examples from Scripture (Abraham and Rahab), theology (demons), hypothetical discussion partners, metaphors (workless faith is like a dead body), and philosophical arguments (words without actions are useless, so claiming to have faith without deeds is worthless). This suggests that when we teach this passage, we may feel the need not only to identify and explain the rhetorical devices that James used but also to use other means—personal examples, other metaphors, different philosophical arguments, and so on—to explain this point since it can be difficult to grasp.

James's harsh language ("you foolish person," 2:20) reminds us that someone who claims to have faith but has no deeds is not easily awakened to the error of their ways. Any of us who have dealt with nominal "Christians" in our churches will recognize this immediately. There is no more difficult group to get through to than the people who claim to be Christians but who have no evidence of real faith in their lives.

Illustrating the Text

Words without works are useless.

Object Lesson: It's great to have architectural plans for a beautiful skyscraper. But plans alone have never raised a single steel girder. It's great to have a gourmet recipe, but recipes never put food on the table. Words can be eloquent. They can be moving. They can be passionate. But words without works do no good. The point may be further illustrated by holding up a recipe card for delicious cookies and saying, "Does anyone want to taste this? It is Grandma's recipe for chocolate chip cookies," to make this point in an engaging and memorable way.

Good works are evidence of genuine faith.

Personal Testimony: In the last days of my father's life, our family sat in the room, watching his chest move up and down as he sometimes labored for breath. We were waiting for the moment when he took his final breath, because this was the sign to us that he had passed to heaven. When he finally did, this was the trigger for my mother to call the funeral home. On the other hand, when the hospice nurse came to check him, she looked for other vitals, including trying to find a pulse. But for the average person, breathing is the sign of life. So too, Christians do not have access to the knowledge God has as to whether someone is a true believer, so in place of being able to see into the heart and mind, we have to rely on outward actions to know whether they are truly alive with God's living Spirit.

Scripture sometimes uses harsh language to wake us up.

Sports: One of the standard legendary moments in sports is the "locker-room speech." This speech is designed to motivate, to move, to unify a team, helping them emerge onto the field of play with a passion that overcomes any obstacle. Perhaps the most revered locker-room speech is the halftime, come-from-behind, claim-the-victory speech. Typically, this speech is loud. It is aggressive. It is not the kind of volume or vocabulary you use at a dinner party. But it can be effective. How many times have we heard a commentator exclaim, "Wow! I wonder what the coach told them in the locker room. They're like another team"? Sometimes, the Lord uses language intended to wake us up and get us moving.

The Tongue and Christian Maturity

Big Idea

The tongue is the best measure of Christian maturity because it is so powerful and naturally untamable and reveals the condition of one's heart.

Key Themes

- What we say is a measure of our maturity.
- Words have power for good or evil.
- The tongue is naturally untamable.
- The tongue is a window to one's soul.
- What we say to others can defile us.

Understanding the Text

The Text in Context

James 1:26 introduced the idea of what we say as a measure of maturity. James 2:12 referenced this as well: "*Speak* and act as those who are going to be judged by the law." Now James is ready to explore in greater detail the idea of what we say to one another. Ironically, having alluded to the fact that words without actions don't do anything (2:14–26), James now addresses the fact that words themselves can do something. Words themselves can be a form of action and therefore a sign of maturity. In fact, in this passage James argues that the tongue is the best measure for evaluating maturity.

James will return to what we say to one another (e.g., 3:14; 4:2, 11–12, 13–15; 5:9, 12, 13, 16), since this is such a prominent theme in his epistle.

Structure

1. The example of teachers and the idea of judgment (3:1)
2. The tongue as the best measure of maturity (3:2)
3. First reason why the tongue is such a good measure of maturity: it is so powerful (3:3–6)

a. Power to do good for others (3:3–5a)
b. Power to destroy others (3:5b–6)
4. Second reason: it is naturally untamable (3:7–8)
5. Third reason: it shows the condition of the heart (3:9–12)

Interpretive Insights

3:1 *Not many of you should become teachers.* While some see no connection between 3:1 and the rest of the passage, teachers are the prime example of the power of the tongue. With their words teachers can guide their students as bridles guide horses or rudders guide ships. Likewise with their words teachers can destroy students as a spark sets ablaze a forest. Because this is the case, not many should become teachers, since with this greater responsibility comes greater accountability to God.[1]

Some commentators, noticing that the imagery points toward how our speech affects others, have gone further and argued that throughout the passage James is alluding to teachers when he uses the word "tongue" and the church when he uses the word "body."[2] But James is not being that specific. The tongue (bit, rudder, spark, poison) represents speakers, of whom teachers are notable examples, while the horse, ship, and trees represent hearers, which can include the church but is not limited to the church.

3:2–4 *We all stumble in many ways.* The NIV has left the explanatory word "for" (*gar*) untranslated, but most other translations leave it in (e.g., ESV, KJV, NASB, NET). "For we all stumble in many ways" is the explanation for why not many people should desire to be teachers. If it is so easy to stumble in what we say, then not many should seek to be teachers, because being a teacher involves a greater level of accountability.

Anyone who is never at fault in what they say is perfect. The word translated "what they say" is the word *logos*, used only here and in 1:18–23, where it is translated as "word." The use of *logos* ties these two passages together. Our "words" are the best indicator of whether we are hearers of the "Word" only or also doers of the "Word." This is why James says that a person who can keep their tongue in check is "perfect," using the same word for "maturity" (*teleios*) from 1:4, 17, and 25.

bits into the mouths of horses . . . steered by a very small rudder. The analogies of bit and rudder are not about how our bodies are controlled by our tongues but about how through our tongues we exert influence over others. It is the rider who controls the horse with the bit. It is the captain who steers the ship with the rudder. Likewise, it is the teacher who influences the student through what they teach (3:1), and it is the snake that poisons its victims (3:8). The broader point in this section is that the tongue is difficult to control (3:8), but if we can control our tongues, we can use our tongues to exert great influence, just like a rider who is trained to control a horse's bit will be able to control the horse and the captain who learns to control the rudder will be able to influence the direction of the whole ship.

3:5 *makes great boasts.* This does not mean that the tongue is always boasting about things. Rather, the tongue boasts great power, or as *The Message* paraphrases it: "A word out of your mouth may seem of no account, but it can accomplish nearly anything—or destroy it!"

3:6 *The tongue . . . a world of evil . . . corrupts . . . sets the whole course of one's life on fire.* A comparison of English translations of this verse will show that this is a notoriously difficult verse to translate. The best translation I have seen is in the NET: "And the tongue is a fire! The tongue represents the world of wrongdoing among the parts of our bodies. It pollutes the entire body and sets fire to the course of human existence—and is set on fire by hell."[3] This translation reflects the fact that in James 1:27 the world is said to pollute a person, using the same word for "world" as in this verse and related words for "pollute/corrupt." It is also important to note that the NET has "sets fire to the course of human existence," while the NIV has "sets the whole course of one's life on fire." The verb "set on fire" brings to mind damage done not to oneself but to others. What we say both pollutes ourselves (as in Matt. 15:11) and destroys others (as in Prov. 16:27; Jer. 5:14).

3:8 *no human being can tame the tongue.* James has written this sentence in such a way as to emphasize the word "no (one)." This is the second reason why it is such a good measure of maturity: no one can tame the tongue without God's help. Those unable to control their tongues are also compared to wild animals in 2 Peter 2:12.

3:9 *praise . . . curse.* If the chief goal of humankind is to glorify God and enjoy him forever,[4] then praising God is the highest and best use of the tongue. Over against this is the cursing of other humans, who are made in the likeness of God (Gen. 1:27); this is one of the lowest forms of use of the tongue. The contradictory nature of these two actions is highlighted by the fact that we bless God and curse God's representatives, people who are made in the likeness of God. The fact that the tongue can do both these things shows again its propensity for both good and evil and its seemingly untamable nature.

3:11–12 *a fig tree bear olives, or a grapevine bear figs . . . a salt spring produce fresh water.* Verses 11–12 contain three images, that of a spring, a fig tree, and a grapevine. Verse 12 gets at the heart of what this imagery is about. It is the same point that Jesus makes in Luke 6:45: out of the overflow of the heart the mouth speaks. The words that one speaks are the best indicator of the state of one's heart. James made this same point more broadly in the previous section, 2:14–26. The works that a Christian does demonstrate whether or not they truly have faith. In this passage, James is saying that the best indicator of whether someone is a mature Christian is the words that come from their mouth. Fig trees cannot produce olives no matter how hard they try.

Theological Insights

The larger overall theme of the Bible when it comes to words is that the right words, spoken at the right time with the right attitude, bring life, while the wrong words, spoken at the wrong time with the wrong attitude, bring death (e.g., Gen. 3; Deut. 30:11–20; 32:46–47; Prov. 11:11; 18:21; Matt. 4:4; John 6:63; Rom. 3:13–14; James 1:18). James's statements that words boast great power like that of a bit and a rudder (3:3–5a) and that the tongue is a fire setting on fire the whole course of life (3:5b–6) fit into this theme of the power of words.

Because words have the power of life and death, evil words defile the one who speaks them (Matt. 5:22; 15:17–20), and each person must give an account of every word they have spoken (Matt. 12:36). James agrees. The tongue "corrupts the whole body" (James 3:6), and teachers will be held to stricter judgment (3:1).

Additionally, because no one is righteous in and of themselves, what one says is evidence of the Spirit's presence in one's life and the measure of the state of one's heart (e.g., Matt. 12:33–37; Mark 13:11; Luke 6:43–45; 1 Cor. 12:3). This is where James makes a significant contribution, arguing that the tongue is the best measure of Christian maturity.

Over against these themes of the power of words, the Bible also presents the idea of the uselessness, meaninglessness, and powerlessness of words (e.g., Prov. 14:23; 29:19; Matt. 21:28–32; Luke 6:46). James 2:14–26 fits into this aspect of the theme of words when it states that merely claiming to have faith is of no value.

Teaching the Text

The primary thing that James is addressing in 3:1–12 is the tongue as a measure of maturity. Often pastors and teachers are looking for "metrics" to help people assess how they are doing in their Christian journey. One of the best assessments for doing this is what we say to others. It is an interesting teaching point to note that it is not the sexual organs (sexual immorality) or the eyes (lust, coveting) or something else that is hardest to keep in check but the tongue. If someone can control the tongue, they can control the other parts of the body as well.

In his argument as to why the tongue is such a good measure of maturity, James gives three reasons, each of which could be its own theme developed from this passage. First, the tongue is powerful. What we say to others can steer their lives in good directions, or it can destroy them. The saying "Sticks and stones may break my bones, but words will never hurt me" is patently false. Second, the tongue is naturally untamable. From this passage and what it says about the tongue, one can easily teach on total depravity and human inability in the face of the powers of sin and hell. Third, the tongue is a window to the soul. Some might take the point of 3:9–12 to be that we should work harder to stop cursing people and to spend more effort trying to bless God. But that is not it. The real point of 3:9–12 is that if we are cursing people and blessing God at the same time, it is a sign that something is wrong at a deeper level with our Christian maturity. In other words, James is not promoting ethical behaviorism but identifying the tongue as eveidence of maturity or lack of maturity.

The theme that what we say also defiles us, though not as prominent in this passage, is definitely present and can provide additional material for teaching.

It is interesting that this passage does not address how to control the tongue. A teacher may want to include material on how to do that, but it does seem to be what James is concerned with at this point in his letter. One might infer from 3:6 that since the tongue is set on fire by hell, it is redeemed and given good things to say from heaven—a point that might be substantiated from 3:17–18. But there controlling the tongue is not explicitly addressed.

Some teach from this passage (usually 3:2–4) that the tongue is how we bring our whole selves under control, in which case the tongue is actually a

---

How to Do Things with Words

In linguistics and philosophy, performatives are words that actually perform an action. The notion of performatives comes from the philosopher and linguist J. L. Austin's book *How to Do Things with Words*.[a] Austin reveals that while we sometimes use words to describe something or make propositional statements, at other times when we talk we are actually doing something with our words.

For example, when my wife says, "You are in charge of the kids this Friday," through uttering those words she is doing the work of putting me in charge of the kids. When a bride says, "I do," she is with those words taking that man to be her husband. Other examples include a student volunteering in class, a judge sentencing someone to prison, or someone calling a friend to wish them well. In each of these cases, words are actually doing the work. In James 3, the performative aspect of words is at the fore. Words praise; words curse. Words are like bits, rudders, and sparks. They accomplish things. Words slander; words encourage; words gossip. Whereas 2:14–15 highlights how words can be inactive, 3:1–10 highlights how active words can be. So in chapter 3, James is concerned first with how our words affect others and then secondly how our words can corrupt us.

[a] Austin, *How to Do Things with Words*.

metaphor for what we think and say. But as argued above, James is focusing on how our tongue affects others (and defiles us), not how it controls our actions. The biblical imagery for controlling the self is usually located in the heart, mind, or will—not the tongue.

Finally, J. L. Austin's idea of performatives (see the sidebar) can be an interesting way to introduce the idea that words have power.

Illustrating the Text

The tongue is the measure of maturity.

Film: *Waiting for Superman.* In this documentary, Oscar-winning filmmaker Davis Guggenheim explores the space between educational aspirations and realities. In it, he advocates for measurable change in the way schools educate. The church faces a similar challenge: trying to close the gap between our stated goal—"making disciples"—and our organizational realities. If we want to do this, then we need accurate assessments for Christian maturity. James tells us the tongue is one of those.

Words matter!

Quote: **Edward G. Bulwer-Lytton.** Popular nineteenth-century English author Bulwer-Lytton famously asserted, "The pen is mightier than the sword."

Human Experience: Blogger Akoshia Yoba provides a secular perspective on just how important a father's words are for daughters. She shares the scars she herself bears:

> When I was about five years old, my father looked at me and offered a stern warning, "You have fat potential!"
>
> At the time, I had no idea what he meant, but I could tell from his tone, and the way he looked at me, it was not good. I eventually learned what it meant and became obsessed with my weight. I was terrified of gaining weight. It took me many years, a handful of therapists and even more self-help books to get myself firmly on the path to reversing the damage inflicted upon my self-image by my father's well-received words.[5]

Peace from God

The Theology

Big Idea

Mature believers do good works in the gentleness and humility that come from the wisdom of God, not the envy, pride, and selfish ambition that come from the world's wisdom.

Key Themes

- The source of our wisdom is related to the attitudes of our heart.
- There are two competing sources of wisdom for a believer.
- Embrace the values of gentleness and peace.

Understanding the Text

The Text in Context

James 3:13–4:10 is one continuous argument addressing the issues of gentleness, peace, and humility in Christian relationships. However, given the length of this section and that a chapter break has been inserted between 3:18 and 4:1, separating this one argument into two parts for the purpose of this teaching commentary seems advisable. Yet the unity of 3:13–4:10 means 3:13–18 and 4:1–10 must be addressed together as much as possible.

James 3:13–4:10 can be broken down into two main sections: the theology (3:13–18) and the application of that theology to the reader's specific situation (4:1–10). Together the whole subsection of James 3:13–4:10 opens with the thesis that mature believers do good deeds in gentleness that comes from wisdom from God (3:13). It closes with instructions about how that is to happen in their situation: by submitting to God (4:7–10).

In the previous section, 3:1–12, James addresses the tongue as the best measure of maturity. He now broadens out that idea and looks more generally at the issue of interpersonal conflicts among Christians as evidence of what is in their hearts and of their relationship to God. What his readers say to one another is certainly part of this, but now the focus is on the gentleness and humility that come from God's wisdom as opposed to envy and ambition that are motivated by love of the world. This continues the larger theme that James has been working with: outward actions reveal what is in the heart. Therefore maturity demonstrates itself in tangible actions of gentleness and peacemaking.

Structure

1. Opening thesis statement: mature believers do good works in the gentleness that comes from true wisdom (3:13)
2. Earthly, unspiritual, demonic wisdom produces pride, envy, and selfish ambition (3:14–16)
3. Wisdom from God produces peace (3:17–18)

Interpretive Insights

3:13 *Who is wise and understanding . . . ?* "Wisdom" and "understanding" are virtually synonymous here. Both refer to the ability to live life well—in other words, being mature. "Wisdom" is knowledge put into practice, and "understanding" refers to "being knowledgeable in a way that makes one effectual in the exercise of such knowledge."[1] James is demonstrating what wisdom looks like as he takes knowledge in 3:13–18 and correctly applies it to his readers' situation in 4:1–10.

by deeds done in the humility. "Deeds" is the same word used twelve times in 2:14–26. James is still concerned about good works, but now he is emphasizing that these good works are done in a spirit of "humility." It is not enough to do good things; they must be done in the right spirit. First Corinthians 13:1–4 says the same thing.

In this context two different words are translated with the word "humility/humble": *praytēs* in 3:13 and *tapeinos/tapeinoō* in 4:6, 10. These are related words, and when they appear together in the New Testament, the NIV translates *praytēs* as "gentleness" and *tapeinos/tapeinoō* as "humility" (Matt. 11:29; Eph. 4:2; Col. 3:12). That is the idea here. James is concerned with gentleness in dealing with others, as seen in 3:17–18 when he focuses on "peace" and the relational aspects of wisdom from above. This gentleness comes from humility, as 4:6–10 will make clear.

comes from wisdom. The fact that true wisdom manifests itself in identifiable actions is perhaps based on Jesus's proverbial affirmation in Matthew 11:19 that "wisdom is proved right by her deeds."

3:14 *bitter envy.* The word "bitter" is used only twice in the New Testament, here and three verses earlier, in 3:11 (translated "salt"). This ties what James is saying here to what came before: boasting and speaking out of bitter envy and selfish ambition are examples of the bitter speech just discussed in 3:11. A related word for "envy" will be used again in 4:2, where it is translated "covet."

selfish ambition. Bitter envy is linked with "selfish ambition," which is the desire to achieve fame, status, recognition, success, comfort, enjoyment, or fortune for oneself. This is not ambition to see the kingdom of God advance but ambition for personal success.

3:15 *from heaven but is earthly, unspiritual, demonic.* What comes down "from heaven" is good and perfect (1:17), but the wisdom that inspires envy and selfish ambition is "earthly, unspiritual, demonic." These three adjectives represent the typical threefold enemies of the Christian: the world, the flesh, and the devil (cf. Eph. 2:1–3 and 1 John 2:15–17 with 1 John 3:7–10). We have a tendency to see evil thinking as coming from just one source, whereas James identifies three different sources of evil wisdom. James has already said that sin comes when we are "dragged away by [our] own evil desire" (1:14), but this is intertwined with "the world" and the "evil one" as well. See the discussion on spiritual warfare in "Theological Insights" in the unit on James 4:1–10.

"Earthly, unspiritual, demonic" also prepare the way for 4:4–7, where James speaks of "friendship with the world" (4:4), the (human) "spirit that he [God] has caused to dwell in us" (4:5), and the need to "resist the devil" (4:7). Earthly wisdom comes from friendship with the world. Unspiritual wisdom comes from the spirit of jealousy that resides within us (see the comments on James 4:5). And demonic wisdom comes from the presence of the devil.

3:16 *disorder and every evil practice.* "Disorder" is a noun used four other times in the New Testament, all with the idea of communal confusion, strife, anarchy, or unruliness (Luke 21:9; 1 Cor. 14:33; 2 Cor. 6:5; 12:20). The opposite of "disorder" is "peace" (1 Cor. 14:33). Given that "disorder" focuses on communal strife, "every evil practice" probably has the more narrow meaning of "disputes between people" (as in 1 Cor. 6:1 and 1 Thess. 4:6) as opposed to every conceivable type of evil. Coveting and ambition lead to interpersonal strife and disputes, which are the opposite of peace.

3:17 *first of all pure.* Wisdom from above is first and foremost "pure," meaning that it is "holy," coming from God and above all set apart from the world, sin, and Satan. God's wisdom and the world's wisdom have nothing to do with each other (cf. 1 Cor. 2:6–16).

peace-loving, considerate, submissive, full of mercy and good fruit, impartial and sincere. The remaining words in the list emphasize communal relationships, and the list itself shows artistic construction. The first four qualities are alliterative with *e*—"peaceful" (*eirēnikos*), "considerate" (*epieikēs*), "submissive" (*eupeithēs*), full of "mercy" (*eleos*). The last three are alliterative with *a*—"good fruit" (*agathos karpos*), "impartial" (*adiakritos*), and "sincere" (*anypokritos*). And the bridging phrase "full of mercy [*eleos*] and good fruit [*agathos karpos*]" has one of each to tie the two lists together. The fact that James has put together two lists in this artistic way carries over into verse 18, which combines the first word in the *e* list ("peaceful," *eirēnikos*) with the first idea from the *a* list ("good fruit," *agathos karpos*): peacemakers who sow in peace reap the fruit of peace.

The result of God's wisdom is that it creates peace within oneself and peaceful relationships with others because it promotes "consideration" of the needs of others and "submissiveness" to the leadership of others and is "full of mercy" for the faults of others. The *a* list, in addition to "good fruit," includes being "impartial" to the differences of others (as in 2:1–13) and "sincere" or genuine in dealings with others.

3:18 *Peacemakers who sow in peace reap a harvest of righteousness.* Note the connection to Matthew 5:9, where peacemakers will be called the children of God. Here James is saying that those whose good works are done in a way that promotes peace reap the righteous life that God desires. "Righteousness" links this verse to 1:20: human anger does not produce the righteousness God desires, but the Word of God—which is wisdom from heaven—produces peace, and this peace brings in a harvest of righteousness. With this statement, James wraps up his theological introduction to God's wisdom. James is returning to the point he started in 3:13. Mature believers produce good works in the gentleness and peace that come from wisdom from God.

Theological Insights

Wisdom, quarrels, and pride. It is fruitful to compare 1 Corinthians 1–4 and James 3:13–4:10. Both passages are dealing with the issue of quarrels and conflicts in the local community; both passages address extensively the issue of human versus divine wisdom; and both passages discuss the themes of pride, envy, humility, and gentleness. The point of both is that when Christians are influenced by Satan, the flesh, and the world's way of thinking, they are given over to pride and envy, which are the source of our conflicts with others in the church.[2]

Proverbs 13:10 affirms, "Where there is strife, there is pride, but wisdom is found in those who take advice." Examples of earthly, unspiritual, and demonic wisdom producing pride and envy that result in human quarrels and conflicts can be seen throughout the biblical narrative: Miriam and Aaron's conflict with Moses (Num. 12); Korah's rebellion (Num. 16); Saul with David (1 Sam. 18); David, Nabal, and Abigail (1 Sam. 25); Absalom (2 Sam. 15); Rehoboam (1 Kings 12); Haman (Esther); the mother of the sons of Zebedee (Matt. 20:20–28); and Ananias and Sapphira (Acts 5).

Teaching the Text

As I have emphasized, 3:13–4:10 is all one section. The teacher of this text is faced with the choice of whether to teach it as one or to break it up. If it is broken up, 3:18 is a good stopping point as long as the teacher recognizes that 4:1–10 makes explicit some of the things that are implied in 3:13–18. For example, until 4:1 it is not explicit that the outward action James is concerned about is conflicts and quarrels in the church. It is only alluded to in the language of "disorder" and "peace." Likewise, the inner attitude that gives rise to conflicts and quarrels is identified in 3:13–18 as envy and ambition, but the issue of pride, which lurks in the background, is not made explicit until 4:6–10. Finally, the notion that the wisdom of the world seeps into a community through loving the world is not made clear until 4:4, even though it is alluded to in the discussion about the two kinds of wisdom in 3:15–17.

With that in mind, 3:13–18 can be a great opportunity to discuss the role of wisdom in determining behavior. Maturity manifests itself in humility, gentleness, and peace in interpersonal relationships. If humility, gentleness, and peace are not present, it is because a person is being influenced by an earthly, unspiritual, and demonic worldview. Where the world's thinking about money, popularity, beauty, and leadership dominates, the result will be conflict. Where God's values of submission, mercy, and unselfishness are present, the result will be peace.

In teaching 3:13–18, it is important to emphasize the communal nature of what James is saying. Too often teachers highlight an individualized approach to the ideas of wisdom from God and wisdom of the world. In other words, if I am trying to figure out whether to apply for a promotion at work, I should use wisdom from God and not worldly wisdom. That is true, but this passage is not focused on that sort of individual decision making. Rather, James is focusing on how the wisdom from God manifests itself in good deeds done in a spirit of gentleness as we interact with others, especially within the Christian community—for example, a preacher trying to decide whether to call out his opponents by name in a sermon, or a church volunteer trying to decide whether to protest a new initiative she was not consulted about.

Illustrating the Text

Conflicts with others start in ourselves.

Human Experience: Road rage stinks. People who turn aggressive in these incidents usually blame "the other guy." They reason, "He cut me off," or "She needs to get over and let me pass." And therefore they determine, "It's my job to make them pay." But the "other guy" really is not the problem. Maybe something that other person did triggered something inside the angry driver. That only shows there was something waiting to be triggered.

Within our hearts are all kinds of dangerous attitudes that only need the right trigger. Just consider how worked up Christians can get about church music. Dangerous attitudes abound: selfish ambition (This is the music I like to sing), pride (The songs that I like are better than those of the younger or older generation), and envy (Why is that generation getting the songs they like to sing and ours is not?). When we find ourselves dispensing with love and humility and replacing them with anger and selfishness, we need to face reality: the problem is in us, not the "other guy."

A lifetime of pursuing peace leads to a harvest of righteousness.

Personal Stories: If possible, share from your own experience of a saint who was a peacemaker. This could include reflecting on how someone was remembered at their funeral. Share how this person's legacy left an impact on many people, pointing many to the path of true righteousness.

Prop: Using a small bell (such as a service bell found on the counter of a hotel check-in), talk about taking shortcuts. Whenever we come up against a situation that is difficult, we can either take a shortcut (ring the bell) or do the right thing. Someone cuts us off in traffic. We can take the shortcut (ring the bell), or we can take a deep breath and pray for them (point finger to the sky). Someone asks for our help one too many times. We can take the shortcut (ring the bell), or we can ask for the kind of divine love that bears all things (point finger to the sky). Someone steps on our toes at work, completely disrespecting us. We can take the shortcut (ring the bell), giving them a piece of our mind and responding in kind. Or we can pause, take a moment to pray, and then engage in an honest conversation aimed at reconciliation (point to the sky). Our spouse complains that we are not doing a good enough job of loving them; we can either take the easy way out and ignore what they are saying or try to disprove their claim, or we can honestly evaluate how we may be falling short of true sacrificial love.

What kind of legacy are you going to leave? Will you be someone whose life was filled with the me-first chaos of always taking the shortcut (ring the bell several times)? Or will you be someone whose godly response to challenging circumstances consistently, peacefully pointed people to the source of your inner peace?

Peace from God

The Application

Big Idea

Submit to God, and he will produce peace in and through you.

Key Themes

- God does not answer prayers offered with selfish motives.
- Friendship with the world creates enmity with God.
- We submit to God by confessing our pride and humbling ourselves before him.

Understanding the Text

The Text in Context

James 3:13–4:10 is one continuous section. It has been broken into two parts here for the sake of more manageable-sized teaching units. The reader is encouraged to look at 3:13–18 for the connection of this section to what came before in James.

Immediately following this section are five case studies of the ways in which our pride/worldliness or humility/submission can be seen: how we speak about others (4:11–12), how we consider God in making our plans (4:13–17), what we do with our resources (5:1–6), how we handle waiting for God (5:7–12), and prayer and community accountability (5:13–18).

Structure

In 4:1–10, the theology of 3:13–18 is applied:

1. Evidence that James's readers are not experiencing peace from God (4:1–3)
2. Their friendship with the world has made them enemies of God (4:4–6)
3. The solution to the problem: submit to God (4:7–10)

Interpretive Insights

4:1 *your desires that battle within you.* Much of the emphasis in 3:13–4:10 is on communal relationships, but James does not ignore the related internal personal issues. The "desires that battle within you" are the internal stress and lack of peace that envious, proud, and selfishly ambitious people experience.

4:2 *You desire but do not have, so you kill.* This is unexpected. There were probably not actual murders in the Christian communities James was writing to. Such murders would merit more attention from James than this. Nor is James just positing the hypothetical situation of actual murder that will happen if they keep envying and fighting. Why would "kill" be listed before quarreling and fighting?

It is best to take "kill" as an allusion to angry speech (as in Matt. 5:21–22). In 3:8–9 James talks of the tongue as "full of deadly poison." Readers are ready for the idea that angry speech "kills." Additionally, James may have in mind what we know of as the Sermon on the Mount, where Jesus redefines two of the Ten Commandments: murder, which now includes anger, and adultery, which now includes lust. The verb "you desire" is the same verb translated "(looks) lustfully" in Matthew 5:28. The idea of asking and receiving from God comes from Matthew 7:7 in the Sermon on the Mount; coveting in James 4:2 would include coveting your neighbor's wife (Exod. 20:17). And James does refer to friendship with the world as adultery. If James is thinking of Jesus's teaching from the Sermon on the Mount, that would add additional support that "killing" is angry speech.

4:3 *When you ask, you do not receive, because you ask with the wrong motives.* We must not miss the connection to 1:5–8. To ask for wisdom from God, one must ask "in faith," meaning not doubting the strength and goodness of God to provide wisdom in the midst of trials. Here, the readers are not asking "in faith" because of pride, coveting, and envy, which cast the strength and goodness of God into doubt. That is what Satan did with Eve in Genesis 3, and James recognizes demonic wisdom inciting the attitudes and actions of the community (3:15; 4:7). To approach God as God is to recognize that he is the God of love who does not show favoritism. The wisdom that he provides makes believers impartial, considerate, and merciful (3:17)—in other words, better able to love their neighbors. James's readers wanted to spend their blessings from God on their own pleasures. God is not a giant vending machine or cosmic genie doling out wishes to those who offer him prayer. James will return to asking God in faith in 5:15.

4:4 *friendship with the world.* First John 2:15–18 is similar. Absorbing the world's values about money, fame, success, recognition, power, and so on will necessarily cause the reader to be envious, proud, or selfishly ambitious, which will in turn create internal stress and external quarrels.

4:5 *do you think Scripture says without reason.* What immediately follows is not a direct quote from the Old Testament, though this introduction would make us expect one. The most plausible explanation is that James has linked a general affirmation of Scripture, namely, that humans are envious creatures, with a specific quotation of Scripture, Proverbs 3:34 in verse 6, and introduced the whole package with the phrase "Scripture says."

he jealously longs for the spirit he has caused to dwell in us? While the NIV's translation is certainly viable, there are three problems with it. First, the Greek word used for "jealously" is always negative and never used of God anywhere else in the Bible. When the Bible speaks of God being "jealous" it uses a different word, one that can be used positively. Second, despite the fact that "friendship with the world" is mentioned, the context is not about God being jealous for Christians but of Christians being proud, envious, and selfishly ambitious toward one another. Third, the next phrase, "but he gives more grace," makes more sense if it refers to the fact that despite all believers' constant natural inclination toward envy and pride, God gives more grace than we have sin. For these reasons the NET (cf. KJV, NEB, GNT, or even 1984 NIV) translation is preferred: "Or do you think the scripture means nothing when it says, 'The spirit that God caused to live within us has an envious yearning,'"[1] with the "spirit" referring not to the Holy Spirit (which James never mentions) but to the human spirit. The meaning is that even though God has given us life, because of our sin natures we are filled with envious desires.

4:6 *God opposes the proud but shows favor to the humble.* The word "opposes" can have the idea of "fight against," and it corresponds to the idea of being an "enemy of God" from 4:4. Proud believers exalt themselves to a level that belongs only to God and by doing so make God their enemy. God's response is to fight to move those people back to their proper position.

4:7 *Submit yourselves, then, to God.* "Then" ties 4:7–10 to 4:6. Because God fights against the proud but gives grace to the humble, the reader should acknowledge God's unique position of authority and come under that authority. How? Verses 8–10 give a series of verbs that provide further explanation: "Come near," "wash," "purify," "grieve," "mourn," "wail," "change," and "humble." These are verbs of confession and repentance.

Resist the devil, and he will flee from you. The devil is seen as being the ultimate source of temptation for pride and envy. He is the source of the "demonic" wisdom of 3:15, which works with believers' own sinful natures to create the "evil desires" that lead to sin and death (1:14–15). It is noteworthy, first, that James takes for granted that *all* believers will experience these kinds of satanic temptations. Second, and more important, James thinks believers have the power to resist Satan. Third, and most important, when believers resist Satan, Satan will be forced to flee and leave them alone. How does one resist the devil? By submitting to God.

4:8 *Come near to God . . . Wash your hands . . . purify your hearts.* See Psalm 24:3–4. Hands represent actions, and hearts represent attitudes. Those who are engaged in envy and quarrels must both stop their contentious actions and change their proud attitudes. "Wash" and "purify" represent the holiness and separateness that are required for drawing near to God. See also Matthew 5:8; 2 Corinthians 6:14–7:1; Hebrews 10:22.

double-minded. The same word is used in 1:8 to speak of the person who is of two minds as to whether God will answer the request for wisdom. Here the immediate context is of readers who have been adulterous by being friends with the world while belonging to God. Many adulterers are of two minds as to what will truly make them happy, their spouse or their lover. James is accusing his readers of being of two minds as to whether following God or their own desires is the best way to achieve the blessings of life.

4:9 *Grieve, mourn and wail.* A truly repentant person not only changes their attitudes and actions (4:8) but experiences emotional pain when they come to understand the effects of their envy and pride on God and others. Other Scriptures describe such emotional remorse: "He . . . wept bitterly" (Matt. 26:75), or "They were cut to the heart" (Acts 2:37).

4:10 *he will lift you up.* This is closely connected to a proverb Jesus uses at least three times in the Gospels (Matt. 23:12; Luke 14:11; 18:14). What is not made clear in this context is what "he will lift you up" refers to. This has to be understood in light of what came before in James 3:13 and 18. In those verses, the mature believer does good deeds in a spirit of gentleness, and the result is a harvest of peace. Such peacemakers are blessed by God and exalted as sons and daughters of God (Matt. 5:9), which includes the honor and reward one reaps from being a peacemaker.

Theological Insights

Spiritual warfare. James 3:13–4:10 is part of a larger discussion of spiritual warfare in the Scriptures. Genesis 3; Job 1–2; Matthew 4:1–11; Luke 11:14–26; John 8:42–47; Acts 13:6–12; Ephesians 6:10–20; 1 Peter 5:8–9; 1 John 4:1–6— these are just some of the many passages dealing with this issue. James 3:15, which refers to "earthly, unspiritual, and demonic" wisdom, fits with the idea that there are three intertwined forms of evil that plague the believer: the world, the flesh, and the devil. This fits with the broader sense we have from the Scriptures.[2] Also, James affirms that believers must resist Satan and that they actually have the power to do so (4:7). Ephesians 6:13 and 1 Peter 5:9 use the same word "resist" to speak of the believer's battle against Satan and the powers of darkness. Such confidence reflects the scriptural idea that

Christ has triumphed over the forces of darkness and given the believer the power and authority to resist in his name.

Teaching the Text

If 4:1–10 is being taught separately from 3:13–18, it is important to remember that the goal of what James is urging is not explicit in this section because it was spelled out in 3:13–18. In 4:1–10 James is moving his readers to embrace their need to submit to God. The positive motivation for doing so, however, is alluded to in this section only because it was made clear in 3:13–18. Submitting to God results in a person doing good deeds in a spirit of gentleness.

James's main application of this passage to fights and quarrels in the Christian community is one that is still incredibly relevant today. But it is important to remember that fights and quarrels are the symptom and not the cause. The cause is assimilating the world's values and wisdom and thereby allowing pride and envy to develop. James's point in 3:16 is that such wisdom creates every kind of disorder, and one example he uses is the fights and quarrels they are experiencing. Fights in church are no less common today than they were then, and it will be helpful for the teacher to point out the role that pride, envy, and selfishness are playing in modern church fights over worship, personalities, disputable matters, building programs, programming, staffing decisions, and so on.

A second idea that can be latched onto from this passage is the "desires that battle within you" (4:1). Many listeners will be experiencing the inner turmoil, worry, and stress that come from absorbing the world's values. Immersion in technology, culture, politics, and media can create a nagging feeling of having to accomplish more, get what someone else has, achieve more success, or fret about what is happening in the world.

A third point that James explicitly mentions is the absence of answered prayer. A church leadership praying for God to double their church in size may actually be praying out of selfish ambition. Such a situation is ripe for what James has to say in this passage.

Fourth, this is a great passage for teaching spiritual warfare. In my experience most people who are experiencing some level of spiritual warfare need to be reminded about submitting to God and resisting the devil. Perhaps there is some way they are doubting the goodness or power of God. Perhaps there is something that God is asking them to do that they are resisting doing. The fears, anger, anxieties, and lack of peace associated with spiritual warfare come when through pride we refuse to submit to God.

Fifth, 4:7–10 provides an opportunity to teach the subject of repentance for sin. The principles James espouses for repenting of pride and envy are applicable to repentance for other sins as well. The teacher should keep in mind that "resist the devil" in 4:7 indicates that identifying and fighting against the source of temptation behind the sin is an important part of true repentance.

Illustrating the Text

You can't be friends with God and the world.

Humor: Have you ever seen one of those funny internet videos of people falling into the water? *America's Funniest Home Videos* has an astonishing collection of people trying to get out of boats and failing miserably. The best examples happen when someone attempts to keep one foot on the dock and one foot on the boat, which is drifting. Eventually, the splits just don't cover the distance. So too, there is peril with trying to find sure footing both in the Lord and in the world, for there is no common ground between the two.

True repentance requires remorse, confession, and submission.

History: In 1969 Norma McCorvey's life was forever changed when she tried to secure an abortion. When her request was denied, she hired some lawyers and pushed her case all the way to the Supreme Court of the United States. When the "right to choose" was finally granted, McCorvey had already given birth. But her efforts led to more than fifty million abortions being performed in the United States alone over the next three decades.

If that is where the story ends, we would have nothing but tragedy. But it does not end there. In 1994, Norma met a pastor who showed her the love of Jesus: while she was taking smoke breaks outside the abortion clinic where she worked, McCorvey struck up a friendship with a pastor who, bit by bit, showed her the way of the cross. Eventually, her heart melted. Her repentance and renunciation of her former ideology were complete and as public as her former advocacy. In 2005, she petitioned the Supreme Court to overturn *Roe v. Wade*.[3]

It's wrong to ask God for his blessing on our selfish desires.

Scenario: Imagine sitting on the board of a foundation famous for providing grant money to worthy causes. Someone has submitted a proposal. On the outside, it looks amazing. Slick cover. Nice design work. When you open it up you find that the person is requesting money not to help treat diseases, educate the poor, or alleviate suffering but to provide for a luxurious new home, expensive car, and round-the-world trip for themselves. How would you react? Do we expect God's reaction to our selfish prayers to be any different?

Bible: **The Prodigal Son.** Tell the story of the prodigal son (Luke 15:11–32). He receives his inheritance from his still-living father. He takes his father's generous gift, meant to help sustain the son for life, only to waste it on selfish living. The wisdom of the world that is guiding his actions becomes obvious as we see the harm his selfish choices inflict on his father, himself, and his brother.

Do Not Slander

Big Idea
Those who speak poorly about other Christians are not submitting to God or loving their neighbor.

Key Themes
- Speaking against another Christian is speaking against God and his law.
- Speaking against another Christian is an attempt to sit in judgment of God and his law.

Understanding the Text

The Text in Context

There is much debate over what to do with 4:11–12. Although there are clear thematic ties to 3:13–4:10 and 4:13–5:6, most commentators recognize that grammatically 4:11–12 is a distinct section. The use of "brothers and sisters" to begin verse 11 and the switch to a negative command ("do not slander") after a string of positive commands in 4:6–10 mark this section off from what comes before. The interjection of the phrase "come now" (NIV: "Now listen") and the change in address from "brothers and sisters" to "you who say" in verse 13 mark this section off from what comes after.

Though grammatically distinct, 4:11–12 is closely connected to what comes before and after. It is the first of five practical applications of the material in 3:13–4:10. In that section, James made his case that pride, envy, and selfishness are from the world, the flesh, and the devil, not God; therefore, believers must submit to God to experience peaceful relationships with others. Those principles are put into action in five practical applications: how we speak of others (4:11–12), how we make our plans (4:13–17), what we do with our resources (5:1–6), how we wait for God (5:7–12), and communal prayer and accountability (5:13–18).

Slandering (4:11–12) is another example of the theme of words that James first introduced in 1:26 and expounded on in 3:1–12.

Structure

1. The command: do not slander (4:11a)
2. The rationale: to slander one's neighbor is to slander and judge the law (4:11b)
3. The danger: to slander and judge the law is to usurp the position that belongs only to God (4:12)

Interpretive Insights

4:11 *slander . . . speaks against.* Both "slander" and "speaks against" are translations of the same Greek word, *katalaleō*. By using two different English translations, the NIV helpfully reminds us that though *katalaleō* includes patently false statements made about another person, it is not limited to false statements. Today's English reader might assume only false statements are in mind if just the word "slander" were used. That *katalaleō* entails more than just verifiably false statements can be seen in Numbers 12:8, where the word is used in the Septuagint to refer to Miriam and Aaron speaking against Moses to others, but not necessarily lying about him. Rather, they seem to be using their questions to undermine his authority, probably out of envy. Likewise, Psalm 78:19 records Israel speaking against God by questioning whether God was able to provide food in the desert. Technically speaking, they did not say he couldn't provide, but their questions implied that God was not strong enough and kind enough to provide.

Slandering or speaking against another is a practical outworking of the envy and pride James addressed in 3:13–4:10. Numbers 16 (read with Ps. 106:16); Psalms 31:18; 56:2; and Acts 13:45 are examples of pride and jealousy leading to slandering and abusive speech.

judges them. "Judge" is the most important word in these two verses. The verb is used four times and the noun twice. The essential theological point is that to speak badly of another Christian is to stand in judgment over them, and humans are not allowed to judge each other in this way. So says Jesus in his famous dictum of not judging others (Matt. 7:1–2). Paul affirms this as well (Rom. 14:3–4, 10, 13), going so far as to say that humans don't even have the right to judge themselves (1 Cor. 4:2–5). Only God has the right to judge. James's contribution to this discussion is the insight that speaking ill of another Christian is a form of judging them.

speaks against the law and judges it. How does speaking against another Christian speak against the law and judge the law? As was noted in discussing 2:1–13 (see "Theological Insights" in the unit on James 2:1–13), "law" for James does not refer to the Mosaic law per se but refers to the new-covenant law. This law is expressed best in the commands to love God and one's neighbor, with the emphasis being on the second half of that formulation. James refers to the command "love your neighbor" as the "royal law" (2:8). Here, by using "law" in 4:11 and "neighbor" in 4:12, James is pointing back to 2:8. James has already said that his readers must "speak and act as those who are going to be judged by the law" (2:12). Those who choose to ignore this commandment to love their neighbor and choose instead to slander their neighbor are speaking against the law and judging the law. Rather than acknowledge that the law is good and right and should be obeyed, slanderers are proclaiming that the law is false and worthless and can be ignored. Such a person is sitting in judgment over the law.

keeping it. The word for "keeping" is used three other times in James, all in chapter 1 (vv. 22, 23, and 25), where James is talking about being doers of the law. Here James is saying, "When you judge the law, you are not doers of the Word but judges over it." Instead of looking intently into the law that gives freedom, the one who speaks evil of others forgets what they have heard, having judged it to be worthless.

4:12 *There is only one Lawgiver and Judge.* James makes one more move in this section. Not only are Christians who speak against other Christians making themselves judges over the law, these people are setting themselves up as judges over God. There is only one Lawgiver, and if you sit in judgment on his law, then you are sitting in judgment over him. Just as in 2:1–13, James has heightened the stakes. There he showed how favoritism was akin to murdering and stealing; here, speaking evil of another person is tantamount to blasphemy!

The close connection between God and his Word can be seen in Hebrews 4:12–13. To come under the judgment of one is to come under the judgment of the other. To stand in judgment over one is to stand in judgment over the other.

the one who is able to save and destroy. The uniqueness of God's position as Lawgiver and Judge is demonstrated in his unique status as the one who saves and destroys. The Scriptures affirm that salvation belongs to the Lord (Jon. 2:9) and that God alone has the power to destroy (Matt. 10:28). His ability to rescue and tear down is unique (Deut. 32:39; 1 Sam. 2:1–10; 2 Kings 5:7; Ps. 75:7; Phil. 1:28; cf. Luke 6:9).[1]

But you—who are you to judge your neighbor? James has placed the "you" in an emphatic position, as if to say to the reader, "And what about *you?* Next to the God who is Lawgiver and Judge, who saves and destroys, what right do *you* have to judge your neighbor?" Pride stands behind the problem of speaking evil of others, as James made clear in 3:13–4:10. This is James's attempt to introduce some humility to his readers and to encourage them to submit to God.

Theological Insights

1. *God as Lawgiver and Judge.* (On the concept of law itself in James, see "Theological Insights" in the unit on James 2:1–13.) Many passages of

Scripture speak of God as the one who gives law to humans (e.g., Exod. 24:12; Deut. 5:31; Isa. 33:22; Jer. 31:33). One trend in Scripture is to distance God somewhat from the giving of the law so that Acts 7:53; Galatians 3:19; and Hebrews 2:2 can say that the Mosaic law was given through angels. James 4:12 provides a counterbalance. Rather than distancing God from his law, 4:12 begins to move closer to the idea that God is himself law. The idea is not that as Lawgiver, God is outside of the law or above the law, but that he is himself the law and therefore the source, norm, and limit of all law.[2] In this way we are to see God's law identified with God himself, just as God is Judge. When James says, "Speak and act as those who are going to be judged by the law" (2:12), he is saying to speak and act as those who will be judged by God, because God does not just wield the law—he is law itself. Whatever God does is by definition right, because he is light and there is no darkness in him at all.

By identifying God more closely with the law, James also is connecting God more closely with his Word, because in 1:22–25 "word" and "law" are referring to the same thing: the Scriptures. If this is the case, then to sit in judgment on the Scriptures—deciding, for example, that because the command to wipe out the Amalekites in 1 Samuel 15 offends modern sensibilities it presents a depraved picture of God—is to attempt to sit in judgment on God. This too is a kind of slander.

2. *To judge or not to judge.* At times, it can be confusing to understand the relationship of different passages that speak of judging others. On the one hand there are passages like James 4:11–12 (and 2:4); Matthew 7:1–2; Romans 14; and 1 Corinthians 4:1–5 that urge Christians not to pass judgment on each other, while on the other hand passages such as 1 Corinthians 2:14; 5:3–12; and 6:1–5 seem to affirm the opposite. The reconciliation of these various passages is that God alone is Judge. Therefore Christians are not to stand in judgment over one another in the sense of being prosecutor, judge, and jury for their neighbors. However, believers are to discern all things and in this sense "judge" whether a person is acting in accordance with God's Spirit (1 Cor. 2:14). Included with this idea of discerning is the idea of rebuke, correction, and accountability. Discernment is necessary for such things. Also, God has committed some level of authority to the local church for dealing with sinful behavior, so some "judging" is necessarily part of the responsibility of those in leadership in the church.

Teaching the Text

With 4:11–12 the teacher must decide whether to teach this section on its own or to combine it with other sections so that there is more material with which to work.

It is important, first of all, to ensure that those who are being taught understand what slander is. Many listeners may be working from a modern, legal definition of slander (or libel), in which the statements made of another person are provably untrue, spoken with malicious intent, and cause quantifiable damage to someone's reputation. For James, slander is much broader and can include rumors, gossip, sarcasm, and undermining questions. Whereas modern slander is difficult to prove in a court of law, slander according to James is an easy sin to commit.

It can be helpful to point out to people just how common speaking evil of others is. Consider how we sometimes speak of other drivers when caught in traffic, for example. Whether or not they can hear us is not the issue from God's point of view. It can be useful to highlight how technology has heightened our ability and motivation to speak evil of others. Examples include cyberbullying, posting mean-spirited comments on a blog post, and saying something through email that we would not say in person.

Second, it is noteworthy that James connects slander to judging and then heightens this further by connecting it to judging the law and God. Because these connections were not immediately obvious before James brought them up, the teacher may find it useful to walk through each move: how slander is actually judging; how judging a fellow Christian is actually judging the law; and how judging the law is actually judging God.

Third, since this material is placed immediately after 3:13–4:10, it will be important for the teacher to bear in mind that lack of submission to God is the underlying issue. This comes out more subtly in 4:11–12 when James speaks about the one Lawgiver and Judge, but when seen against the backdrop of 4:7–10, submission to God is a central idea. The solution, then, for slander is found in the previous section: submit to God, resist the devil, and repent not only of slander but of pride and envy.

Illustrating the Text

Slander is pervasive.

Popular Culture: To see how prevalent speaking evil of others is, simply scroll down to the bottom of any internet page that allows comments. Often the comments section will devolve into people slandering one another rather than engaging with the issues presented on the page. You might want to project a page of comments from an internet site (making sure they don't get inappropriate).

Slandering is sitting in judgment.

Cultural Institution: In some communities, there is a tradition that many engage in for Sunday lunch. They refer to it affectionately as having "roast preacher" for lunch. This means Sunday lunch is the opportunity to discuss all the failures and shortcomings of the sermon that they just heard. To do so is to sit in judgment over the sermon, rather than to submit to what God might be saying to them through it. The same thing happens when we ignore the law and choose to speak evil of others. Rather than submitting to God, we sit in judgment over him and his law.

Slander is a manifestation of an attitude of pride and envy.

Sports: In 2014 a Twitter exchange took place between Anthony Kalla, a twenty-four-year-old Lions fan, and Brandon Marshall, a wide receiver for the Chicago Bears, in which Kalla slandered Marshall for disparaging comments Marshall made about the Lions a year earlier. Marshall responded by challenging Kalla to a fistfight. When you listen to his quarrel, Kalla's comments seem motivated by envy—he would like to be a Pro Bowl wide receiver as Marshall is. Marshall's comments seem motivated by pride. His team is doing poorly, and this fan has insulted him. Here is pride and envy at work in causing people to speak evil of one another.[3]

Church History: The Heidelberg Catechism has some powerful insight into the true nature of slander. When defining the meaning of the sixth commandment ("You shall not kill"), the Heidelberg Catechism (question 105) has this to say:

> Q. What is God's will for you in the sixth commandment?
> A. I am not to belittle, hate, insult, or kill my neighbor—not by my thoughts, my words, my look or gesture, and certainly not by actual deeds—and I am not to be party to this in others; rather, I am to put away all desire for revenge.

In other words, slander shares the same root as murder!

Future Plans

Big Idea
Stop boasting about the future, and submit your plans to God since you cannot control your own life.

Key Themes
- Live under the sovereignty of God's will.
- Life is fleeting and humanly uncontrollable.
- Beware of self-sufficiency, arrogance, and pride in one's future plans.

Understanding the Text

The Text in Context

James 4:13–17 is the second of five practical applications sourced in the theology of 3:13–4:10. James 3:13–4:10 demands submission to God as a means of experiencing peace in life. The first practical application in 4:11–12 dealt with speaking against others. This is the second, and it deals with making plans for the future either through submitting to God's will or by ignoring it.

James 4:13–17 is strongly tied to 1:2–12 and especially 1:9–11, which speaks of the rich fading away while they go about their business. Asking God for wisdom in the midst of trials and patiently enduring is how a believer submits to God's sovereignty during difficult times. Seeking and acknowledging the Lord's will over future plans is the same principle applied during the good times.

Structure

1. The ongoing practice among James's readers of discussing and formulating their future plans apart from God's will (4:13)
2. The futility of such thinking since humans cannot control their own lives (4:14)
3. The alternative: submitting future plans to God for his approval and blessing (4:15)
4. Upping the ante: charging the reader not just with folly but with the sin of pride (4:16)
5. Closure: a general statement about obeying God (4:17)

Interpretive Insights

4:13 *we will go*. Note the communal element in this passage. In Luke 12:13–21 Jesus tells a parable about a rich fool. That parable, in many ways similar theologically to what James is saying, is focused on the individual. Jesus uses the language of the individual: the rich man "thought to himself" and wondered, "What shall I do?" James uses the language of "we" rather than "I." James is not simply addressing people who are overconfidently planning their futures quietly to themselves. He has in mind the arrogant boasting about the future taking place in the midst of the community. Remember, 4:13–17 is the practical application of 3:13–4:10, which focuses heavily on the negative effect of the world's wisdom on communal relationships. The word "will" in 4:13 emphasizes the supreme confidence of the speakers in their plans. In their minds, there is no "maybe" or "perhaps" in their thinking. What they have planned is what they assume is going to happen.

carry on business. This verb is related to the noun "business" in 1:11, where James said the rich will fade away even while they go about their business. Here James expounds on the fleeting, uncontrollable nature of life as it relates

James 4:13–17 and Ecclesiastes

There are four strong parallels between James 4:13–17 and the book of Ecclesiastes, which will help make clear some things in James 4. (1) The key term for the book of Ecclesiastes is the Hebrew word *hbl*, often translated "meaningless," but which has as its most basic meaning "vapor, mist." Most modern commentators on Ecclesiastes insist that both the ideas of "meaninglessness" and "vapor, mist" must be kept in mind when reading Ecclesiastes.[a] James is picking up on the "vapor, mist" theme when he says in 4:14, "you are a mist." (2) The theme of toiling and working in business is prominent throughout Ecclesiastes, and this is the specific example James raises in 4:13. (3) A central theological point of Ecclesiastes is that God is the one who actually controls life, something James draws out in 4:15.

(4) The epilogue of Ecclesiastes summarizes the point of the book: "Fear God and keep his commandments" (Eccles. 12:13). James closes this section with instructions related to fearing God (4:15) and obeying his commandments (4:17). Because of these connections, the background of Ecclesiastes illuminates this short passage in James. The everyday aspects of life—work, pleasure, relationships, money, and so on—are outside of our control, but they are under God's control.[b] This is the point of Ecclesiastes. But Ecclesiastes's solution—to fear God—is fleshed out a little more in James. To fear God means to allow God's will to guide and direct us through life, to ask him for wisdom (James 1:5), and to not make plans without consulting him (cf. Isa. 30:1–2).

[a] On the use of *hbl* in Ecclesiastes, see Treier, *Proverbs and Ecclesiastes*, 122–26.
[b] See the very helpful introduction to Ecclesiastes and the discussion of *hbl* in Curtis, *Ecclesiastes and Song of Songs*, 1–7, 11.

to business. The connection to 1:11 indicates that 4:13–17 is especially aimed at the wealthy. One of the dangers of wealth is that it deceitfully conveys the perception of control. Money can create a false feeling of autonomy from God. Positively, this passage becomes an important foundation for thinking about business as a way of serving God.[1]

4:14 *You are a mist.* This is the idea from Ecclesiastes that life (apart from God) is not only meaningless but also a vapor or a mist (see the sidebar). The basic sense of "vapor, mist" is that life cannot be controlled, grasped, possessed, or extended. James is saying to his readers, "You cannot control your lives any more than you can control what happens to the vapor you breathe out on a cold winter's morning. You make plans, but whether those plans will come to fruition is not within your power to control."

appears for a little while and then vanishes. Although James is using the metaphor of a mist, we are to see reference to our birth ("appears") and death ("vanishes" = disappears). These are the two events in our lives that most demonstrate our lack of control over our own lives. We cannot control when our lives begin or when they end, or under what circumstances they do so. The two events in our lives that we often most strongly desire to control are clearly beyond our control. Jesus made this same point about death in a related passage: "Who of you by worrying can add a single hour to your life?" (Luke 12:25).

4:15 *Instead, you ought to say, "If it is the Lord's will."* On the concept of the Lord's will, see "Theological Insights" below. James does not have in mind simply adding the phrase "Lord willing" to whatever statement we make about the future, any more than praying "in Jesus's name" means simply saying "in Jesus's name" at the end of every prayer. To pray "in Jesus's name" means to pray in accordance with Jesus's lordship over all things—that is, in accordance with his glory, power, honor, and love for us. To say, "Lord willing," means to approach our lives, plans, and future from the perspective of God's sovereignty over all things.

4:16 *boast in your arrogant schemes.* It is not simply that the business people James is addressing were coming up with grandiose and arrogant business plans, as if more moderate plans would be acceptable. Any attempt by the reader to envision their future apart from the sovereignty and lordship of God is, for James, the height of arrogance.

All such boasting is evil. Here is the explicit connection to pride. James 3:13–4:10 identified pride and a lack of submission to God as the prime problem. "Boasting" represents this pride. To confidently plan for the future without taking into account God's sovereignty over all things is to position oneself as equal with God.

4:17 *If anyone, then, knows the good they ought to do and doesn't do it, it is sin for them.* James closes this section with a general statement about obedience and submission. This is the contrast to the boastful pride of making plans without God. It fits with the broader theme of James, espoused in 1:22–25, of not just hearing the Word but doing it.

There is an interesting connection to the ending of the book of Ecclesiastes (see the sidebar). Ecclesiastes ends, "Fear God and keep his commandments" (12:13). James ends this section essentially by saying, "Submit to God, and keep his commandments."

Theological Insights

1. *Tomorrow.* Jesus's teaching in Luke 12:22–31 (// Matt. 6:25–34) presents an important parallel in relation to the idea of tomorrow. Whereas James is focused on boasting about tomorrow, Jesus is focused on worrying about tomorrow. But both overconfidence and worry regarding the future spring from the same error: a lack of submission to God and a lack of faith in his sovereignty and goodness. Because both boasting and worry arise from the same issue, often the person who boasts about tomorrow one day will be worried about tomorrow the next. The strong connection between worrying about the future and boasting about the future can be seen in how Luke links Jesus's parable about the rich fool in Luke 12:13–21 with the teaching in 12:22–31.

2. *God's will.* The concept in the Scriptures of God's will is tricky to deal with. At its most basic level, "God's will" refers to what God wants to happen. Sometimes this is used in Scripture of the inviolable plans of God being executed in human history, especially with regard to salvation (e.g., Isa. 53:10). Sometimes it is used in Scripture of God's violable moral demands for humans (e.g., 1 Thess. 4:3). Sometimes it is used of God's guidance and approval of human decisions outside the realm of specific revealed moral commands of God (e.g., 1 Chron. 13:1–4). It is to this third usage that 4:13–17 belongs.

In this third usage of seeking guidance from God, there are examples from Scripture where believers have no preconceived plans regarding a specific decision and inquire of the Lord for guidance (e.g., Gen. 24; Acts 1:12–26). There are also examples where believers have a specific plan that they are submitting to God for his approval (e.g., 2 Sam. 7:1–17). James 4:13–17 fits in the latter category.

The wide variety of ways God's will is conceptualized and referenced in Scripture can lead to a variety of understandings of passages such as Psalm 37:4; John 7:17; Romans 12:2; 2 Corinthians 8:5; Ephesians 5:17; and 1 Peter 4:2. The general point that James 4:13–17 helps make clear is that all of life is to be lived under the sovereignty of God, not just with regard to moral issues but business and travel plans as well. How this works itself out in each and every situation will vary, but the attitude of submission to God as Lord will be constant.

Teaching the Text

In the West, our economic situation is such that the number of people in the audience to whom 4:13–17 is directly applicable has grown substantially from the time James wrote the passage. Most of us today are financially independent enough to be able to make the kinds of plans and decisions that James is speaking of in 4:13. For this reason, the teacher may decide to stay simply within the realm of financial decisions when teaching this text. If, however, it is necessary to broaden the application, decisions about whom to marry, what educational path to follow, and so on, are all fair game.

As is often the case in this epistle, James employs two arguments against overconfident boasting about the future. He begins with the wisdom argument: What control do you have over your life? He then moves to the sin argument: speaking and acting in such a way sets yourself up as claiming power that belongs only to God. Therefore, the person teaching this passage should address both arguments. The foolishness of being overconfident about the future can be illustrated easily (see below) and should receive wide acceptance, but the more important point is not just that things never seem to work out as planned but the idolatrous claim that such boasting makes about who we are in relation to God. Most people will see it as harmless to plan their own futures apart from God's guidance; some will agree that it is foolish to do so, but the majority will not think of it as evil.

The tendency of many Christians to sometimes habitually and thoughtlessly add the phrase "Lord willing" (or DV, which stands for the Latin *deus volent*) to any future plans means that anyone teaching this passage should address the underlying issue of outward obedience to this command versus obedience in heart. Anyone can add the words "Lord willing" to future statements, and likewise, most people can tack on a few thoughts about God's sovereignty after all their plans have been made. But James has in mind a life lived at all times in awareness of God's will and who God is. To submit to God is to submit all our future plans to him. That will entail a radical reordering of how we go about planning for the future.

It also seems wise when teaching this passage to make note of the communal nature of what James is saying. His concern is not just with private plans of individuals but with the kind of arrogant boasting about the future that comes out in the midst of community. Those who discuss and plan in the community for the future apart from God contribute to deceiving others into believing that the future is in our hands and not God's.

Illustrating the Text

Being overconfident about the future is foolish.

History: There are many examples of people who made confident claims that turned out to be completely wrong, sometimes with comedic effect and sometimes with tragic consequences. Mathematical economist Irving Fisher confidently proclaimed in 1929, three days before the Great Depression: "Stocks have reached what looks like a permanently high plateau." In 1977, Ken Olsen, founder of Digital Equipment Corporation, stated, "There is no reason anyone would want a computer in their home." Darryl Zanuck, a movie producer at Twentieth Century Fox, said in 1946 that television wouldn't last because "people will soon get tired of staring at a plywood box every night." "The Beatles have no future in show business," a Decca Records executive told the band's manager, Brian Epstein, in 1962. "We don't like your boys' sound. Groups are out; four-piece groups with guitars, particularly, are finished." Phillip Franklin, vice president of the White Star Line, which had produced the *Titanic*, stated, "There is no danger that *Titanic* will sink."[2]

Don't make plans without consulting God.

Personal Testimony: A few years back I was returning from Israel with a group from our church. It was February. We had just arrived in Newark. It was about six in the morning on a Tuesday. We found out that our flight to Grand Rapids had been cancelled because of snow. We also found out from the airline that the whole East Coast was going to be shut down for the next few days because of snow and that they were rebooking us on flights for Friday, three days later. It was amazing that although we had just spent ten days in Israel studying the Bible, the natural inclination of most in our group was not to gather to pray. Instead, almost everyone hurried to rebook flights on other airlines. When that option didn't look possible, it was off to the rental car companies to try to rent cars to drive home. When that option looked way too expensive, people began to call around the city looking for passenger vans that we could rent that would be less expensive. The whole time people were on their smartphones trying to figure out weather patterns and which airport hub to fly into in order to give us the best chance to make it home if we could get a flight. None of these options opened up. After all our efforts, we gathered together as a group to pray. When we finished praying, twenty-five seats (just enough for our group) opened up on a different flight back to Grand Rapids, and we made it home safely. God was merciful, but we should have consulted him first.

Robbing Your Workers

Big Idea

Believers who selfishly pay their employees unfair wages must repent or face God's judgment.

Key Themes

- Hoarding wealth and possessions is dangerous.
- God is concerned for the financially oppressed and mistreated.

Understanding the Text

The Text in Context

This is the third practical application following the basic teaching of 3:13–4:10, which stressed that pride, envy, and selfish ambition destroy peace in the community. James 5:1–6 applies that teaching to the issue of selfish employers robbing their employees through unfair wages so that they themselves might live luxuriously. While this topic is related to the second application in 4:13–17 in that both have something to do with wealth and business, this is clearly its own topic. That can be seen in 5:1 from the repetition of the phrase "come now" (NIV: "Now listen") from 4:13 and the change of address from "you who say" to "you rich people."

Money and mercy are favorite topics for James, and to this point he has discussed luxury and trials (1:9–11), favoritism toward the rich (2:1–13), and helping those in need (1:27; 2:14–16).

Structure

James 5:1–6 begins with a call for repentance, followed by two roughly parallel sections, each with warnings of danger followed by accusations of guilt.

1. Call for abusive rich landowners to repent (5:1)
2. Warnings of danger: the possessions of the rich will testify against them and eat away at their lives (5:2–3a)
3. The primary accusation: storing up wealth in the last days by defrauding employees (5:3b–4a)

4. Heightened warning of danger: the Lord Almighty has heard the cries of the defrauded (5:4b)
5. Expanded accusation: living in selfish luxury and oppressing the poor (5:5–6)

Interpretive Insights

5:1 *you rich people.* Is James addressing believers here? Commentators are divided on this issue. On one hand James's comments seem overly harsh—more in the style of prophetic diatribe against the nations—and there is seemingly no encouragement to repent. If these are not Christians, then the purpose of this section is to encourage the Christians experiencing oppression from their nonbelieving bosses and/or to warn nonbelievers in the community.[1]

On the other hand, the arguments for seeing these as rich Christians are stronger. First, while the language is harsh, James has already accused his believing readers of being murderers (4:2), adulterous enemies of God (4:4), and double-minded sinners (4:8)—hardly gentle language. Jesus is just as harsh when he addresses wealthy Christians in Revelation 3:14–18. Second, the Old Testament prophetic diatribe style James draws on was applied equally to Israel (cf. Amos 8). Third, the passage does include a call to repentance in 5:1 (see below). Fourth, James is furious that his readers have hoarded wealth "in the last days" (5:3). For a Christian this would add to their guilt, but why add this comment if James is speaking about nonbelievers? It is also important to note that James is addressing not all rich Christians but specifically rich Christian landowners who are hoarding wealth by failing to pay proper wages.

weep and wail because of the misery that is coming on you. "Weep" is the same word in the exact form as in 4:9. James is calling his readers to repent and begin the process of submitting to God in 4:7–10. There is misery coming, because God "opposes the proud" (4:6).

5:2 *Your wealth has rotted, and moths have eaten your clothes.* This is perhaps a reference to the teaching of Matthew 6:19–20, but it is used here in a more condemning way. Jesus was speaking about the potentiality and eventuality that moths and rust will destroy one's possessions. In James, because the landowners have stolen their resources by failing to pay the workers, moths and rust have *already* destroyed their possessions. To the human eye, the landowners are dressed in luxurious clothes, but in God's eyes they are wearing filthy, moth-eaten robes.

5:3 *Your gold and silver are corroded.* "Corroded" means "completely rusted through" and worthless. This is how we know James is speaking metaphorically and not literally about their possessions. Gold is the most nonreactive of all metals and cannot be eaten or rusted away. Silver too is remarkably durable.

Their corrosion will testify against you and eat your flesh like fire. There are two problems with the money and possessions the rich have stored up. (1) The corrosion testifies to the guilt of the rich person. It is almost as if the rich person's gold and silver will take the witness stand and testify against the rich in a court of law. (2) This corrosion will destroy the rich. The word for "corrosion" can also be translated "poison," as it is in 3:8. Not only does corrosion make possessions worthless; it also makes them dangerous if the corrosion is acidic or poisonous. James is saying that the money and possessions you have stolen are eating away at you, destroying your life. Job 20:12–29 is a vivid picture of this destruction for those who oppress the poor, including the imagery of the rich person's own possessions being self-destructive poison and fire.

When does James envision this happening? For some, "the last days" and "fire" in 5:3 point to judgment day, with 5:7 as the confirmation of this. Surely James is not excluding judgment day, but the immediate future is primarily in view, just as it is in Job 20:12–29. "Fire" represents the damage that hell can do to and through believers *now* (3:6); the cries of the harvesters have reached the ears of the Lord Almighty *now* (5:4); and God opposes the proud *now* (4:6). The prophetic imagery is that when God arises and responds to the cries of the harvesters—which can be at any time—the rich person's possessions will testify against them and bring about their downfall.

You have hoarded wealth in the last days. This is the main accusation. The problem is not wealth. It is the rich person's selfish desire to hoard wealth, which led them to steal from their employees through underpayment. This is intensified because these are "the last days," a reference to the fact that the blessings of the hoped-for future promised in the Old Testament have begun to occur in the here and now (e.g., Isa. 2:2; Hosea 3:5; Mic. 4:1). This use of "last days" for James may recall the unforgettable event of Pentecost, when Peter quoted Joel 2:28–32 and declared believers to be living in the last days (Acts 2:17). One of the memorable characteristics of the early church in Jerusalem was their willingness to share their possessions (Acts 2:45; 4:32–37). Surely this made a huge impact on James. For Christians to hoard wealth and steal from other community members in the last days was intolerable (cf. Acts 5:1–11).

5:4 *wages you failed to pay.* Another way to translate this is, "the wages that have been stolen by you." James uses the word for steal that in Mark 10:19 refers to "appropriating someone else's possessions" and is effectively parallel to "You shall not steal."[2] (It is also used in 1 Cor. 6:7 of one Christian monetarily cheating another Christian.) Given James's propensity to cite the Ten Commandments and another allusion to the sixth commandment in 5:6, we should see this accusation in terms of a direct violation of the eighth commandment.

cries of the harvesters. The cries of the harvesters and the crying out of the stolen wages in 5:3 link to 5:1, where the rich are told to weep and wail (or "cry out"). Although different words are used, the connection is that just as those who were oppressed cried out to the Lord, so the rich need to cry out in repentance to God. Also, if by reading this somehow the rich could be encouraged to cry out in repentance before the cries of the workers reach the Lord, the rich would spare themselves great trouble.

Lord Almighty. Or Lord *Sabaōth*,[3] or the Lord of hosts. The title points to God as the commander of the armies of Israel and ruler over all. This militaristic language about God links this section to 4:6, where James used militaristic fighting language in the phrase "God opposes the proud." When the cries of the harvesters reach the Lord of hosts, he gathers himself for battle to bring down the proud oppressors (cf. Exod. 2:23–25).

5:5 *luxury and self-indulgence.* In 5:5–7 James piles accusations one on top of another, each building on the original accusation of hoarding wealth (5:4). Living in luxury and living self-indulgently are the first two. For the rich, their own pleasure and comfort are their only priority. They live lavishly, well beyond the bounds of what is appropriate. Their desire to spend what they get on their own pleasures is the embodiment of the attitude of 4:3.

You have fattened yourselves in the day of slaughter. Can you imagine a sheep trying to make himself look as fat as possible on slaughtering day when the fattest lambs are the ones that are killed? James is saying to the rich, "You think that you have provided for yourself a comfortable lifestyle that is free from trouble, but you are actually earnestly begging for trouble. You have chosen the path that puts you directly into the line of God's fire. God is preparing to hand out judgment, and you are jumping up and down yelling, 'Pick me, pick me!'"

5:6 *You have condemned.* "Condemned" brings to mind passing judgment in 4:11–12 and 2:4. To fail to be generous to those who work for you is to judge them as less worthy than you to receive fair compensation.

murdered. As in 4:2 the "murder" is most likely not literal. On the trajectory of things considered murder, withholding good from the poor and failing to pay proper wages are somewhere between cursing and actual murder. This is James's regular pattern of naming sins in the starkest of terms: cheating one's workers and hoarding wealth are stealing and murder.

the innocent one, who was not opposing you. A few commentators believe "the innocent one" refers to Christ, but this is highly unlikely—especially if James is talking about Christians, as we have argued here. This phrase does position James's teaching within the larger realm of the righteous sufferer who is being oppressed, of which Christ is the ultimate example. But its use here seems more pedestrian—the poor who are being exploited through improper wages have done nothing wrong that would merit such treatment.

Theological Insights

Beginning especially with Israel's captivity in Egypt (e.g., Exod. 1:11–12; 3:9; 22:21–27), God's care for the poor and oppressed and hatred of economic oppression of the poor are major themes in the Scriptures. Job 20; Psalms 82:2–4; 147:5–9; Proverbs 22:16; Isaiah 10:1–4; Ezekiel 18; Luke 4:18; 20:47; and 1 Corinthians 6:7–8 are just a few of the many passages that address this theme. Within this broader theme, there is also the idea of the destructive nature of hoarding wealth and living in abundance (e.g., Job 20:12–29; Prov. 30:8; Eccles. 5:12–13; Luke 12:13–21; 16:19–31).

Teaching the Text

The link to 3:13–4:10 is very important when teaching this text. The call to repentance in James 5:1 is not clear unless one realizes that "weep and wail" is a reference to "grieve, mourn and wail" in 4:9. So too, the implicit warning of 5:4 that "the cries of the harvesters have reached the ears of the Lord Almighty" is made explicit through the connection to 4:6, where God is said to actively oppose the proud. Finally, it is easy to surmise that the rich are hoarding wealth and oppressing the poor because of selfish desires, but 3:13–4:10 links those selfish desires to being influenced by worldly wisdom and satanic manipulation. The teacher may not have to explicitly draw out those connections for the hearers but should at least know that they are there.

One must also decide to whom 5:1–6 applies today. I have argued here that this passage was originally aimed at James's Christian readers, but the prophetic warnings against economic injustice can also be applicable to non-Christians. Further, what specific modern situations are relevant? Clearly, wealthy employers who fail to pay proper wages to those who work for them are directly in view. This can be everything from the minutia of refusing to tip wait staff at restaurants to corporate decisions to outsource work to sweatshops. What about fair-trade goods? What about unnecessarily laying off employees in a recession to maximize profits? What about overworking exempt employees? What about using temp workers or keeping people just below full time so you don't have to pay for benefits?

It may be necessary for the teacher to point out that the emphasis in 5:6 on the "innocent one" excludes situations where an employer has to fire an employee who has been embezzling money, for example. It may also be necessary to emphasize that this passage is not talking about employers who are struggling to pay the bills and unable to give raises. It is about those who are growing rich by unfairly compensating those who work for them.

Although dealing with fair compensation provides plenty of material and is the primary application of this passage, this text can be used to address the broader problem of the rich hoarding wealth, living luxuriously, and refusing to be generous even apart from work situations.

As for the strategy of teaching the material, James has arranged his material such that there is a call to repentance followed by two sets of warnings and accusations. Some Western audiences may relate better to this order: accusations, warnings, then call for repentance; but regardless of the order, all three elements should be present to truly teach what James has here.

Illustrating the Text

God cares for those who have been financially victimized.

Bible: **Luke 16:19–31.** Tell the story of the rich man and the beggar Lazarus. This biblical story is probably the best illustration of how God feels about those who are victimized and those who ignore them.

Those who store up their own wealth at the expense of the poor will face God's punishment.

History: History is replete with examples of rulers who lived high on the hog while their people starved. "Let them eat cake," Marie Antionette is (wrongly) reported to have said when told her people were starving (historians have now shown that the callous statement predated her rule). A similar statement is often attributed to an ancient Chinese emperor who, being told that his subjects didn't have enough rice to eat, replied, "Why don't they eat meat?"[4] The ongoing power of these statements, whether actually uttered or not, shows how history itself heavily censures those indifferent to suffering that they are in a position to alleviate.

It is far better and more lasting to expend our resources in worthwhile, heaven-oriented pursuits than in selfish endeavors.

Humor: Have you heard the one about the man who hoards money all his life and begs God to allow him to bring something with him? God says he can bring whatever he can fit into one suitcase. Thinking the best thing to take would be gold bricks, the man buys a dozen, loads them into the suitcase, and arrives in heaven. As he brings the gold bricks through the pearly gates, Peter asks him, "I was wondering, of all the things in the world you could bring in your suitcase, why would you bring pavement?"

Literature: **The Hunger Games Trilogy, by Suzanne Collins.** In this series of novels and related movies, a near-starving population is kept in check by a ruthless government. Each year, they are made to face the horror of "The Reaping," when young people from each district of the empire are dragged away from their homes and forced to fight to the death in the Hunger Games. The entire population of young people from the districts is put into a lottery, and names are chosen for representatives from each district, who will be transported to the capital to participate in the elaborate games, with great fanfare. But in James, those who hoard worldly wealth and show no generosity are like the affluent and frivolous people in the capital in The Hunger Games Trilogy. They are people who expend untold sums for oppression and for their own entertainment instead of using that money to alleviate the suffering of others.

Quote: **Pliny the Younger.** In one of his letters, the Roman statesman Pliny writes, "An object in possession seldom retains the same charms that it had in pursuit."[5] His words remind us that the *promise* of wealth always falls short of our hopes. How tragic it is, then, to risk our very souls in accumulation!

Wait for God

Big Idea

Wait patiently for the Lord's coming without complaining or trying to control things.

Key Themes

- Have patience and persevere in the midst of suffering.
- The Lord's coming is near.
- Do not grumble against others.
- We cannot guarantee the future, though we try.

Understanding the Text

The Text in Context

James 5:7–12 and 5:13–18 draw to a close the application sections from 3:13–4:10 as well as begin to draw to a close the entire epistle. These two sections are connected through the idea of the presence of God. In 5:7–12 the focus is on God's future presence manifested in and through the second coming of Christ. Because the focus is on the future, the key idea that is stressed is patience. In 5:13–18 the focus is on God's current presence and availability to his people, and therefore the key ideas that are stressed are prayer and community.

James 5:7–12 performs three functions. First, it continues on from 5:1–6 to discuss the broader concept of suffering (see the comments on James 5:6). Second, in returning to the issue of suffering that began the epistle, 5:7–12 begins to close the whole epistle, while the admonition against grumbling recalls the theme of appropriate speech that has been so important in James. Third, 5:7–12 functions as the fourth application of the truths of 3:13–4:10 about pride and submission to God, this time within the context of difficult situations.

Structure

Three commands make up the skeletal structure of 5:7–12: (1) be patient and stand firm (5:7–8); (2) do not grumble (5:9); and (3) do not swear (5:12).

The first command is primary, and the two negative commands support it. In other words, "be patient and stand firm, not complaining or swearing while you wait." Three examples provide flesh for the bones: farmers (5:7), the prophets (5:10), and Job (5:11).

The relationship between the two negative commands is important. Many have assumed 5:12 is a stand-alone verse. But in Greek, 5:9 reads, "do not grumble . . . so that you might not be judged," and 5:12 reads, "do not swear . . . so that you might not fall into judgment." Further, when it is understood that swearing is a means to assert control (see the comments on James 5:12, below), the parallels between 5:9 and 5:12 become clear: be patient in the midst of suffering, and do not complain about others or try to take control of the situation and usurp God's place.

Interpretive Insights

5:7 *Be patient.* Patience is the key idea in this passage. The verb "be patient" (*makrothymeō*) appears twice in 5:7 and once in 5:8, and the noun "patience" (*makrothymia*) appears in 5:10. Related words, the verb "persevere" (*hypomenō*) and the noun "perseverance" (*hypomonē*), each appear once in 5:11. Is there a difference between "patience" and "perseverance"? Potentially "patience" emphasizes the time element, in the sense that "waiting patiently" means waiting longer than one would like in adverse circumstances. With "perseverance" the pressure and stress are emphasized: to persevere is to endure great difficulties.

then . . . until the Lord's coming. "Then" connects this section not only to the rest of the letter (see "The Text in Context," above) but also to the previous section, 5:1–6. There are probably two aspects of the previous section that lead to this one. First, if James is aware of those who are rich exploiting others for financial gain, he is probably aware of those among his readers who have been exploited for financial gain. This allows him to return to the broader theme of patiently enduring suffering, with which he began his writing. Second, conceptually God's acts of judging/saving in history are linked to God's judgment/salvation at the end of history. James's warning of God's impending judgment and discipline of the rich for their exploitation of the poor in 5:1–6 provides the opportunity as well to turn to the broader theme of the Lord's second coming in relation to suffering now. This is because, while God does discipline oppressors and help the oppressed in the here and now, the ultimate solution to the problem awaits Christ's return.

autumn and spring rains. Israel experiences three seasons of rain, but the two most essential for the farmer are mentioned here: autumn rains in October–November and spring rains in March–April. The spring rains were especially anticipated in that they were necessary for wheat and barley harvests in late spring.[1] The image of rain brings to mind absolute dependence on God, who controls the weather. Israel was given not a land fed by the Nile but one that drinks in rain from heaven, so that they would stay dependent on God (Deut. 11:10–12).

5:8 *the Lord's coming is near.* A double meaning is intended here. "Near" means near in time, that is, "soon" (as in Rom. 13:11–12; Heb. 10:25). But "near" also means near in space, that is, "nearby" or "at hand" (as in Matt. 3:2; Luke 10:9–11). The word for "coming" (*parousia*), when used of Jesus, almost always refers to the second coming, which is in the future. And the primary frame of reference thus far in 5:7–12 has been the future. But the verb "is near" is in the perfect tense, which usually indicates something that has already been put into place and that has continuing effects. So besides the emphasis on Christ's future second coming, there is also a sense that James is saying the Lord is nearby his readers now, that they should wait for him to rescue them from their sufferings in some ways before the second coming. This ambiguity of Jesus (or his kingdom) being both already present in some sense and not yet present in another runs through much of the New Testament. While 5:7–12 has a stronger emphasis on the "not yet" aspect, 5:13–20 emphasizes the "already" aspect.

5:9 *Don't grumble against one another.* James 5:9 is closely linked to 4:11–12. Both mention speaking against other believers as well as the concept of judging and the Judge. One of the great temptations during times of trial and suffering is to grumble and complain against others, as Israel in the wilderness repeatedly did to Moses and Aaron (Exod. 15–16; Num. 14; 16; 17). Instead of waiting for the Lord to bring help, it is easier to look around for others to blame.

you will be judged. The Judge is standing at the door! Here again one can see the already / not yet of Jesus's presence in 5:8. In one sense the concept of Jesus as Judge pictures the final judgment at the second coming. But this Judge is already standing at the door, and this language emphasizes the reality of experiencing Jesus's discipline now (see the parallel in Rev. 3:19–20). James's point is that those who grumble will experience discipline from Jesus in part now and some level of judgment from Jesus at his second coming.

5:11 *The Lord is full of compassion and mercy.* This phrase is linked in Greek to the previous phrase, so that it could read, "what the Lord finally brought about because the Lord is full of compassion and mercy." James wants his readers to know that everything that happened to Job, both good and bad, happened because the Lord is full of compassion and mercy. The same is true for them while they wait for God to act.

5:12 *Above all . . . do not swear.* "Swear" refers to swearing oaths, not the use of vulgar profanities. But why does James bring up the swearing of oaths? The issue is authority and control of the future. To swear the kind of oath James has in mind is an attempt to assert one's control of the future with regard to a particular situation.

Hebrews 6:13–20 is illuminating in this regard. In that passage the writer says that God wanted to promise Abraham descendants, and to confirm his intentions he swore by himself. In the midst of his argument, the author of Hebrews tells us that is why humans swear too—to confirm that what they said will happen actually will happen. Interestingly, in Hebrews 6:15 it says, "so after *waiting patiently*, Abraham received what was promised." Abraham could not control the future, so he had to wait patiently for God, who could control the future. Abraham doesn't say, "I swear to God, I am going to have a baby." Instead, God says, "I swear by myself that you are going to have a baby." When it comes to dealing with life, the one who swears is the one who controls the future; the one who waits is the one who can't control the future. To wait is to trust God to make things right; to swear an oath is to trust yourself to make things right.

Swearing oaths as a means of wrongly claiming control can be seen in Matthew 5:33–37, which records Jesus's teaching on swearing that James is referring to. In that statement, Jesus commands believers to refrain from swearing by heaven, earth, Jerusalem, or your own head, since "you cannot make even one hair white or black." In other words, since you can't control what happens to you, do not swear and try to assert that you can. (On what swearing an oath might look like in times of trouble, see "Illustrating the Text," below.)

This is the same idea that underlies James 4:13–17. If a Christian making plans for the future without acknowledging the Lord's will is bad, then certainly oaths regarding the future are even worse. Both are forms of a lack of submission to God.

This is why James prefaces his statement with "above all." Whereas grumbling and complaining about suffering are bad (5:9), the worst thing someone can do in the midst of suffering is to attempt to usurp God's place and claim control over the future.

Otherwise you will be condemned. Matthew's version of Jesus's statement on swearing ends with "anything beyond this comes from the evil one" (Matt. 5:37). Satan's modus operandi is to displace God, and this is an expression of his primary sin, that of pride. When we swear oaths, we are exercising pride and insubordination as we attempt to usurp God's place in determining our lives.

Theological Insights

On the idea of Christ's coming being "near in time" and "near in space," 5:7–12 is part of a larger theme in the Scriptures often referred to as an "already/not-yet" framework or "inaugurated eschatology." An example of this already/not-yet framework can be seen in Jesus's presentation of the kingdom of God as something that is both present (e.g., Matt. 6:33; 11:12; 12:28; Mark 10:15; Luke 17:21) and future (e.g., Mark 9:47; 10:23–25; 14:25; Luke 13:28).[2] Likewise, there is already new creation in Christ (2 Cor. 5:17), and we are awaiting the new creation (Rev. 21:1–5); we know God in part, but we will know him fully (1 Cor. 13:12); and we have been saved (Eph. 2:8), but we are still awaiting our future salvation (Phil. 3:20).

Teaching the Text

With one overarching command (be patient and stand firm), two supporting commands (do not grumble, and do not swear oaths), and three examples (farmers, prophets, and Job), 5:7–12 provides a straightforward structure and ready-made illustrations for teaching this material. The two supporting commands fit nicely with the overarching command, because the two strongest temptations while one is suffering are to complain (grumble) and to try to control the situation (swear an oath).

James 5:7–12 also fits well with 5:13–20 for a two-part series on the presence of God, with 5:7–12 focusing on the future coming of Christ and the need for patience and 5:13–20 focusing on the present reality of God's presence and the need for prayer.

The two biggest hurdles facing the teacher of this text are (1) explaining the meaning behind swearing oaths in 5:12 and (2) deciding how to handle the dual perspectives on the nearness of God. With regard to swearing oaths, the commentary explained that this is an attempt to guarantee the future and supplant our need for trusting with self-reliance. We all want to take matters into our own hands when we are suffering and to fix the problem. Such oaths are attempts to take the future out of God's hands and put it into our own. There may be a need to stress that it is not the exact wording that makes something an oath but the attitude of trying to guarantee the future to oneself or others.

The second hurdle is deciding how to approach the dual perspectives on the nearness of the Lord. On the one hand, the teacher can focus only on the "near in time" perspective and preach or teach this passage in light of Christ's imminent second coming. At that time patience will be rewarded, suffering will end, and judgment will come upon those who have grumbled or sworn oaths. On the other hand, the teacher may feel compelled also to address the "near in space" perspective that God is already near to us and therefore the rescue that we are waiting for from God and judgment for grumbling and swearing will come to some extent before Christ's second coming. After all, not only was Job waiting for the day of the Lord; he also was waiting for God to show up in his life at some point before that and bless him—and God did.

While both perspectives are in this text, the near-in-time/second coming is emphasized and shouldn't be excluded. The teacher may choose to leave the near-in-space perspective for 5:13–20, where it is the focus.

Illustrating the Text

Swearing an oath is an attempt to control a situation of suffering.

Bible: See 1 Samuel 25:22, where David makes an oath, showing that he has resolved to take matters with Nabal into his own hands instead of waiting for God (1 Sam. 14:24 would be another example). A modern-day example is a person who has been betrayed by an adulterous spouse saying, "I swear to God I will never let that happen to me again."

Waiting is the hardest part.

Film: *Waiting for Guffman.* This movie is a fictional "documentary" about a small town's sesquicentennial celebration, featuring a local theater troupe attempting to produce a musical they unrealistically hope will make Broadway. Early in the film, the director of the musical receives a confirmation letter that a representative of a New York City production company will send someone to review the musical: Mr. Guffman. The rest of the drama unfolds around the deep tension created by pairing outsized hopes with subpar writing, terrible acting, and what-one-would-expect production values. Waiting for Mr. Guffman makes everything else much more difficult.

Human Experience: Describe different situations of waiting: for example, purchasing a gift you can't wait to give a good friend, waiting to see what your new hair color will look like, the time between engagement and marriage, hungrily waiting for a table in your favorite restaurant, waiting for results from a cancer-screening test.

Situations that require patience tend to strain relationships.

Scenario: Have you ever been part of a company "team-building exercise"? The object is to help a group of coworkers band together, overcome obstacles, and realize that each member of the team is a valued player in achieving common objectives. These lessons are typically taught by putting participants in situations that require extra measures of patience and careful communication. The tasks can vary—fitting five people on a stump the size of a soda can, blindfolding the team and forcing them to untangle a rat's nest of rope, and, of course, doing trust falls. Inevitably, participants are forced to deal with impatience. Hard-charging competitors have to slow down and listen to thoughtful, deliberate doers. Lone rangers learn that tasks can be completed only through teamwork. Sounds a lot like life, doesn't it?

The Power of Prayer

Big Idea

Earnest prayer is powerful and effective, and those who are sick and troubled, especially, should engage with God through the community in prayer.

Key Themes

- Prayer is powerful and effective.
- God brings healing through prayers of faith.
- Faith is submitting to God's plan in our sickness.
- Confessing sins to one another in community brings healing.

Understanding the Text

The Text in Context

James 5:13–18 is the penultimate section of the epistle and the mirror image of 5:7–12. James 5:7–12 focuses on waiting for the future coming of the Lord and stresses patience; 5:13–18 focuses on the present availability of the Lord to his people and stresses prayer. Both sections have the undercurrent of submission to God and his will. James 5:13–18 also concludes the five areas of application of pride or submission to God coming out of 3:13–4:10.

As the first of the concluding sections of the letter, 5:13–18 picks up themes from the opening two sections, including troubles, prayer, and faith (1:2–12), and sin (1:13–18). Elijah is also the final example from the Old Testament and connects 5:13–18 with 5:7–12 (Job and the prophets) and 2:14–26 (Abraham and Rahab). This section prepares the reader for the closing section, 5:19–20, as it discusses healing/saving and sin.

Structure

The opening verse, 5:13, introduces prayer as the activity for believers during the present time. The next two verses, 5:14–15, provide specific instructions regarding prayer by elders for the sick. From there, James transitions to more-general comments about the power of prayer in 5:16–18.

Interpretive Insights

5:13 *Is anyone among you in trouble? Let them pray.* The opening question marks the thematic transition from 5:7–12. Instead of grumbling (5:9) and trying to take control of difficult situations (5:12), believers should not only wait patiently for the Lord's coming but also pray for God's help now. "Trouble" is a general category intended to cover a broad range of issues, just like "trials of many kinds" in 1:2.

sing songs of praise. These four English words translate one verb in Greek. It is used three other times in the New Testament, all connected to corporate worship (Rom. 15:9; 1 Cor. 14:15; Eph. 5:19). Note especially 1 Corinthians 14:15, where singing and prayer are tightly linked, as they are here. Singing songs of praise is a form of prayer.

5:14 *Is anyone among you sick?* For modern Westerners, the word "sick" usually conjures up images of germ-induced illness or physical problems with natural causes. But James is working from a worldview in which sickness can be mental, physical, emotional, or spiritual and is often viewed as the result of satanic power. (Note, for instance, Acts 19:12 and 2 Cor. 12:9–10, where the same word translated here as "sick" is used of that which is caused by demonic forces.)[1]

Let them call the elders of the church. The responsibility for seeking help is placed on the shoulders of the person who is suffering. Of course James wouldn't rule out leaders taking the initiative to seek out those who haven't specifically requested healing (e.g., John 5:1–15; Acts 3:1–10). But here he is emphasizing the need for the sick to call the elders of the church. To do so is an act of submission and obedience on the part of the sick and therefore a tangible expression of faith. The elders are not called because they are more spiritually mature than everyone else in the church, but because they were responsible for shepherding and caring for God's flock (Acts 20:28; 1 Pet. 5:14). This responsibility included healing the sick (cf. Ezek. 34:4). Additionally, elders were part of the authority structure that God set up and therefore in some ways they represented Jesus and the authority Jesus has given to the church.[2]

anoint them with oil. Mark 6:13 is the other passage in the New Testament that connects miraculous healing with anointing with oil. The oil symbolizes three things: (1) Oil is medicinal (Luke 10:34) and is associated with joy (Ps. 45:7; Isa. 61:3) and so provides a natural symbol for healing. (2) Anointing with oil symbolizes the power and presence of the Holy Spirit (1 Sam. 16:13; cf. Luke 4:18; Acts 10:38), so that the joy of healing is connected with the work of the Spirit. (3) In the Old Testament, anointing with oil symbolizes that something is set apart as belonging to the Lord (e.g., Exod. 29:21; 40:9; Lev. 8:10–12, 30). The person who is anointed with oil belongs to God, meaning that God is responsible for taking care of them.

in the name of the Lord. This phrase imbues the elders' actions with spiritual authority and power. "In the name of the Lord" appears just a few verses earlier, in 5:10, to refer to prophets commissioned by the Lord to speak in his power and authority. Here James envisions the elders of the church having access to the same power and authority to ask for healing in Jesus's name (cf. Matt. 18:19–20) as well as to deal with any satanic influences that might be contributing to the suffering (cf. Luke 10:17–19; Acts 16:18; 19:13).

5:15 *the prayer offered in faith will make the sick person well*. Is James guaranteeing that the sick person will be healed? Inherent within the concept of praying *in faith* is the idea of submission to God and his will (as in 4:13–17). To offer a prayer in faith is to approach God with the attitude that God knows whether or not healing is best for us. However, as in 1:5–8, to ask God for something in faith means believing that he will respond. In the New Testament, healing is often linked to faith, and the stronger the faith, the better (Matt. 9:22; 15:28; Mark 10:52; Luke 17:19; Acts 14:9).

Mark 9:14–29 provides an important illustrative story for understanding what James means by "the prayer offered in faith." In Mark 9 Jesus's disciples are unable to cast the demon out of a certain man's son who was experiencing epileptic-like seizures. Jesus's rebuke of the disciples ("you unbelieving generation," 9:19), his interaction with the boy's father ("Everything is possible for one who believes," 9:23), and his grace to take even the weakest of faith and make it stronger ("Help me overcome my unbelief," 9:24) all demonstrate the necessity of faith. At the end Jesus declares that this kind of demon comes out "only by prayer" (9:29), which makes this an example of the "prayer offered in faith" and its power to heal.

Whose faith is James referring to? The elders'? The sick person's? That of friends who may be accompanying the sick person? At first pass, we might think it is the elders', since they are the ones praying and in Mark 9 it was the disciples' lack of faith that was the problem. On the other hand, it was the father's faith on behalf of his son that Jesus ultimately used. And if the son was able to have faith, we should imagine that this would have been sufficient. So the point is that God can work through anyone engaged in the time of prayer who has the faith to believe.

If they have sinned, they will be forgiven. "If" indicates both that sin is a possible cause of the sickness and, at the same time, that this is not automatically the case.

5:16 *confess your sins to each other and pray for each other so that you may be healed*. The scope now broadens to a more general principle: communal confession and communal prayer bring healing. This broadening will continue in 5:17–18, so perhaps we are to see James indicating that elders praying for the sick, including confession, is a specialized and more powerful form of general prayer for one another, which is a specialized form of prayer in general. Higher-profile or more-difficult cases of sickness may require the higher level of authority invested in the elders, but communal prayer and confession can still be effective in other cases.

5:17–18 *Elijah was a human being, even as we are.* James preemptively dismisses a possible objection to his use of Elijah: "Of course God answered Elijah's prayers. Elijah was a spiritual superstar and an important prophet, but I am a nobody." There is no difference between Elijah and James's readers when it comes to prayer. As in 1:5, where *anyone* could ask God for wisdom and God would answer *all* who asked him, so here there are no extraordinary humans with unique access to God, just an extraordinary God whose power is available to all who are willing to pray.

He prayed earnestly. Note the emphasis on earnest prayer. In 1 Kings 18, Elijah sends his servant to look for rain seven times, presumably continuing to pray more and more earnestly each time the servant returned and there was no rain. In the immediate context, 1 Kings 18 is a puzzling choice of example since it is not a healing story. Yet in a broader perspective, the miracle of rain provides a tie back to 5:7 and the patient farmer waiting for God to provide rain. That picture is now complemented by the earnestly praying prophet who has the power to stop the rain and then to have it begin again. By citing such an extraordinary example with regard to rain and drought, James raises the expectations of his readers as to what they can accomplish through prayer. It would have been hard for James's readers to hear 5:17–18 and think any Old Testament miracle was off-limits to them. The other effect of James's choosing a nonhealing miracle is that we understand he is now talking about all prayer and not just prayers for healing.

Theological Insights

James 5:13–18 makes an important contribution to broader scriptural themes on three fronts. First, 5:13–18 is an important teaching on the issues of healing, sickness, and sin. Sometimes sickness is a result of sin (e.g., 2 Kings 5:27; John 5:1–15)—whether because of God's discipline (e.g., 1 Cor. 11:30) or through the influence of Satan (e.g., 2 Cor. 2:10–11; Eph. 4:26–27). Sometimes sickness is not a result of sin (e.g., Job 2:1–10; John 9). James helpfully articulates the middle way: *if* it is the result of sin, confessing that sin in the context of the elders or Christian community is a part of the healing process.

Second, 5:13–18 is relevant to any discussion of faith, prayer, and healing. Other passages, such as 2 Corinthians 12:7–10 and 2 Samuel 12:15–18, must be considered lest we conclude that all prayers offered in faith will result in healing. While prayer and faith do not guarantee healing, they are a major factor in healing.

Third, since James envisions this healing taking place within the local church, 5:13–18 gives clear teaching regarding the role of community in the process of care and healing. More specifically, certain levels of divine power and authority have been invested in the church and its leaders (cf. Matt. 16:18–19; 18:15–20; 28:18–20; Acts 8:17; 1 Cor. 5:4–5; 2 Tim. 1:6).

Teaching the Text

Since 5:13–18 presents both specific teaching on prayer for healing and broader teaching on the power of prayer, the teacher can choose either or both of these emphases to focus on.

If teaching specifically on prayer for healing, there are four issues the teacher should consider. First, modern notions of "sickness" are narrower than what James had in mind. Sickness for James included physical, emotional, mental, and spiritual weakness—struggles like depression, cancer, overwhelming struggles with anger, hearing evil voices in one's head, and so on. Much of this is connected to spiritual warfare for James, as it still is today.[3]

Second, the connection between sin and sickness is tricky but important. There is not always a direct link, but many times there is, especially when operating with a view of sickness that includes demonic influence and oppression. Sins like anger and an unwillingness to forgive are doorways through which Satan brings sickness into our lives.

Third, the role of the local church may also be a stumbling block for listeners. Verse 16 affirms that confession and prayer among a generic group of Christian friends are helpful in bringing healing, but James also gives specific instructions regarding calling the leadership of the local church to pray and anoint them with oil. It may be necessary to address this as an issue of obedience and submission to God whether we understand or agree, much like in the story of healing from 2 Kings 5:11–14.[4]

Fourth, how should 5:15 be handled? Often our tendency is to want to qualify what James is saying about the prayer offered in faith making the sick person well. This is understandable since we know the damage that is caused when someone thinks God has committed himself to heal all prayers offered in faith when God has not. And the teacher needs to deal with this. However, James's point is *not* why God doesn't always heal but to convince his readers to pray to God for healing. Our teaching of this material should accomplish the same by emphasizing that God does heal through prayer.

If you are teaching more generally on prayer, there are two important points to keep in mind. First, my experience in teaching this material is that James's insistence that Elijah is just like us is incredibly important. Most believers today feel that people in the Bible were special people living during unique times and that such power is not available to us. James explicitly attacks that notion, and the teacher should too. The listener should leave with the sense that God's arm is not too short and there is nothing beyond the power of God, which is available to the one who prays earnestly.

Second, it may be important to flesh out what earnest prayer looks like. For me, earnest prayer is emotionally engaged (e.g., Heb. 5:7; 1 Sam. 1:1–20; Neh. 1:4), physically exhausting (Gen. 32:22–32; Luke 22:39–44), persistent (1 Kings 17:19–22; Matt. 15:22–28; Luke 18:1–8; 2 Cor. 12:8–9), and time consuming (Deut. 9:18–19; Luke 6:12–16). Mark 14:32–42 is a beautiful picture of all these.

Illustrating the Text

Confession is a critical part of healing prayer.

Human Experience: Many who have suffered a serious wound have recognized the need to have the wound cleaned and dressed so that healing can take place. For example, if the wound is the result of imbedded broken glass, healing will not take place until the glass is removed. Even after removing the glass, it is still necessary for the wound to be cleaned and for the one doing the cleaning to be free from contaminants, lest the wound become infected. In the same way, when a Christian needs healing prayer, confession is necessary—both because confession removes any sin that might be directly causing the sickness and because confession causes the sick person and those asking for healing to be pure so that true healing can take place.

Prayer is powerful.

Quote: **Charles Spurgeon.** Spurgeon tells this interesting story on the power of prayer:

> I have reminded you before of the father who had prayed for many years for his sons and daughters, and yet they were not converted, but all became exceedingly worldly. His time came to die. He gathered his children about his bed, hoping to bear such a witness for Christ at the last that it might be blessed to their conversion; but unhappily for him he was in deep distress of soul, he had doubts about his own interest in Christ. He was one of God's children who are put to bed in the dark; this being above all the worst fear of his mind, that he feared his dear children would see his distress and be prejudiced against religion. The good man was buried and his sons came to the funeral, and God heard the man's prayer that very day, for as they went away from the grave one of them said to the other, "Brother, our father died a most unhappy death." "He did, brother; I was very much astonished at it, for I never knew a better man than our father." "Ah," said the first brother, "if a holy man such as our father found

it a hard thing to die, it will be a dreadful thing for us who have no faith when our time comes." That same thought had struck them all, and drove them to the cross, and so the good man's prayer was heard in a mysterious manner.[5]

Just as in the days of Elijah, God still heals.

Personal Testimony: Roughly a decade ago, our church began to implement James 5:13–18 in earnest. Our elders make themselves available for healing prayer with anyone in the congregation who wants it, either during a scheduled time or as part of a walk-in session on the first Tuesday of every month. We ask people to bring friends and family and think through if there is any sin in their life; we anoint them with oil and pray and ask God to heal them. Although we don't keep statistics, my sense is that over the past ten years we have seen about 25 percent healed miraculously with no medical intervention, another 25 percent healed through medical intervention, and another 25 percent for whom God provided some level of miraculous spiritual healing, guidance, reconciliation, or something else that was being asked for. And about 25 percent received no healing but great peace from God as they walked through their trials. Among those miraculously healed, we have witnessed God remove cancer, eliminate back pain, cast out demons, overcome insomnia, remove panic, heal kidneys, and much more.

Rescuing Sinners

Big Idea
Christians must care for each other by working to restore those who wander from the faith.

Key Themes
- Believers can experience physical death because of their sins.
- Restore those who wander from the faith.
- Wandering from the faith is the ultimate sign of immaturity.

Understanding the Text

The Text in Context

James 5:19–20 is the closing section of the book. If its ending seems abrupt, it is because we are used to the more personal endings of many Pauline Epistles. But other, nonbiblical letters from the time of James lack a letter closing.[1] In this regard, James is similar to 1 John—another letter written for wide circulation that lacks a formal letter close.

The last two verses of James tie together both the theme of God's presence in 5:7–18 and the entire letter. With regard to 5:7–18, through patience and prayer believers experience God's presence. The opposite of this and the worst thing one can do in dealing with the struggles of this life is to wander away from the truth.

With regard to the entire book of James, those believers for whom trials create doubts about God (1:2–12), who are drawn away by sin and enticed (1:13–18), who are hearers but not doers (1:22–25; 2:14–25), who favor the rich of the world (2:1–13), who cannot control their tongues (3:1–12), and who are overly influenced by satanic, worldly wisdom and refuse to submit to God (3:13–5:6)—it is these who are in danger of walking away from the faith. Additionally, the fact that 5:19–20 addresses not those who are walking away from the faith but those who can turn a person from the error of their ways reemphasizes that James is writing about maturity lived out in a communal setting. The readers of James are responsible not only for themselves but for helping others.

Structure

1. The twofold condition: if someone walks away from the truth and someone brings them back (5:19)
2. The result: saving a sinner from death (5:20)

Interpretive Insights

5:19 *if one of you should wander from the truth.* The Greek that James has used to form the conditional clause is purposefully as general as possible,[2] so we should be careful not to narrow down too far what this means. James must have in mind Christians being swayed by false teaching, since the other use of the word "wander" is in 1:16, where he speaks about being deceived regarding the goodness of God. However, it is safe to assume from the rest of the letter that anything James has discussed is fair game: being eager for money (cf. 1 Tim. 6:10), pride, envy, coveting, impatience

Restoring Christians or Saving Non-Christians?

Is James speaking of believers in the community who have wandered away from the faith and are restored to true fellowship? Or is he speaking of nonbelieving community attenders who wander away from their interest in Christianity but are ultimately sought out and brought to faith? Or could it be that James has in mind Christians who leave the faith, lose their salvation, and then are saved again?

The lack of clarity comes from the dual meanings of the phrases James uses. "If one of you" sounds like it refers to believers, but the phrase can also mean "if one among you" and might indicate non-Christians in the community (cf. Matt. 13:24–30; 1 Cor. 14:23; 1 John 2:19). "Wander" is a word that is used sometimes to refer to the state before conversion (e.g., Matt. 18:12; 1 Pet. 2:25) and sometimes to refer to postconversion wanderings (e.g., Luke 21:8; Heb. 5:2). "Sinner" can refer to either a Christian (e.g., 1 Tim. 1:15) or a non-Christian (e.g., 1 Pet. 4:18). Likewise, "save from death" can refer to a non-Christian being saved from eternal separation from God or a Christian being rescued from physical death because of the consequences of sin.

While the language can be ambiguous, the context of this passage in James clarifies it. Although it is possible that 2:1–12 envisions rich and poor non-Christians visiting the community, James's primary concern has been the successes and failures of Christians in the community (even in 5:1–6). "Sinner" is used one other time in James and refers to believers (4:8). Equally important, the major discussion of sin and death in 1:13–18, the only other time James uses the word "death," refers to believers. "Save" is used by James for both eternal salvation (2:14; 4:12) and rescue for believers (1:21; 5:15), but the proximity of 5:15 and the connection of 1:21 to the discussion of sin and death in 1:13–18 are decisive. As a result, it is best to understand James as talking about Christian believers wandering from the truth and being restored again to fellowship.

or disappointment with God in the face of suffering, or being lured by sinful desires.

someone should bring that person back. The verb "bring back" and the verb translated "turns" in 5:20 are the same verb (*epistrephō*). James doesn't say explicitly how a believer or group of believers goes about bringing back a Christian who has wandered from the truth. But there are a few things we can infer from the process.

First, the close relationship of 5:19 to 5:13–18 indicates that fervent prayer is key to the process. Luke 22:32 may provide confirmation of the role of prayer. In a tradition James probably knows, Jesus predicts Peter's denial and says to him, "But I have prayed for you, Simon, that your faith may not fail. And when you have turned back [*epistrephō*], strengthen your brothers."

Second, there is probably an allusion back to 3:3–5a. To turn a sinner back to God is like steering a horse or turning a ship. Using speech effectively to steer someone back to God is key as well. James may have in mind Jesus's teaching in Matthew 18:15–20 (cf. Luke 17:3–4) about believers confronting those who sin, since the notion of "winning them over" in Matthew 18:15 is similar to "bring that person back." This would provide an example of speaking to an erring brother or sister. If not Matthew 18, then surely James's own example of instruction and vigorous argumentation in this letter provides the guideline as to what he intends with regard to bringing back erring believers.

5:20 *will save them from death*. James 1:13–18 is central to understanding what is meant here. In that passage James informs his readers that believers are susceptible to temptation, which leads to sin and finally death. "Death" in 1:15 cannot mean eternal separation from God. What it does mean is the loss of everything that one might think of with regard to life: fellowship with God, meaningful relationships with others, fruitful labor, joy, health and strength, peace, and even physical life. That a Christian can experience this kind of death even while still physically living is clear from Romans 6–8 (cf. 1 Cor. 5:4–5; Rev. 3:1–2; see also the comments on James 1:14–15 above). Moreover, Acts 5:1–11 and 1 Corinthians 11:30 make clear that a Christian may experience physical death as well, as a result of sin.

The notion that sin leads to death comes from the theology of the Old Testament, crystallized in Deuteronomy 30:11–20, where Moses lays before the Israelites the offer of life if they obey God and death if they disobey God. An aspect of that death for Israel was exile from the land (Deut. 30:18). With this background, 5:20—the last verse in James—forms a powerful inclusio with the first verse in James and the reference to "the twelve tribes scattered among the nations" (1:1). The twelve tribes were scattered because they wandered from God. Believers must not make the same mistake. Even though their sin will not result in eternal separation from God because of their faith in Jesus, decisions to sin in this life still result in discipline, suffering, pain, distancing oneself from God, and quenching his Spirit.

As background, Ezekiel 3:20–21 is also noteworthy. Based on the same Deuteronomic framework of life and death, God acknowledges that righteous people can turn from their righteousness. If they do, God says he will place a stumbling block before them and they will die. Ezekiel is urged to help turn the righteous from their sin to save them from death (see also Ezek. 18:24–32). Interestingly, God says that if Ezekiel turns a righteous person from their sin and back to God, Ezekiel will have saved himself. This has caused some commentators to think that the phrase "save them from death" in James 5:20 applies to the person who restores and not to the one who is restored, which is possible in Greek. But the NIV has given the right sense in the translation. The one saved from death is the sinner, just as the emphasis throughout Ezekiel is on sinners being saved from death, not Ezekiel saving himself from death.

cover over a multitude of sins. The sins being covered are those of the rescued sinner, not the rescuer. Some have seen an allusion to Proverbs 10:12, but there is a more likely connection to Psalm 32:1: "Blessed is the one whose transgressions are forgiven, whose sins are covered." This psalm describes the experience of death on the part of the one who has walked away from the Lord (32:3–4) and the blessings of experiencing full and free forgiveness for all the sins that have been committed. This is the promise of grace that James says is available to those who have walked away from the Lord. The use of "multitude" lets the reader know that no matter how many sins have been committed in walking away from the Lord, they are all taken away when one turns again to God.

If Psalm 32 is connected to David's sin with Bathsheba, as traditionally thought, this adds further depth to the parallel in that David wandered away from the truth through the sins of adultery and murder and Nathan is the one who turned him back. This is what James is urging his readers to do—to care enough about others in the community of faith who are wandering away from the truth to help rescue them from sin and death.

Theological Insights

James 5:19–20 fits theologically with other texts about confronting and restoring believers who have fallen into sin or error. There are many narrative accounts of this throughout the Scriptures (e.g., 1 Sam. 25; 2 Sam. 12; Neh. 13; John 21:15–19; Gal. 2:11–14). Most of the prophetic tradition is applicable to this as well.

Whereas 5:19–20 does not give instructions on what to do in case the believer does not return and repent, such instructions can be found in Matthew 18:15–20; 1 Corinthians 5:1–5; and Titus 3:9–11, among other places.

Galatians 6:1 and Jude 22–23 provide warnings regarding the process that are also absent from James 5.

Teaching the Text

Teachers who wish to use 5:19–20 as an opportunity to summarize and close out the entire letter need to look at wandering from the faith as the end point of the spectrum of immature and sinful behavior James has been speaking about. Not being patient in suffering, being polluted by the world's wisdom, showing favoritism, speaking against other believers, and the rest lead one down a path away from the faith. Conversely, seeking to restore a wandering brother or sister can be seen as the epitome of a mature Christian. Only a mature Christian can control the tongue and use it for this kind of good; it would be a demonstrable act of faith and an opportunity to exercise the power of prayer, and it would make one a doer of the Word. In this way, the teacher can tie together much of what James has taught in this last section.

Along the same lines, 5:19–20 can provide an opportunity to emphasize the communal nature of maturity and the need for fellow believers to look out for one another. In this way too the passage provides an opportunity to address the fact that believers in the community are responsible for one another. Favoritism, slandering, robbing the poor, quarrelling, and refusing to help those in need tear a community apart, but restoring wandering sinners builds community.

Another way to use 5:19–20 to close the letter is to realize that James is closing by telling his readers to do what he has been doing. In writing this letter, James has been attempting to turn wandering Christian sinners from the errors of their ways as well as to protect others from making those same mistakes. Now the readers are instructed to do likewise. The whole letter of James becomes an illustration for how to correct, rebuke, and encourage with great patience and careful instruction, as 2 Timothy 4:2 says.

If the focus in teaching 5:19–20 is more on explicit content of the passage and less on the passage as a conclusion to the letter, it is important to note that James is addressing the rescuers and not those who need to be rescued. The teacher most likely should do the same.

There are two ideas that James seems to want communicated to the rescuers: (1) It is a great thing to rescue another believer. Sometimes there is so much emphasis on saving the lost that we lose track of the greatness of rescuing someone who has wandered from the truth. (2) Compassion and grace are central to the act of rescuing another. On the one hand, it is the rescuer who must be unselfishly motivated by compassion and grace. It is often easier to leave alone those who wander lest we provoke their anger or say something that risks our relationship with them. But James's point is that the wandering sinner is experiencing and will experience death. On the other hand, James is drawing on the compassion and grace of God. His mention of covering a multitude of sins is important because those who wander from the truth can accumulate staggering amounts of sinful behavior and may believe the lie that there is no way back for them. There is no one in the book of James who needs more mercy or who will experience more hardship and oppression than one who has wandered from the faith.

Finally, this question may need to be answered: how does a Christian go about turning a wayward believer? While much more can be said from the rest of the New Testament, from James alone it seems that the answers must be prayer—5:19–20 follows after 5:13–18 for a reason—and speaking words full of wisdom from heaven (chap. 3), exemplified in James's own presentation.

Illustrating the Text

Our sins can lead to physical death.

Anecdote: Shortly after being called to serve a church, a young pastor was asked to perform a funeral for the relative of a church member. New to the community, the pastor did not know this family, but he was more than willing to help in their time of need. He learned that this relative had not been a church member and, in fact, had led a life far from church. He had died in his fifties. During a segment of the service, the friends of the deceased stood and shared memories of him. One thread wove its way through it all: "He liked to have a good time." After the service, the young pastor walked around, looking at the collections of photographs the family had assembled. In every single picture, the man was holding a drink in his hand—beer, whiskey, or some other alcoholic drink. In most, a hazy, glazed-eye face grinned at the camera. It was so sad to see how a "love for the good time" had ended.

Wandering is a sign of immaturity.

Film: Up. In this animated film, a mad genius has fitted a pack of fierce dogs with a collar that allows them to speak and express themselves like humans. These dogs are like the man's minions, doing his diabolical bidding. But there is one thing he could not unprogram from the animals: they are still easily distracted by squirrels. This gives way to some funny scenes. One of the dogs will be midsentence then suddenly stop, jerk his head, and shout "Squirrel!" In the same way, immature humans can have their attention diverted by all kinds of things. It is a mark of maturity to be able to shut out the distractions that can divert us, misdirect us, or lead us to wander away from God, the one who should be our focus.

We must restore those who wander.

Bible: Tell the story of Mark. This disciple was an early travel companion of Paul and Barnabas. However, we read that at one point he abandoned them midmission. When it came time to head out again, Paul was unwilling to take Mark. Barnabas, on the other hand, did not want to give up on the young man. So they parted ways (Acts 15:36–40). Barnabas invested in Mark. Eventually, his work must have paid off, for Paul himself would later praise Mark as a helpful brother (2 Tim. 4:11). Other scriptural examples of restoring those who wander include Nathan rescuing David from his sin with Uriah and Bathsheba (2 Sam. 12), and Paul helping Peter and Barnabas recognize their sin of discrimination with regard to eating with gentiles (Gal. 2).

Introduction to 1 Peter

First Peter explores the gift of salvation with special attention to God's sovereignty and Christian suffering. God's call makes believers elect exiles in this world, requiring us to live differently, resulting in suffering as we wait for Christ's return. This suffering is an opportunity to prove our faith, follow the example of Jesus, win others to Jesus, and experience God's unique grace through the Spirit and in the community of faith. The goal of 1 Peter is to form a community of people who live in submission to God's will and are faithful witnesses to God's salvation in a hostile world.

Importance of 1 Peter

The value of 1 Peter cannot be overstated. Other than Jesus, no other person is mentioned as often in the New Testament or plays as large a role in the establishment of Christianity as Peter. Peter is prominent in the Gospels and Acts. The sense of importance that Paul attributes to him in 1 Corinthians and Galatians is unparalleled among the other disciples. In addition he wrote two epistles of his own. Such sustained overall prominence is unmatched by Paul, James, or even John. There is no one else whose successes and failures are catalogued so completely for us. Peter was also present at major key events of Jesus's life, including the transfiguration, the Last Supper, the resurrection, and the ascension. He heard firsthand the Sermon on the Mount, the Olivet Discourse, and Jesus's private interpretation of his parables. To have two epistles from this apostle is a blessing. First Peter is the more complete epistle, addressing a range of important topics, like the already/not-yet character of salvation, fearing God, the church, God's sovereignty and grace, spiritual gifts, elders, hospitality, evangelism, submission, governing authorities, husbands and wives, spiritual warfare, and more. As a whole, 1 Peter covers many of the important topics of the faith. It does so in a way that shows clear connections with Jesus's teaching, is built on the Old Testament, and complements masterfully the teaching of Paul and the other writers of the New Testament.

Although 1 Peter covers a wide range of topics, the twin themes of God's sovereign plan and the suffering of Christians tie the whole epistle together. Given that Peter struggled so mightily with the notion of righteous suffering (Matt. 16:21–27; John 18:10–11; cf. John 9:1–2) and experienced so much suffering himself, to have an epistle written by him on the role of righteous suffering is truly wonderful. Furthermore, since suffering is such an integral part of every true Christian's experience, 1 Peter is an invaluable book for every believer to spend time working through.

Author, Setting, and Date

While some scholars dispute that the apostle Peter was the author of 1 Peter, there are no substantial reasons for denying the claim of the letter itself (1:1). Concerns about the quality of Greek in 1 Peter overlook the fact that he probably grew up in a bilingual context, speaking Greek fluently.[1] Being "unschooled" (Acts 4:13) indicates a lack of formal theological education and not an inability to read or write Greek. Referring to Rome as Babylon (5:13) does not require a post-70 date (see commentary at 5:13).

Peter's theology complements Paul's more than it reproduces it. Peter's reading of Isaiah 53 (1 Pet. 2:21–25), his theology of the church (2:4–9), and his emphasis on wives married to non-Christian husbands (3:1–6) are just a few of the many examples.

Most likely 1 Peter was written from Rome (Babylon in 5:13 = Rome) to believers in provinces in Asia Minor, many of whom were gentiles who may have been experiencing some level of state-sponsored localized persecution but were more generally simply experiencing suffering in many different forms. The probable dates are in the early 60s, given that this is when Peter was in Rome. Church tradition tells us Peter was martyred under the emperor Nero, who himself died in AD 68.[2]

Theological Themes and Suggestions for Teaching

Theologically, 1 and 2 Peter fit well together, and the teacher may want to consider teaching them together if possible.

The primary themes in 1 Peter are summarized in 5:10–11: (1) salvation / God's grace; (2) God's sovereignty; (3) God's glory, including the evangelistic emphasis Peter gives to the notion of God's glory in his epistle; (4) union with

Christ and following the example of Christ; (5) the necessity of suffering, and the fact that suffering precedes glory; (6) God creating a holy people, including a strong theology of church as a witness to the world and a place where God's people receive grace to endure suffering. (See the unit on 1 Pet. 5:10–14 for more on these themes.)

Utilyzing the stories we have from Peter's life can be effective when teaching 1 Peter. For example, Peter knows what it is like to suffer at the hands of governing authorities (Acts 3–4; 12) and to be informed that it was God's will for him to suffer in ways different from other apostles and that God's glory would be manifested in his suffering (John 21:18–23). Peter knows the need to have one's faith tested and refined so that it shines like gold (Matt. 14:22–33). Peter understands the choice between a life of suffering for the sake of Christ and a life of pleasure (Mark 10:17–31), the value of hospitality (Mark 1:29–31), what serving each other in love looks like (John 13:1–17), and the reality of spiritual warfare (Luke 22:31–34). Peter knows what it is like to fail miserably (Matt. 16:22–23; 26:69–75; Gal. 2:11–13).

Because suffering is such a prominent theme in 1 Peter, it is important to think about what kind of suffering 1 Peter can rightly be applied to. Clearly, suffering persecution for being a Christian (4:14, 16) should be included. And it is just as clear that what 1 Peter has to say about suffering does not apply to those who are suffering as the consequence of immoral choices (2:20; 3:17; 4:15). But is there more?

Suffering for being a Christian includes not only outright persecution but also more subtle forms. Those who speak maliciously against your good behavior (3:16) and heap abuse on you (4:4) for good behavior may do so not explicitly because you are a Christian but simply because they are making fun of the behavior itself. Likewise, being accused of doing wrong (2:12) can include accusations of intolerance, narrow-mindedness, or unenlightened foolishness for believing biblical truths.

Taking this a step further, Peter seems to imply a general level of suffering that wives will experience if their husbands are not Christians. This would include loneliness at not being able to share a common commitment to Christ and difficulties of living with a man whose character is not being reformed by the Spirit. Similarly the "unjust suffering" (2:19) from a harsh master must include being subjected to abusive tirades at work or being discriminated against for refusing to sacrifice one's family for work. The fact that non-Christians may also be abused or discriminated against by the same boss does not nullify the suffering.

Furthermore, there seems to be suffering associated with being a part of the Christian community. This includes persecution that a community of faith might experience through being subject to burdensome or anti-Christian governmental regulations and the shared suffering that comes from loving others in the community who are being persecuted for their faith. This also includes the suffering Christian leaders experience when trying to shepherd the flock God has entrusted to them or that believers experience when leaders are not acting like true shepherds.

Finally, when Peter says believers suffer grief in "all kinds of trials" (1:6) and speaks of suffering as a result of Satan's attacks (5:8–9), this opens the door to realizing that suffering can include sickness, weakness, hardships, difficulties, and spiritual warfare.

So while suffering persecution for being a Christian should receive pride of place in teaching 1 Peter, the text should also be taught with a broader application of suffering in mind.

Opening Introduction

Big Idea

God, having chosen believers for salvation and alienating them from the world, is accomplishing this through the Spirit, who applies the blood of Christ to them, bringing about their obedience.

Key Themes

- Believers are exiles in the world.
- God the Father planned salvation.
- Jesus Christ made possible believers' participation in the new covenant through his blood.
- The Holy Spirit applies Christ's blood to believers and brings about obedience to God.

Understanding the Text

The Text in Context

First Peter 1:1–2 follows standard letter-writing procedure in naming the author and the recipients of the letter as well as offering grace and peace to them. In addition, the way that the author and recipients are introduced, including the discussion of Father, Son, and Holy Spirit in 1:2, provides an introduction to some of the main themes that will appear in the letter. Specifically, 1:3–12 will expand on some of the ways in which the Father, Son, and Holy Spirit have been and are at work in bringing about the believer's salvation.

Structure

1. Author and recipients of the letter (1:1)
2. An introduction of salvation being brought about by Father, Son, and Holy Spirit (1:2)

Interpretive Insights

1:1 *Peter.* "Peter" is the Greek translation of the Aramaic nickname Cephas that Jesus gives to Simon in John 1:42. Both Peter and Cephas mean "rock." As with other divine name changes, such as Abram to Abraham and Jacob to Israel, the new name has meaning associated with it. Peter is given the name in John 1:42, but it is not infused with meaning until Jesus correlates the name Peter (Greek, *petros*) with the word for "foundation rock" (Greek, *petra*) (Matt. 16:18). While Peter himself identifies Jesus as the cornerstone of the building in 2:7, Jesus affirms that Peter is foundational to what he is building.[1] This affirms both 1 Corinthians 3:11, where Jesus is the foundation, and Ephesians 2:20, where the apostles are part of the foundation, with Jesus as the cornerstone.

Jesus's declaration in Matthew 16:18 is no small matter. While the other apostles will be part of the foundation, no other disciple is ever singled out by Jesus for such a proclamation. The name Peter, then, has less to do with his character when it is given. Rather, it is a promise that he will become "rock solid" and the lead apostle, a first among equals. Peter's unique status is evidenced in that (1) in the four Gospels Peter holds a unique place of being the authoritative disciple; (2) in John 21 Peter alone is commissioned by Jesus to feed the sheep; (3) Peter receives his own individual resurrection appearance before the other apostles (1 Cor. 15:5; cf. Luke 24:34); (4) Peter is recognized by Paul as holding a unique position among the apostles (e.g., 1 Cor. 9:5; Gal. 1:18; cf. Gal. 2:9); (5) in the early chapters of the book of Acts it is Peter who is clearly the lead apostle; and (6) Peter is mentioned more times in the New Testament than any other human besides Jesus.

Therefore, Peter is not the foundation of the church, but he is foundational to the church. He also grows into his name in that, by the time of the writing of this epistle, Peter is now strong, firm, and steadfast—a rock that his readers can lean on for support in the midst of suffering.

an apostle of Jesus Christ. Given that Peter is the first among the apostles, the fact that he identifies himself as simply an apostle of Jesus Christ is an expression of the humility that Peter will urge on his readers in 5:5–6. The main role of an apostle is that of an authoritative witness testifying to who Jesus is and what God is doing in and through him (cf. Acts 1:8).

To God's elect. "Elect" is further defined by the context of 1:2—"chosen according to the foreknowledge of God the Father." With "God's elect" Peter sounds the first note of a major theme for his epistle, that of the sovereignty of God. Those who are believers in Jesus are so because God has selected them to be believers—something Peter learned from Jesus (e.g., Matt. 11:27; 22:14; Mark 13:20; Luke 18:7; John 13:18; 15:16–19).

exiles. Because Jesus has chosen believers out of the world, the world hates believers (John 15:19). Peter fleshes out that teaching here, using the language of "exiles." God's elect necessarily must be "exiles," or strangers and foreigners in this world. The word's other two occurrences in the New Testament are in 1 Peter 2:11 and Hebrews 11:13.

Peter is writing to believers "scattered throughout the provinces of Pontus, Galatia, Cappadocia, Asia and Bithynia" (1:1).

scattered throughout. The word for "scattered" is the Greek word *diaspora,* from which we get the English term "diaspora." Diaspora Jews were displaced people living as foreigners in countries not their own because of the reality of foreign empires oppressing Israel. By using such a word in connection with "exiles," Peter is saying that Christians are living in exile even in their countries of origin (see Heb. 11:13–16).

Pontus, Galatia, Cappadocia, Asia and Bithynia. These are five provinces in what is today Turkey. "Asia" refers not to the continent of Asia but to a specific Roman province on the western side of Turkey. Jewish people from Cappadocia, Pontus, and Asia were present at Pentecost and heard Peter's gospel presentation there (Acts 2:9). As a result, there would have been some knowledge of Peter in that region from the beginning of Christianity. How exactly the gospel came to some of these regions and to what extent, if any,

1 Peter 1:1–2

Peter was involved in the initial evangelization is unknown.[2] Paul did bring the gospel to Ephesus (which is in the province of Asia) and to southern Galatia, but he was prohibited by the Spirit from entering Bithynia (Acts 16:6–7). Some overlap between the ministry of Peter and Paul in these regions might account for the mention of both Silas and Mark (1 Pet. 5:12–13), who were connected with both apostles.

1:2 *who have been chosen according to the foreknowledge of God the Father.* With this phrase, Peter begins one of the great trinitarian passages in the New Testament. While the church will have to wait a few centuries to iron out the more formal language used for the Trinity, the willingness to acknowledge one God eternally existing in three divine persons comes out of passages such as this one where all three persons of the Trinity are presented together, with each fulfilling a distinct role in salvation. As is usually the case, Peter begins with God the Father. The Father has planned and decreed all that is happening, a concept already invoked by the use of the term "elect" in 1:1. Peter's other use of the term "foreknowledge," recorded in Acts 2:23, gives the sense that everything that has happened is a result both of God's preordained plan and of the actions of accountable humans (see the comments on 1 Pet. 2:8). Here the emphasis is not on human action but on God's planning. It is vitally important to Peter that those who are suffering for being Christians understand that God is in control of all things, and so Peter emphasizes at the beginning of his letter that God is working everything out in accordance with his plan.

through the sanctifying work of the Spirit, to be obedient. Although Jesus is often mentioned second, here it is the Holy Spirit. The sense here, throughout Peter's letter, and in the wider context of Scripture is that the Holy Spirit is God's empowering presence, who enacts the plans that God the Father has made.[3] The Spirit is the one who takes those the Father has chosen, sets them apart from the world, and works out their salvation in accordance with God's plan.

The NIV (and ESV) translate 1:2 so that believers are obedient to Jesus. But, it is more likely that the NET, HCSB, and NLT are right in connecting obedience to the Holy Spirit (i.e., "set apart by the Spirit for obedience and for sprinkling with Jesus's blood") so that the end goal of his sanctifying work is bringing about obedience to God the Father. This fits with 1:14–19, which refers to "obedient children" (1:14). "Children" implies obedience to the Father, whose judgment is the subject of 1:17. This obedience is possible because of the blood of Christ (1:19), the same truth present here. Of course believers are to obey Jesus, but in Peter's epistle the theme of obeying the will of God the Father, especially as it relates to suffering for the faith, is important, and that theme is foreshadowed here.

sprinkled with his blood. Peter closes his trinitarian introduction with the mention of being sprinkled with Jesus Christ's blood. Although Peter is talking now about Jesus, what he is saying is still within the domain of the sanctifying work of the Spirit, meaning that God the Father planned salvation; Jesus accomplished God's plan through his life, death, resurrection, and ascension; and the Holy Spirit enacts or applies what Jesus has done to the lives of believers.

The Greek word for "sprinkled" appears one other time in the New Testament, in Hebrews 12:24, where it is used in connection with the new covenant. Both 1 Peter and Hebrews are alluding to Exodus 24:8, where Moses sprinkles the blood of the covenant on the people of Israel. This was a covenant ratification ceremony showing that Israel accepted the terms of the Mosaic covenant and responded to God's offer to make them his treasured possession—a kingdom of priests and a holy nation (Exod. 19:3–6). Peter will apply Exodus 19 to his readers in 2:9–10. By mentioning sprinkled blood he is saying that through the Spirit believers in Jesus have signed the contract of the new covenant. Jesus uses this same "blood of the covenant" language during the Last Supper as he introduces the rite of communion, commemorating their participation in the new covenant (Matt. 26:28; Mark 14:24). Peter will return to this idea in 1:19 with his only other use of the word "blood" in this epistle (see the unit on 1 Pet. 1:13–25).

Theological Insights

The Trinity. First Peter 1:2 provides a concise picture of the working of the Trinity with regard to salvation. God the Father is the one who plans salvation, God the Son accomplishes the work of salvation, and God the Holy Spirit applies Christ's accomplishments to the life of the believer, bringing about the obedience that God desires. This fits with the fuller explanation found in Ephesians 1:3–14. Additionally, by mentioning all three members of the Trinity at the same time, 1 Peter 1:2 shows their unity, but in such a way that each must be distinct from the others. Other passages like this are Matthew 3:16–17; Mark 1:9–11; Luke 3:21–22; John 14:16–17; 1 Corinthians 12:4–6; 2 Corinthians 13:14; and Ephesians 4:4–6.

Teaching the Text

Some teachers may not feel the need for a separate teaching on the introduction to the letter. Admittedly, it is only two verses, and all the themes present in 1:1–2 reappear throughout the letter. It does, however, present an opportunity to introduce the five major "characters" of the epistle—Peter, the readers, the

Father, the Son, and the Holy Spirit—and this can be a good way to structure the teaching of this section.

When the teacher introduces Peter, it is notable that he chooses to use not his personal name, Simon, but his Greek nickname, Peter. This recalls Matthew 16:13–20, where Jesus infuses Simon's nickname with its meaning. It can be an important teaching point to note that in Matthew 16 Peter, the rock, is more of a potential stumbling block to Jesus (16:21–23) than a foundational rock for God's people. This tendency toward being a potential stumbling block is not an isolated incident (see also Matt. 26:31–35 [and 69–75], 36–46; Luke 9:28–36; John 18:1–14; and even Gal. 2:11–16). However, through the narrative of the Gospels and especially in Acts, we see Peter being transformed from a stumbling block to a rock-solid Christian. By referring to himself as Peter, the author may be calling attention to the fact that he has been transformed by God's saving power and his readers will be too. It also may be interesting to point out that as far as we know, this man is the first person ever called by the name Peter,[4] highlighting the completely new person that Jesus was making him. It also allows the teacher to introduce the fundamental role that the apostle Peter plays in the history of Christianity as the first apostle among equals. In many Christian traditions, Peter is underappreciated. Yet with Peter we have a man who was with Jesus from the very beginning and who heard everything that Jesus taught and saw everything of significance that he did. Finally, it is not an accident that after Peter's confession in Matthew 16 (and its parallels) Jesus introduces the idea of the suffering Messiah, to which Peter reacts so poorly. While the idea of suffering that is so central to this epistle can be connected to "exiles" or to Jesus's sprinkled blood, it can also be connected to the meaning of Peter's name and the discussion at Caesarea Philippi.

When the teacher introduces the readers, it may be helpful to note that while there were first-century readers to whom 1 Peter was originally addressed, all those who come to 1 Peter today are in mind when we think about the readers of this epistle. For readers today, drawing the connection between being elect and being exiles is important. John 15:19 is helpful in this regard. All believers who come to 1 Peter are coming to it as strangers in this world, and it is on this basis that Peter is addressing us. Those who are listening to 1 Peter today may not be able to articulate exactly why we feel estranged from the world, but in so many areas believers can feel lost in this world. This may be true in regard to moral standards, how the world spends its time and money, anti-Christian sentiment, incivility, where technology seems to be taking us, politics and war, or living in a world driven by selfishness and greed. Knowing that God has planned for us to be strangers in this world and addresses us directly in that position of being foreigners can be very helpful.

When the teacher introduces the Trinity, notice that Peter has summarized the role of each person of the Trinity in a way that can help listeners get a better grasp on how the Trinity works with regard to our salvation. The teacher may want to explain that the Father is the one who plans salvation; the Son is the one who executes the plan by becoming one of us, suffering, dying, being resurrected, and ascending to heaven; and the Spirit is the one who takes the results and applies them to us. Many of the major themes of the epistle are present here as well: God's sovereignty, union with Christ, the new covenant in Christ's blood, and the Spirit's work in bringing about obedience to God.

Illustrating the Text

Election and free will are different perspectives on the same event.

Human Experience: Ask most couples how they met, and you will hear two different takes on the same event, one told from the husband's point of view and one from the wife's (a literary example of this is Marilynne Robinson's *Gilead* [husband's point of view] and *Lila* [wife's point of view]). Both are true, but they can sometimes sound pretty different. The same is true for describing our salvation. "Elect" describes from God's point of view how we ended up having a relationship with God. It is Jesus telling Peter, "You did not choose me, but I chose you" (John 15:16). From our point of view, we may describe it differently, for example, "My brother told me about Jesus, and I soon came to believe he is Lord"—which is essentially how John describes Peter entering a relationship with God in John 1:40–42. Both perspectives are valid, though they sound different.

The exile experience is not easy.

Personal Testimony: My wife and I lived overseas for a few years. While there are many things that we enjoyed, we always felt like we didn't quite fit in—we didn't really understand people's worldview, how to interact with others was confusing, being American was not viewed favorably where we were (Europe) when we were there (beginning of second Iraq War), and our natural instincts of how to react to stressful situations were usually wrong. So too, being Christians in a world that is antithetical to God is difficult. The more you feel like a Christian, the less you feel like you fit into this world and its systems.

The Trinity accomplishes salvation.

Scenario: It takes a number of people to build a house. First, there are those who plan the whole thing (architect and general contractor). Second, there are those who must actually build the house (builders). Third, there are those who then make it possible for you to move into the house (realtor, banker, moving company). In this analogy, God the Father is the designer—choosing us for salvation and determining for our salvation to happen through Jesus's death and resurrection. God the Father is the one who has planned when Jesus will return. Jesus, then, is the skilled tradesman—accomplishing the work of salvation. He is the one who becomes human, gathers and trains disciples, dies on the cross, and is raised from the dead. He is the one who will return at the end to set up God's kingdom on earth. Finally, the Holy Spirit is the realtor, banker, and moving company that gets us into the house. He teaches us who God is and convinces us that our current living situation is terrible and that we should accept this offer of salvation from God. He is the one who helps us believe and understand what Jesus has done. The Holy Spirit helps us to pray and obey. He is the one who dwells with us, empowering us to enjoy and experience the salvation God planned and Jesus enacted. God the Trinity has every aspect of the process of salvation covered.

Our Present/Future Salvation

Big Idea

Believers should rejoice in God's salvation despite current sufferings, since these sufferings are all part of God's plan, testified to by the Old Testament prophets.

Key Themes

- Jesus's suffering and glorification are a model for our suffering and glorification.
- Present and future aspects of our salvation are accessed by faith.
- Experience joy in the midst of trials.
- God is keeping our future inheritance safe for us and preparing us for it.
- God's plan of salvation has been prophesied in the Old Testament.

Understanding the Text

The Text in Context

Having introduced his letter in 1:1–2 as being written to the elect who were chosen by the Triune God, Peter now dives into a section that explores the theme of election—namely, the salvation that God has chosen believers to participate in. Because these elect are also exiles in this world, Peter discusses their salvation in terms of both its present and its future dimensions. The next two sections, 1:13–25 and 2:1–3, will address Christian ethics that are necessary as a result of this salvation. Many of the themes that will play a role in future sections of the epistle are present here, including joy, sufferings, Jesus's own story, and God's sovereignty over all things.

Structure

"Joy" and "praise" are key markers of the subsections in 1:3–9. "Praise" opens verses 3–5; "greatly rejoice" in verse 6 transitions from verses 3–5 to 6–7; "praise, glory and honor" closes verses 5–7; and "rejoice/joy" in verse 8 is the center of that final subsection.

The connection of 1:10–12 to 1:3–9 is very important. Verses 10–12 tell us that our stories of suffering and salvation follow the pattern of Jesus's. Because Jesus's sufferings and subsequent glories were accurately predicted by the Old Testament prophets, we can have confidence that all of salvation is happening just as God has planned and therefore what Peter says in 1:3–9 will happen as well.

1. The present/future framework of salvation (1:3–9)
   a. The concept of salvation (1:3–4a)
   b. The future aspect of salvation (1:4b–5)
   c. The present aspect of salvation (1:6–9)
2. Salvation in its historical context: Jesus's story of suffering followed by glory, prophesied ahead of time (1:10–12)

Interpretive Insights

1:3–5 *Praise be to the God and Father of our Lord Jesus Christ!* This is the exact phrase that begins Ephesians (1:3) and 2 Corinthians (1:3).

has given us. Some translations have "gave us" (e.g., NET), but the NIV is correct that the context demands more of a sense of having been born into a new situation as opposed to viewing the new birth as a one-time gift given at some point in the past.

new birth into a living hope . . . into an inheritance. Salvation is defined by Peter as new birth into two things: a living hope and an inheritance. "A living hope" speaks to a future ("hope") characterized by life ("living") as opposed to a future characterized by death. This living hope is a result of Jesus's resurrection from the dead. "An inheritance" has a slightly different nuance. "Inheritance" usually refers to some tangible thing like money, possessions, or land (e.g., Matt. 21:38; Luke 12:13; Acts 7:5). Together "a living hope" and "an inheritance" represent the intangible and tangible aspects of salvation: eternal life, new relationships in the family of God, and a new purpose in life, as well as a kingdom, heaven's riches, and spiritual power. Just as being born into a biological family brings with it both physical life and access to the family's possessions and resources, so being born again into God's family brings both eternal life and access to the riches of heaven.

kept in heaven for you, who through faith are shielded by God's power. Here Peter employs two synonyms, "kept" and "shielded," to form a parallel: God is keeping our inheritance in heaven safe for us and keeping us safe for our inheritance. The point is that although suffering will happen in this life, believers will be shielded from experiencing more than they can handle (cf. 1 Cor. 10:13).

the salvation that is ready to be revealed in the last time. For people experiencing persecution and suffering, life often appears to be out of control. But God is fully in control. Our salvation is not dependent on present circumstances. It has already been accomplished. God is just waiting for the right moment to reveal it.

1:6–7 *in all kinds of trials . . . the proven genuineness of your faith.* In James 1:2–3 these same Greek words are translated, "trials of many kinds" and "the testing of your faith." In both passages trials are connected to the testing of one's faith, but James emphasizes the process of development and refinement. The testing of faith produces perseverance. Peter focuses on the final product: the faith that has been proved genuine.

praise, glory and honor. Whose? God's, ours, or both? Probably both. When the proven genuineness of believers' faith is made known, the God who has shielded believers by his power will receive praise, glory, and honor, and the believers whose faith it is—"your faith"—will likewise receive recognition for that faith. Both God's glory and believers' participation in that glory are strong themes throughout this letter.

1:8 *you love him . . . even though you do not see him now.* God expresses his love to believers by shielding them and caring for them during times of suffering. As a result, even though believers do not see Jesus during this time, they grow in their love for him through suffering.

you believe in him. Peter writes "believe in him" rather than simply "believe him." This observation, together with his use of the verb "love," highlights that Peter has in mind personal trust in Jesus in the context of a relationship with him. This is not just a statement that the readers are Christians. It is a statement that they are actively depending on Jesus in the midst of the sufferings and trials of daily life. The result of this active trust is joy. Joy in the midst of trials is the experience, not of all believers, but only of those who are loving Jesus and placing their trust in him in the midst of such trials.

1:9 *you are receiving the end result of your faith, the salvation of your souls.* Here the present and the future aspects of salvation merge almost paradoxically. How can believers be receiving *now* the *end result* of their faith? Because the future salvation promised in 1:5 is now becoming a reality in the lives of the readers through the reality of suffering and trials in life.

1:10–11 *searched intently and with the greatest care, trying to find out.* Three verbal elements are used: searched for, made careful inquiry, and inquired. Using three verbs emphasizes the intensity of the prophets' searching and heightens the sense of importance as well as the detailed nature of God's plan for salvation.

Spirit of Christ in them. All three persons of the Trinity are mentioned in 1:3–12, and Peter shows their interconnectedness by identifying the Holy Spirit as the Spirit of Christ, just as he identified God as the Father of our Lord Jesus Christ in 1:3. The Holy Spirit is said to have been "in" the prophets and not just having "come upon them."

when he predicted the sufferings of the Messiah and the glories that would follow. The fact that "glories" is plural allows for the fact that this refers not only to the resurrection, ascension, and return of Christ but also to the glory that results from Jesus's followers enduring suffering and being shown to have genuine faith (see 1:7). This ties the readers' sufferings and glory to Jesus's, so that our current sufferings can be seen as part of God's plan and incorporated into the story of Jesus (see 4:13).

What Old Testament passages does Peter have in mind when he speaks of the predicted sufferings and glories of the Messiah? Looking through the Epistles of Peter and Peter's speeches in the book of Acts, we can see a number of passages that Peter connects to either Jesus's sufferings, his glories, or both. These include Psalm 118:22 plus Isaiah 8:14; 28:16 (cited in 1 Pet. 2:4–6; Acts 4:11); Isaiah 53 (1 Pet. 2:22–25); Psalms 69:25; 109:8 (Acts 1:20); Joel 2:28–32 (Acts 2:17–21); Psalm 16 (Acts 2:31); Psalm 110:1 (Acts 2:34–35); Psalm 34:8, 12–16 (1 Pet. 2:3; 3:10–12); Deuteronomy 18:15–19 (Acts 3:22–23); Psalm 2:1–2 (Acts 4:25–28); and perhaps Deuteronomy 21:23 (1 Pet. 2:24; Acts 10:39; cf. Gal. 3:13). More broadly, Peter's comment recorded in Acts 3:24 that "indeed, beginning with Samuel, all the prophets . . . have foretold these days" reveals a much broader range of prophecies applicable to this situation, but these are surely a starting point.

1:12 *Even angels long to look into these things.* First, the mention of angels adds a numinous sense to what Peter is saying. So exciting is what God is doing that all of creation is interested, including celestial beings.[1] Second, it emphasizes the union of believers with Jesus. While angels are normally messengers involved in announcing God's plans, here they seem left out. Believers are suffering with Jesus, and believers will be glorified with Jesus. Salvation is not available to the angels.[2] Both of these aspects of salvation, the numinous and the exclusive, heighten its value.

Theological Insights

1. *Present/future salvation.* The biblical perspective on salvation is that it exists in an already/not-yet framework (see "Theological Insights" in the unit on James 5:7–12). Already the future has begun, but it has not yet been consummated. We have already been saved (Eph. 2:8), and we will be saved (Phil. 1:28). The kingdom has already come (Luke 11:20), and the kingdom is still coming (Luke 22:18). All things are already new (2 Cor. 5:17), and all things will be made new (Rev. 21:5). We already have eternal life (John 3:36), and we will inherit eternal life (Matt. 19:29). First Peter 1:3–12 is important in the way it presents this framework in one passage.

2. *Old Testament prophecies.* The prophecies of the Old Testament provide verifiable evidence of the truthfulness of the gospel and assurance of God's ability to bring about the salvation he has promised. This is an important theme for Peter (1 Pet. 1:10–12; cf. 2 Pet. 1:19–21; Acts 3:21–24) as well as for Jesus (Luke 24:44–47).

3. *Interpreting Scripture.* Rather than the oft-cited view that human authors were writing only with their original audiences in mind and therefore Scripture must be interpreted in light of its original context only, 1:10–12 suggests that Old Testament writers were conscious of their future audiences (see also Rom. 4:23–24; 15:4; 1 Cor. 9:9–10; 10:11). Such a thing is possible only if the Scriptures are divinely inspired, which makes interpreting the Bible unlike interpreting any other book.[3] On the broader theme of Scripture in Peter, see comments at 2 Peter 1:12–21 and 3:16.

Teaching the Text

First Peter 1:3–9 and 10–12 could easily form the basis of two complementary teachings. Verses 3–9 introduce the concept of salvation in its present/future framework, while verses 10–12 root our salvation in history, particularly in the story of Jesus and the prophecies of the Old Testament.

First Peter 1:3–9 is an especially good passage for addressing the question, how can believers have joy despite the sufferings of this life? Peter's answer comes in recognizing that joy is connected to salvation (both appearances of "rejoice/joy" in verses 6 and 8 are tied to the word "salvation" in verses 5 and 9). Because the present and future aspects of salvation are so closely tied

1 Peter 1:3–12

together, joy occurs in the midst of suffering for three reasons. (1) Through suffering believers experience God's shielding power (1:5). Most Christians who are suffering can identify ways in which God has protected them from the suffering being worse or provided strength to endure. Such active care and protection during the present shows that our inheritance is safe in heaven and that we will make it there. (2) Through suffering, believers receive evidence that their faith is genuine (1:7). Those who suffer and still believe in God can know that their belief is not simply mental assent, nor is it present merely because of peer pressure, cultural upbringing, or family influence, or for health and wealth. Since their faith is genuine, believers can be sure that on the day that Christ appears there will be praise, glory, and honor as a result of their faith. (3) Through suffering and the care believers receive from the invisible Jesus, they grow to love him more and to put their faith in him, which means that believers are getting now what they have been promised in the future, an ever-increasing love relationship with their Father in heaven through Jesus.

When you teach 1:10–12, it is important to show that Jesus's sufferings were part of the plan of God, not simply the result of human actions done against Jesus. This is evidenced by the fact that God prophesied about Jesus's sufferings hundreds of years before they happened. It may be important to teach some of the Scriptures that prophesied the sufferings and glories of Christ (many are listed above). But Peter is not bringing up the fact that Jesus's sufferings were predicted ahead of time just as an interesting apologetic for the truthfulness of the gospel. The teacher should tie together God's sovereignty over Jesus's sufferings with God's sovereignty over our sufferings.

Furthermore, the teacher could make the point that just as the Scriptures spoke of Jesus's suffering hundreds of years before it happened, they also spoke of our sufferings long before they happened. When we read the Scriptures and God speaks to us about our particular situation, we can know that what we are going through is not just the result of human actions against us or seemingly random bad luck, but it is a part of the plan of God. Since so much of Jesus's suffering is predicted in the Psalms, one practical thing a teacher can recommend to those who are suffering is to start reading in Psalm 1 and keep reading until you find your psalm—meaning the psalm that God has sovereignly chosen by the power of the Spirit to speak directly to you and your specific situation.

Illustrating the Text

Focusing on our promised inheritance will make perseverance possible.

Scenario: Imagine a man promising his twenty-five-year-old son that when the time is right he will inherit the company. How would that promise change the son's approach to work? Difficult assignments would become opportunities for joy because he is the future owner of the company. He would know that each assignment was given to him by a father who was preparing him for a promising future. And each challenge would draw him closer to the father who had such incredible plans for him. Likewise, when we think about our sufferings in light of the inheritance that God has promised to us, we realize that God is preparing us for our future, and this helps make sense of our present difficulties.

God's Word can bring joy.

Personal Testimony: A few years ago my dad died after a long, slow decline because of dementia. How does the interconnectedness of our present and future salvation bring joy in the midst of suffering? First, as difficult as my dad's slow death was, I look back and realize that if he had died quickly, I wouldn't have been able to handle it emotionally. When I did the funeral service for my dad, I felt God's sustaining grace. I can see now that although this was a hard event, God was shielding me from the full effect of it (1:4–5). Second, my dad's death proves the genuineness of my faith. I watched someone I love very much die, and it did not destroy my faith. I still believe that God is good. Therefore, my faith must be genuine, and I am not left wondering what will happen when I stand before Jesus (1:7). Third, my dad's death has taught me to love Jesus more. I don't know that I can explain how this happened, but it had something to do with the fact that throughout my dad's death God was so incredibly faithful. God never left me. He sent me home from work the day before my dad died to spend time with him. God wrote the funeral for me the night before my dad died. God was there with me when the funeral home came and took my dad's body away. Suffering gave God a chance to show me how much he loves me. And I grew in my love for him in return (1:8). For these reasons I experienced joy through suffering.

God gave us new birth into a living hope.

Humor: A group of men were sitting together at a restaurant. One of the men was in his early thirties, another in his early forties, and the third was fifty. The thirtysomething was as fit as could be, and the other two looked on while he consumed three meals' worth of food. The man in his forties turned to the man who had just turned fifty and said, "I can't eat like that anymore." The fifty-year-old replied, "Wait until you turn fifty."

In the natural world, as we get older we feel the coming of death in our physical bodies, our social relationships, our mental health, and more. But for Christians we have a living hope, which means our physical bodies will be resurrected, our social relationships in Christ will keep going into eternity, our labor in the Lord is not in vain, our eternal relationship with God will continue to deepen, and we will become more and more like Jesus with each passing year.

Be Who You Are

Big Idea

Believers in Jesus are already obedient children of God. Now they must live up to who they are by setting their hope on Christ's coming, being holy, fearing God, and loving one another.

Key Themes

- Set your hope on Jesus's return.
- Be holy because God is holy.
- Fear God, and love one another.
- The imperishable and enduring is far better than the perishable and fading.

Understanding the Text

The Text in Context

Having introduced in 1:3–12 the concept of salvation with its present/future framework that is rooted in the past, Peter begins to work out the consequence of such a framework—namely, the need to live out our salvation now. God has already declared us to be his children; he has redeemed us, and we have purified ourselves in obedience by believing the truth preached to us in the gospel.

Now Peter moves to the ethical imperatives that such an election to salvation demands. In this section Peter spells out the four central commands that believers must obey in light of this salvation: set our hopes on the coming grace, be holy, live in the fear of God, and love one another. The following section, 2:1–3, will spell out specific behaviors that flow out of these four commands as well as urge believers to embrace the spiritual growth that should come as a result of being chosen as a child of God. The major themes of the four imperatives will all resurface in 1 Peter: setting our hope on the coming grace (4:12–19; 5:10), being holy (2:4–10, 11–12), fearing God (2:13–17; 3:8–22; 5:1–9), and loving one another (3:8–22; 4:7–11).

Structure

The passage is organized around the four primary imperatives, with each command expanded by connected clauses.

1. "Set your hope," which is a way of preparing our minds; we do this by being mentally disciplined (1:13)
2. "Be holy," which includes not being conformed to our former evil desires (1:14–16)
3. "Live in reverent fear," which happens when we consider God as impartial Judge and realize that we have been redeemed by the blood of Christ (1:17–21)
4. "Love one another," which is the goal of our purification and has eternal value because we've been born again (1:22–25)

Interpretive Insights

1:13 *with minds that are alert and fully sober, set your hope.* Given the underlying Greek verbal elements (aorist participle, present participle, aorist imperative), the translation I favor here is "Prepare your minds for action by being mentally disciplined, and set your hope completely" (cf. NET). The main command is "set your hope completely," which is a more specific form of what "prepare your minds for action" means. Preparing one's mind for action—and, consequently, setting one's hope—happens through a process of mental discipline; that is, readers prepare through consciously forcing themselves not to dwell on their current circumstances, adversity, or character issues and not looking to money, politics, or personality to solve their problems. Instead, they are to focus their hope completely and totally on God's grace. See Psalms 33:12–22; 62:5–12.

1:14 *As obedient children.* The present/future framework from 1:3–12 can be seen here too. By setting our hope *now* on Jesus's *future* coming, we bring into focus what will be revealed at that coming—our status as obedient children of God. By urging his readers to not "conform to the evil desires you had when you lived in ignorance" (1:14) and to "be holy" (1:15), he is telling them to be who they will be and who in fact they already are. In other words, "You are a child of God—now live like one!" And, "You will be obedient children when Christ comes; be obedient children now."

do not conform to the evil desires. Compare this with Romans 12:1–2, the only other place this Greek word "conform" is used. For Paul, believers must not be conformed to the world. They must be transformed into being like Christ. For Peter, believers are not to be conformed to the evil desires we once had but to become like our Father.

1:15–16 *be holy in all you do; for it is written, "Be holy, because I am holy."* "Holy" has two related aspects to it: pure and set apart. This can be seen from the surrounding context in Leviticus of the verse Peter quotes. In Leviticus 11:44–45 the command to be holy refers to not eating certain animals. What one eats or doesn't eat is not an inherently moral issue, since Jesus declared all food as inherently clean (Mark 7:19; cf. Acts 10:15; Rom. 14:20). Rather, these laws have to do with being set apart from animals associated with certain things, like death. However, in Leviticus 19:2 the command to be holy refers to being pure with regard to inherently moral issues, like dishonoring parents, stealing, and lying. Both aspects—set apart and pure—are present in 1 Peter 1, because the main command to be holy follows on from a statement about obedience (i.e., purity) and leads to a command about living as foreigners (set apart) in this world.

1:17 *live out your time as foreigners here in reverent fear.* Peter continues to draw on Old Testament language and ideas. The fear of the Lord is one of the central themes of the Old Testament. Because God is holy (Isa. 8:13), to fear the Lord entails trusting the Lord only (Exod. 14:31), serving the Lord only (Josh. 24:14), loving the Lord only (Deut. 6:2–5), and obeying the Lord only (1 Sam. 12:14). Furthermore, fearing the Lord makes the Lord's people holy because it sets them apart as belonging to the Lord and causes them to obey him (Ps. 33:9–14). The notion of being foreigners is also connected to the Old Testament idea of fearing the Lord and being holy. Because Israel was set apart as God's people, when they went to Egypt they were foreigners there. This caused them to suffer and be mistreated, but they had an eye to a coming salvation that God would bring about (foretold in Gen. 15:13).

Because Christians are children of God, we are set apart as holy and are therefore to act holy—which means above all to fear God, trust God, love God, serve God, obey God, and look to God alone for help. As a result we are foreigners in this world, suffering mistreatment.

1:18 *handed down to you from your ancestors.* The word being translated here means "inherited from one's father or ancestors." Note the parallel with the child/father language of 1:14, 17. Children inherit patterns of behavior from their parents. Before Christ these were patterns of disobedience, but now, having been given a new Father, Christians are the recipients of patterns of obedience and holiness from God.[1]

1:19 *a lamb without blemish or defect.* To this point, Peter has alluded to Israel's sojourn in Egypt and time in the wilderness in the phrase "with minds fully alert and sober" (1:13),[2] in the quote from Leviticus 16:16 (1:16), in the reference to "foreigners" (1:17), and in the reference to "redeemed" (1:18). These allusions continue with a reference to Passover. During Passover, God redeemed the children of Israel through the sacrifice of a male lamb without blemish or defect (Exod. 12:5), which was a symbol of the coming sinless but still crucified Christ.

1:22 *love one another deeply.* Here is the fourth command in this passage. It is another example of "be what you are," since the phrase that immediately precedes it declares that believers already have sincere love for one another.

1:23 *you have been born again, not of perishable seed, but of imperishable.* What is the connection between being born again and loving one another deeply from the heart? Being born again places us into God's family, where we immediately have a connection with all other "newborn babies" (2:2). Since all believers are born of imperishable seed, we are all going to be in the same family forever. Even the very best and most glorious things that nonbelievers do for one another will ultimately fade away, just like the flowers—the most glorious part of the grass—will fade (1:24). But believers' relationships of love and acts of Christian kindness to one another will last forever since they are born out of the living and enduring word of God, the gospel (1:25).[3]

1:25 *the word of the Lord endures forever.* This quote from Isaiah 40:6–8 ties together a theme that Peter has been drawing on since 1:4 dealing with that which perishes (using words like "perish," "spoil," "fade," "perishable," and "withering") versus that which is imperishable (using words like "living," "genuineness," "imperishable," and "enduring"). Peter's point is profound: the imperishable word of God (1:23, 25), which is the gospel message of Jesus's imperishable blood (1:18–19), is preached to perishable people (1:24), causing them to be born again into an imperishable inheritance (1:4) through their imperishable faith (1:7).

Theological Insights

1. *Be who you are.* Why would obedient children need to be encouraged to obey (1:14)? Why would those whose faith and hope are in God (1:21) need to set their hope on God? Why would those who have a sincere love for one another be commanded to love one another (1:22)? And why would believers who have already purified themselves (1:22) be commanded to be holy (1:15)? This is part of a larger theme in the New Testament of believers being encouraged to be who they are, something that arises out of the already/not-yet framework of salvation.[4] Other examples of this include Galatians 5:16–18, where believers are commanded to "walk by the Spirit" and declared to be those who are "led by the Spirit," and the fact that Christians are regularly declared to be holy (Eph. 1:1; Col. 3:12; 1 Pet. 1:2) and also commanded to be holy (e.g., 1 Thess. 4:3–7; Heb. 12:14; 1 Pet. 1:15).

2. *Fearing God.* The commentary above lists some important Old Testament passages regarding fearing God, but these commands are not limited to just the Old Testament. There are also relevant New Testament texts on this theme (e.g., Luke 18:2–4; 23:40; Acts 9:31; Rom. 11:17–24; 2 Cor. 5:11; Phil. 2:12; Rev. 14:7; 19:5). Fearing God entails more than simply respecting or honoring God or holding him in high esteem. On the one hand it is a holistic idea, paired with loving God. To love God is to fear him, and to fear him is to love him. On the other hand, fearing God draws more on the concept of God

as the impartial Judge who cannot and will not tolerate sin. Such a view of the holiness of God creates within his children a healthy fear of defying God.

But doesn't perfect love cast out fear (1 John 4:18)? Yes. But only with regard to the security of our relationship with God, not with regard to the way we interact with him within the context of that relationship. In other words, no Christian should fear that God will cast them away because they are not good enough or continue to struggle against sin. But every Christian should fear God's discipline and his displeasure when we choose to live selfishly rather than for God.

Teaching the Text

The structure of four central commands—set your hope, be holy, live in fear of God, and love one another—is a great way to organize the teaching of this text. Explaining the logic of the order of these four commands can be helpful too. We begin with setting our hope on the future grace that is to come to believers. When we do that, we realize that we are different from the world around us and that God commands us to be holy and therefore separated from the world in which we live. Disentangling our identity and behavior from the world prepares us for the command to fear God, which means to submit to him, trust him, put our hope in him, love him, obey him, and serve him alone. Having a right orientation in our relationship with God then prepares us to love our neighbors as ourselves.

It may also be useful to show how each of the subsequent three commands (be holy, live in fear, and love one another) is enabled by setting one's hope on the grace that is coming when Jesus returns, so that "set one's hope" becomes the key command that unlocks the rest of them. When Jesus returns, the world and its values will be destroyed, and we will be children of God; therefore, we are free to be holy now. When Jesus returns, God will impartially judge all believers; therefore, we should give ourselves to serving and obeying him now. When Jesus returns, the relationships that we have with other believers will continue for eternity; therefore, we should devote ourselves to loving those people now. Pointing out that "set your hope" is the very first command in the entire epistle may be helpful as well.

The teacher would also be wise to pay attention to the clauses supporting each command, because these flesh out further the what, how, and why of each command. Setting our hope on the grace to come is a more specific way of preparing our minds for action and happens through a process of mental discipline whereby we take our focus off of ourselves and our present circumstances, focus instead on the future, and allow our future to determine our present. Being holy includes not conforming any longer to the lifestyle we had before Christ. Understanding that God is Judge is central to being able to live in fear of God and God alone. Fearing God comes about by realizing the depth of God's love for us—even before the foundation of the world, God purposed to redeem us using the infinitely precious blood of his own Son. And finally, in order to love one another fervently, we must realize that this is the goal of purifying ourselves through the gospel and is the only thing that is lasting.

Of the four commands, living in the fear of God is most easily misunderstood. It may be helpful to explain that fearing God and loving God are two sides of the same coin (cf. Deut. 6:2–5). That's why 1:17 mentions fear and 1:18–20 speaks of God's willingness to redeem us at the cost of his own Son. The best example of this may be a healthy parent-child relationship, where the child feels totally and completely loved but also knows that if they step out of line or hurt a sibling, there will be very real and painful consequences.

Illustrating the Text

Be who you are.

Popular Culture: A popular aphorism in American culture today is "Anyone can be a father; it takes a real man to be a dad." Someone who fathers a child biologically is technically a dad, but we recognize that such men still have to live up to what they now are. So too, when we accepted Jesus as Lord, we were declared by God to be obedient children, but now we have to live up to that title that we have received.

Our hope for the future impacts us today.

Human Experience: We see the power of focusing on the future when we are working to get out of debt. Seeing ourselves as debt free in five years can bring comfort as we suffer under the burden of debt as well as encouragement to curb our spending now so as to achieve that goal.

It takes effort to focus on the future.

Lyrics: "Don't Stop," by Fleetwood Mac. This song was written during the time of Christine McVie's divorce from her husband, and the chorus especially is about putting your focus on the future.

Set your hope on the grace that is coming when Jesus is revealed.

Film: *The Lion King.* In this Disney animated film, when the young lion Simba concentrates on who he is going to be in the future, it gives him great confidence and encouragement to become the king that he is supposed to be. When he loses sight of who he is going to be, he wanders off and stops acting like the king. When he rediscovers the vision of his future near the end of the movie, his behavior changes accordingly. When we as Christians focus on who we will be at Christ's coming, that will dramatically change our behavior in the present.

Hope frees us to love extravagantly.

Personal Testimony: I once did a funeral for an older man who had died of ALS (amyotropic lateral sclerosis). At the funeral three young girls read Scripture because they had formed a deep friendship with the man and his wife after he had been diagnosed with ALS. These girls were free to invest their time and energy in him rather than just be concerned about themselves because death would not end their friendship. From a worldly point of view, investing this kind of time and energy in a person with a terminal illness makes no sense. Couldn't these girls have better used their time and energy forming friendships with other girls, or studying for school, or doing something else? But given the fact that when Christ returns this man will be resurrected, they were free to love him, make cards for him, and spend hours with him without fear that they were wasting their time. In this way Christ's return frees us to love one another deeply from the heart.

Become Who You Are

Big Idea

Believers grow spiritually as we put off malicious practices and experience God.

Key Themes

- Malicious attitudes and actions cause great damage.
- We grow as believers through our experiences of God.

Understanding the Text

The Text in Context

Having finished imploring his readers to *be who they are* (1:13–25), Peter now wants to encourage them to *become who they are*. The "therefore" that begins 2:1–3 follows on logically from 1:13–25 in that once the goal of the process has been spelled out, Peter shifts focus to emphasize the process itself. His readers have been declared to be obedient children (1:14) and have been commanded to be holy (1:16). Now Peter wants them to think about the process of becoming holy. Focusing on the process of growth for them individually in 2:1–3 will allow Peter to transition to what they are growing into corporately in 2:4–10.

Structure

First Peter 2:1–3 follows the same structure as 1:13–25: a controlling command modified by a participial phrase that fills out the command. In this case the participle is in verse 1 and the command is in verse 2.

1. Put off evil (2:1)
2. Crave the Lord (2:2–3)

Interpretive Insights

2:1 *rid yourselves.* This is a verb commonly used by New Testament writers in moral exhortation to speak of ridding oneself of evil practices (Rom.

13:12; Eph. 4:22, 25; Col. 3:8; Heb. 12:1; James 1:21). A literal usage in Acts 7:58 shows that it is commonly used in the world of clothing, with the sense of "put off." "Putting off" also implies "leaving off," since no one puts off dirty clothes only to put them right back on. Likewise, Peter does not intend for his readers to rid themselves of all malice, deceit, and so on, only to take them back up again. Working together with the controlling command of the section—"crave" in 2:2—gives this participle the sense of a command, so that "rid yourselves" and "crave" are two actions that go together. Both verbs are in the aorist tense, which means that Peter is not highlighting the ongoing nature of these actions. But cravings by definition are ongoing. Therefore, we should see "rid yourself" as an ongoing decision to put off and not take up evil practices, so that we are constantly rejecting evil practices and constantly craving the Lord.[1]

all malice and all deceit, hypocrisy, envy, and slander of every kind. The NIV's translation reflects the fact that there are three sections of words, each marked off by the word "all/every." The first section is "all malice." This is the general, overarching category. The word can mean any kind of evil or wickedness, and Peter will employ it in its most general sense in 2:16 when he says, "Do not use your freedom as a cover-up for evil." However, given that the rest of the nouns in 2:1 have to do with interpersonal conflict as opposed to every evil practice, the NIV has rightly translated the word as "malice," indicating antagonistic, mean-spirited, or spiteful attitudes or actions toward others.

The second section of words is "all deceit, hypocrisy, envy." "Deceit" is trickery or falseness. Peter uses this word twice more, in 2:22 and 3:10. "Hypocrisy" refers to actions that do not match one's words (as with Peter and Barnabas in Gal. 2:13) or the attitude of those whose hearts do not match their words and actions (as with the Pharisees in Matt. 23:28). "Envy" is jealousy or coveting, a longing for something that God has not given. Such envy contrasts with what Peter will say in 2:2 about longing for God. Taken together, "deceit," "hypocrisy," and "envy" form the second group and have in common that they are all attitudinal issues, pretending to be something that one isn't or desiring something that one doesn't have.

The last phrase listed is "slander of every kind." If "malice" is any antagonistic attitude or action and "deceit," "hypocrisy," and "envy" are malicious attitudes, then "slander" represents malicious actions. It is interesting that of all the malicious actions that Peter could have chosen, slander is the only one he mentions. This is similar to James, who places high emphasis on the tongue and avoiding slander. For a discussion of slander, see the unit on James 4:11–12, above.

2:2 *Like newborn babies, crave pure spiritual milk.* The controlling metaphor for this section is not clothing but human development, the most common biblical metaphor for spiritual growth. Within the context of this metaphor for spiritual growth, milk is explicitly mentioned in 1 Corinthians 3:1–2 and Hebrews 5:13–14, but in both cases it represents baby food as opposed to adult food, which is not Peter's point here. Just as newborn babies crave their mother's milk, so believers should crave "pure spiritual milk."

The word translated as "spiritual" (*logikos*) is used one other time in the New Testament, in Romans 12:1. There it has the sense of "fitting" or "true and proper." That is most likely the sense here too. Just as a baby craves the milk that is fitting for her, that is, her mother's milk, so a believer should crave the milk that is fitting for us, that is, pure milk that comes from the Father. Such milk will be "spiritual," since God is spirit, but Peter uses *logikos*, not *pneumatikos*, the word normally translated as "spiritual." Peter knows the word *pneumatikos*, since he will use it twice in 2:5, so the fact that he doesn't use it here is evidence that "fitting, true, and proper" is what he has in mind.

What does "pure, fitting milk" refer to? Many have seen this as a reference to the Word of God, meaning the Scriptures, or the word of God, meaning the gospel, since *logikos* sounds similar to *logos*, an important word from 1:23.[2] It is certainly true that the Word/word of God feeds believers, but Peter has something broader in mind here: God himself. After all, 2:3 says, "You have tasted that the Lord is good." While every interaction with Scripture is an engagement with God, God does engage with his children outside of the Scriptures. For example, prayer, a word of encouragement from a fellow believer, experiencing God in nature, and listening to the testimony of another believer are all ways that God can be experienced outside the canonical Scriptures. Peter is urging his readers to crave engagement not just with the Scriptures but with God himself.

so that by it you may grow up in your salvation. The result of engaging with God is a process of spiritual maturation. To "grow up in your salvation" is a slightly different way of formulating this process than what Peter used in 1:9, where he said that believers are in the process of receiving the salvation of their souls. In 1:9, the language pictures salvation coming to believers, like an inheritance coming to an heir. In this passage, the language envisions believers growing up to be people who are worthy of their inheritance. Peter will also use the word "grow" in 2 Peter 3:18, where he speaks of growing in the grace and knowledge of the Lord Jesus Christ.

2:3 *now that you have tasted that the Lord is good.* This is a quote or allusion to Psalm 34:8 (33:9 LXX; Peter also quotes from Ps. 34 in 3:10–12), with two related changes. First, in Psalm 34 "taste" is a command. For Peter it is something that has happened. Second, Peter drops the "and see" from Psalm 34:8. Since tasting the Lord has already happened, there is no need for the command to perceive that the Lord is good. Peter's readers, who are believers, already know it. Together these two changes reflect Peter's theology from 1:23–25. Believers have already been born again through the living and enduring word of God; that is, they have already tasted God and found him to be good. Peter's point is that the initial taste should cause believers to continue to crave God.

"Taste" can be used literally of eating food, either of a small taste (e.g., John 2:9) or actually consuming completely (e.g., Acts 20:11). When it is used metaphorically, it means "experience," as in the common phrase "taste death" (Matt. 16:28; John 8:52; Heb. 2:9). The closest parallel use to Peter's is Hebrews 6:4–5, where the author speaks of tasting the heavenly gift, sharing in the Holy Spirit, and tasting the goodness of the Word of God and the powers of the coming age. The use in Hebrews means to have experienced the fullness of God, which is what Peter is aiming for here. Believers have experienced God in a real and powerful way in their conversion, and now Peter wants them to continue to experience God so that they might grow in their salvation.

The word translated "good" in other contexts has the idea of "loving and kind" (Luke 6:35; Rom. 2:4; Eph. 4:32), which functions in the background here. God is good in the sense of being morally good, kind, compassionate, and loving.

Theological Insights

Sanctification and spiritual growth. First Peter 2:1–3 is not lengthy, but together with 2 Peter 1:4–11 it gives some sense of Peter's theology of spiritual growth. Whereas 2 Peter 1:4–11 focuses much more on the process of growth, this passage gives the overall framework: putting off evil and engaging with God in order to become like him (which comes out of 1 Pet. 1:14–16). In this sense, Peter's theology of spiritual formation is similar to what we see in Romans 12:1–2, where believers are to no longer conform to this world but be transformed into the image of Christ.[3]

Teaching the Text

A few things about this text stand out for the teacher to consider when teaching. First is the relationship of this text to what comes before and what follows. By placing this passage where it is, Peter is transitioning from a discussion about the goal of the process of sanctification to a discussion about the process itself for individuals. This will then lead to a discussion in 2:4–10 about what God is doing corporately among believers within the local community. Missing this little section can cause readers to jump over a crucial logical step: thinking and talking about the spiritual growth of individuals.

Second, some traditions and theological systems do not lend themselves as easily to discussing spiritual growth. Justification can sometimes drowned out sanctification. Practically speaking, it can mean that if one believes (rightly) that we are at the same time justified and still sinners, it can lead (wrongly) to the idea that we must remain in the same state of ungodliness as when we were saved lest believers in any way be seen to earn our salvation. To preach and teach our role in sanctification can be, for some, to preach law instead of gospel. Because we have no part in our justification, we must not have any part in our sanctification. Peter takes a different approach. He commands believers to get rid of evil and to crave the Lord so that we can grow.

Another reason why some find it difficult to talk about spiritual growth is because it implies inequality. Under the gospel, we all equally are wretched sinners, and no one can be better than another. When it comes to spiritual growth, some are further along in the process of growing into their salvation, and many people today chafe against the idea that someone else might be further along than they are. But just as a baby who feeds constantly from her mother's breast will grow more than a baby who feeds only occasionally, so a Christian who craves the Lord and regularly experiences him will experience more-sustained and healthy growth as a believer.

Third, when you are teaching this text, it is important to notice that Peter's key to spiritual growth is the ongoing experience of God. Spiritual formation is often seen as a set of spiritual disciplines where one trains for godliness as though training for a marathon.[4] There are passages of Scripture that take that approach (1 Cor. 9:25–27; 1 Tim. 4:7–8), but the overarching theme that Peter draws out is one of experiencing God. Prayer brings growth, not because it is a good discipline, but because in prayer one experiences God. Scripture reading is good for spiritual growth for the same reason. To be in God's presence and to experience God cause a person to be transformed to be like God.

Finally, it is important to note that in some ways the first step in experiencing God and therefore growing is to get rid of malicious attitudes and actions. Peter tells us to put off certain things before he tells us to crave the Lord. It is important to realize that our malicious actions and attitudes not only hurt others; they also hinder us from being able to engage with the Lord and therefore to be able to grow into our salvation.

Illustrating the Text

God brings growth to the believer.

Human Experience: One of the questions that first-time parents have when holding their newborn is, how does this parenting thing work? That's because we live in a manufactured world. Cars sit still until you figure out how to drive them; toys that come at Christmas need to be assembled and are constantly breaking; stoves won't turn on by themselves unless we program them. But dealing with a baby is different. A baby is created by God. We don't have to figure out how to make a baby want food, go to the bathroom, or cry. Nor do we have to figure out how to make a baby grow. Babies grow. Sometimes we think that everything must be perfect: the baby must eat this amount of food, burp this many times, sleep for this long, and be held just right, or else the child will not develop. But babies grow.

So it is with our spiritual life. If you are a believer in Jesus, God has given you new birth. You are born again. You have life in you. You don't have to make spiritual growth happen. It is designed into who you are in Jesus. You don't have to get some formula just right: if I read my Bible this many times and pray for this long and go to church this often, then I will grow a specific amount. It is more organic than this; Christians grow. Parents take comfort in the fact that their baby will grow with time. In the same way, it can be comforting to us as Christians to realize that we are designed to grow into the people God has designed us to be. Does that mean that we have no role to play? Of course not. A parent doesn't just leave a baby sitting around and say, "Well, you're designed to grow. Get going." Babies need milk to grow. Well-fed babies grow better than undernourished babies. The same is true for our spiritual life.

We must surrender things that keep us from connecting with God and experiencing true growth.

Nature: Plants that don't receive sunlight will never grow as they should. They will either remain stunted and small, or they will eventually grow distorted, as they reach out for the light that they so desperately need. Show the congregation one plant that has been placed in the sun and another that has been kept in a dark closet for a few weeks. It is clear which one has gotten sun. Talk about how this can be true in our spiritual lives: we must stay connected with the light of God.

A Spiritual House

Big Idea

Through Jesus, God is building a community of believers who will bring glory to his name.

Key Themes

- Jesus, the living Stone, is now the cornerstone.
- We grow not only as individuals but as a community.
- God has a plan for the church within salvation history.

Understanding the Text

The Text in Context

Having begun with election in 1:3–12 and moved to ethics in 1:13–2:3, Peter now transitions to community in 2:4–10. As believers grow into their salvation, getting rid of malicious attitudes and actions and craving Christ more and more (2:1–3), they will be drawn closer to one another, becoming a spiritual house and a royal priesthood.

This section on community prepares for the transition to the section on mission, which begins in 2:11–12. As God's temple and as a kingdom of priests, the church plays a vital role in drawing others to God.

Structure

1. Main point: Jesus the living Stone makes believers into a temple of living stones offering sacrifices of praise to God (2:4–5)
2. Support and explanation of the main point from three chained quotes from the Old Testament (Isa. 28:16; Ps. 118:22; Isa. 8:14) (2:6–8)
3. Further implications and explanations of the communal language of the main point in fulfillment of Exodus 19:5–6 and Hosea 2:23 (2:9–10)

Interpretive Insights

2:4 *As you come to him.* "Come" is present tense, and so is "are being built" in 2:5. This gives the sense of ongoing activity. In other words, it is not primarily about conversion but about the constant drawing nearer to God that happens as a part of the sanctification process. When we crave God (2:2), we are drawn closer and closer to him.

the living Stone. Peter moves from a metaphor about babies (2:1–3) to one about buildings. The connection seems to be in the Hebrew idea that to have children is to build one's house (see, e.g., 2 Sam. 7). The same thought pattern is in Ephesians 2:18–22, where the concepts of God's fatherhood, household, temple, and cornerstone are all present. If God has children, then he has a house. If God's children are growing, then God's house is growing. The notion of Jesus as the living Stone probably arises from Psalm 118, quoted in 2:7 and alluded to in the phrase "rejected by humans" in this verse. The rejection of the stone stands for Christ's death, and God making Christ the cornerstone happened when God raised him from the dead, something Psalm 118:17–18 predicts. Hence Jesus is the living Stone, and those who trust in him receive life and become themselves "living stones" (2:5).

2:5 *are being built into a spiritual house to be a holy priesthood.* In Greek "spiritual house" is not the direct object of the verb "being built up." Rather, "spiritual house" further describes the subject that is being built up. In other words, "you, as a spiritual house, are being built up" (cf. ESV, NET). Peter is not saying readers will someday become a spiritual house. They are already a spiritual house but are becoming more so.

This is communal language, since Peter says, "you [pl.] are a house [sg.]," not, "you [pl.] are houses [pl.]." This is like 1 Corinthians 3:16, which says "you [pl.] are God's temple [sg.]"—speaking about the church—as opposed to 1 Corinthians 6:19–20, which says, "your body [sg.] is the temple [sg.] . . . therefore glorify God with your body [sg.]" (NET)—speaking of individual Christians.

But to what does Peter refer here, the local church or the universal church? Certainly the local church is to be included since Peter will speak directly to elders of local churches (5:1–6). But his language probably also includes a referent to the universal church since Peter uses the "people of God" language that was used in the Old Testament to refer to all Israel. Most likely Peter is mimicking the use of *ekklēsia* in Matthew 16:18–19 and 18:15–20, where Jesus moves seamlessly from speaking about the universal church to speaking about the local church. The fact that Jesus has defined the church not as a building but as where two or three are gathered coheres well with Peter's move from spiritual house to holy priesthood. It is the people who are the temple, not a building.

The language of "spiritual house" recalls the tabernacle. In and through the church, God is uniquely present with his people, just as he was in Israel through the tabernacle (and temple).

offering spiritual sacrifices. This refers to believers' praise of God, referenced in 2:9. Such praise comes not only in the form of words but in song, testimony, financial gifts, prayers, proclamations of truth, and so on.

2:6 *a chosen and precious cornerstone.* This is a quote from Isaiah 28:16. "Chosen and precious" ties the whole passage together (see also 2:4, 7, 9). Verse 7 says that what characterizes believers is the fact that what is precious to God is precious to us, namely, Jesus the living Stone. In verse 9, those who regard Jesus as "precious" are those who are God's "chosen" people. Therefore, everything hinges on how people view Jesus the cornerstone. Those who put their trust in him, meaning they view Jesus as precious and invaluable, become the holy people of God because God views Jesus as precious and invaluable.

2:7 *The stone the builders rejected has become the cornerstone.* On at least three distinct occasions in the New Testament, this verse from Psalm 118 is quoted. First, in the parable of the tenants (Matt. 21:42 // Mark 12:10 // Luke 20:17) the emphasis is on Israel's rejection of Jesus and God's plan to take away the kingdom from ethnic Israel and give it to believers who will produce its fruit. Second, the verse is quoted in Acts 4, where the emphasis is on the turning-everything-on-its-head nature of Jesus's crucifixion and resurrection. A man lame from birth can now walk, two unschooled apostles know more about God than the religious leaders in the land, and salvation has come to the unlikely rather than to the expected.

First Peter 2:7 is the third use. Both the rejection of Israel and the turn-everything-on-its-head motifs are present. Believers in Jesus have become the people of God rather than physical descendants of Abraham only. Corporately they are offering back to God the fruit of praise that is due to him. But everything is also now turned upside down—the foreigner in the world is the one accepted by God; the one who is outwardly suffering is actually being made ready for an inheritance.

2:8 *they disobey the message—which is also what they were destined for.* Here Peter displays the same compatibilist approach that he is depicted as displaying in Acts 2:23 and 4:28, where Peter holds to both free will and determinism at the same time. In this verse, Peter uses both an active verb ("disobey") and a passive verb ("destined for") in the same sentence! Those who do not believe stumble because they refuse to believe (free will), but at the same time God has destined that they would not believe (determinism).

2:9 *a chosen people, a royal priesthood, a holy nation, God's special possession.* Peter refers to the most important event in the history of the nation of Israel, their experience at Mount Sinai, where God made his covenant with them. God says to Israel in Exodus 19:5–6, "Out of all nations you will be my treasured possession . . . you will be for me a kingdom of priests and a holy nation." With Israel, God wanted to create a community of people who believed in him, who would be unique among all nations and be able to minister God's grace and truth to them. This is now happening, not through ethnic Israel, but through the community of believers in Jesus. The goal of priests in Deuteronomy 10:8–9 makes clear God's intentions. Priests stand before the Lord and then go out from his presence changed and pronounce blessings to those outside God's presence. That is what believers in Jesus now do.

2:10 *Once you were not a people, but now you are the people of God.* This is a reference to Hosea 2:23. Together with Exodus 19, these two texts declare God's purpose and desire to create for himself a people. The use of Hosea 2:23 reminds us that God's plans will not be thwarted through Israel's infidelity and unbelief. God's mercy and love will overcome human sinfulness and unfaithfulness. Through those who have faith in Christ, God is creating for himself not a collection of saved individuals but a holy and united people to be priests ministering his grace to a lost world.

Theological Insights

1. *Ecclesiology.* First Peter 2:4–10 informs our understanding of the church as being the fulfillment in this age of God's plans for Israel. This connects the church to the biblical ideas of tabernacle/temple and the assembly (*ekklēsia*) of God. The church is the means by which God is present among his people in a unique way. Other passages that make a significant contribution to this connectedness between the church and what was happening in Exodus 19 and following are Matthew 16–18; 1 Corinthians 3:16–17; Ephesians 2:18–22; and Hebrews 12.[1]

This theme of the church as the people of God is one aspect of the larger theology of church in the New Testament that includes the church as a new creation (in which the Christian community is viewed from the perspective of God's plan to redeem the world and make all things new), fellowship in faith (in which the Christian community is viewed from the perspective of individuals in relationship with one another), and the body of Christ (which focuses on the church's ability to incarnate Jesus in this world).[2]

2. *Priesthood of all believers.* One of the tenets of the Protestant Reformation, in reaction to the clerical elitism that was part of Roman Catholicism at the time, was the assertion that all Christians are priests and therefore able to interact with God and represent him to the world. First Peter 2:4–10 presents useful language for such a discussion with its mention of Christians as a royal/holy priesthood (2:5, 9), but this text is talking corporately rather than

individualistically. In addition, this passage must be balanced with 5:1–6 and its discussion of elders. Otherwise the belief in the priesthood of all believers can easily be perverted into a no-leadership theology.[3] Such a view comes from the all-too-human desire to be freed from submission to authority, something that neither Peter nor the early Reformers would affirm.

Teaching the Text

The structure of this passage can be a big help to the teacher. The theological richness of the entire passage can seem overwhelming, but it is helpful to remember that 2:4–5 contains the main point: believers who are coming to Jesus are growing together as a spiritual house, offering sacrifices of praises to God.

But this is such an important theological idea for Peter that he bolsters it with no fewer than five direct quotations from the Old Testament, many of which are alluded to in 2:4–5. To properly teach this text, then, it is important to present what is happening with regard to the Christian community in terms of God's plans for Israel in salvation history. For teaching purposes, reordering the texts in salvation-historical order might be helpful. This would mean beginning with Exodus 19:5–6, where God indicates his desire to form a covenant people who will uniquely belong to him (Gen. 18:18–19 can be helpful for explaining why God wanted such a people: to enable him to fulfill his promise to Abraham to be a blessing to all nations through him—the same point Peter will make in 2:11–12). Hosea 2:23 would be next, revealing Israel's unfaithfulness to God and God's promise to make a new people. From there Psalm 118:22 brings Jesus into the discussion of God's historical plan. When Israel rejected Jesus, God raised him from the dead and made him the chief cornerstone of the new people that he was building. Isaiah 8:14 and 28:16 follow after Psalm 118 in that they tell of how those who accept Jesus are incorporated into God's new-creation people and how those who reject him are separated from them. Rooting what is happening with Christian believers in God's plan from the Old Testament is of central importance for Peter (1:10–12), and it should be for the teacher of this text as well.

One danger teachers must be aware of is that this is a theological passage. There are no commands for readers to do anything. It is a description of what is being done to us with regard to our communal identity. But there are practical implications from this theology: (1) We rest in the fact that the church is what God is doing, not solely dependent on our actions. (2) God is not building his house simply so that we can enjoy his presence. We are becoming a kingdom of priests to be able to go out and share Jesus with those who don't know him. (3) The church is Jesus's plan for rescuing the world in this age. (4) Believers cannot become the priests God wants us to be without the church, since the church is an integral part of the means by which we are transformed and grow. (5) If you are looking for God, you can find him in the midst of those who gather in his name.

Illustrating the Text

The church plays a role in salvation history.

Testimony: Identify a family in your church that has three or four generations of faith and passionate following of Jesus. Have someone in that family (maybe even two or three generations) tell about how being part of your church, or another congregation, has strengthened their faith. You might want to project pictures of baptisms, professions of faith, or landmark faith decisions in the lives of this family. Connect these to the power of being part of a local church. Being an active part of a local church strengthens faith and grows people into spiritual maturity—let this family be a living illustration of this reality.

The cornerstone is central to the foundation of the house.

History: The metaphorical use of "cornerstone" to indicate something of fundamental importance derives from an architectural practice that goes back to ancient times. The cornerstone would be the first stone laid in a masonry project. It was critical that this stone be set perfectly, because it would become the reference point for all the stones to follow.

As a kingdom of priests, we are called to reach out and share Christ.

Popular Culture: In the video game *Age of Empires 2* (but not in later versions) users could create one unit called a "priest." Because this game character was capable of "converting" the opposition, a viable strategy for winning games was creating not hordes of mighty warriors but an army of priests. Then, the user would send an army of priests into battle to convert all of the enemy warriors, buildings, and everything else in sight. We as Christians are to be just such an army: not overpowering people with force, but winning them to Jesus with love.

God chose the rejected cornerstone.

Lyrics: "**Rudolph the Red-Nosed Reindeer.**" Talk about the story of Santa coming and picking Rudolph to guide his sleigh because of his unique nose. He was the reindeer that had been despised and rejected, but Santa recognized that the very thing they were rejecting him for was actually the most important thing for successfully guiding a sleigh. While it is rather trivial to compare Jesus to Rudolph, everything in all of creation is supposed to point to him, and the lesson is that the idea of someone choosing what had previously been rejected is embedded in certain stories that are culturally acceptable to us. Look at Jesus and identify some of the reasons he was rejected, and clarify that these very things are what lead to our salvation and make him the cornerstone of our faith and lives.

Live Godly Lives under Government

Big Idea

Living godly lives among the lost, which includes submitting to and honoring governmental authorities, will bring glory to God.

Key Themes

- Christians need to live godly lives in a non-Christian world so that people might come to faith.
- Believers are to submit to nonbelieving governmental authorities.

Understanding the Text

The Text in Context

Having addressed election (1:3–12), ethics (1:13–2:3), and community (2:4–10), Peter moves his focus to mission—namely, how God's people can function as a kingdom of priests, drawing the lost to faith in Jesus. Peter's use of "dear friends" plus "I urge you" to begin 2:11 signals this shift toward the evangelistic outworking of their Christian behavior and community.

Verses 11–12 give the programmatic overview for how believers' behavior can result in others coming to faith in Christ. Peter will then take this general principle and apply it to specific situations: submission to governing authorities (2:13–17), slaves and masters (2:18–25), husbands and wives (3:1–7), and the community (4:7–11). While 2:11–12 can stand alone, for the sake of this commentary it is included with 2:13–17, where Peter addresses Christians' responsibilities with regard to the state.

Structure

1. Peter's overarching ethical commands to abstain from evil desires and to live good lives for the missional purpose of bringing glory to God (2:11–12)

2. More specific outworking of the overarching ethical commands with regard to the realm of state authorities (2:13–17)

Interpretive Insights

2:11 *foreigners and exiles.* "Exiles" appears in 1:1, and "foreigners" is related to the word Peter uses for "foreigner" in 1:17. By bringing them both together here in 2:11, Peter is highlighting the background against which these exhortations come: Christians living in the midst of a non-Christian world. The other use of the word "exile" in the New Testament is in Hebrews 11:13 (NIV: "strangers"), an important parallel passage. In Hebrews the discussion about being exiles comes in the context of the story of Abraham, and that may be underlying Peter's thoughts as well (cf. 3:6) since in the Abrahamic narrative the pattern of election, ethics, community, and mission is first laid out (see the sidebar).

abstain from sinful desires, which wage war against your soul. Just as in 2:1–3, there is a negative command ("abstain from sinful desires") and a positive command ("live good lives") in 2:11–12. The negative command to stay away from sinful desires pictures these desires as attacking the Christian from the non-Christian world outside, as opposed to James 1:14 (see the comments on James 1:14–15), where they are seen as coming from within.

2:12 *among the pagans.* This phrase also could be translated "among the nations." The NIV's translation, while accurately representing that Peter is talking about unbelievers, threatens to conceal the connection with the prominent Old Testament background of declaring God's glory among the nations (e.g., 1 Chron. 16:8–36; Ps. 96:3–7; Isa. 62:2; 66:18–19; Dan. 7:14; cf. Luke 2:29–32; 1 Tim. 3:16; Rev. 15:4).

Election, Ethics, Community, and Mission

Throughout the Bible there is a pattern of election, ethics, community, and mission. The pattern is first spelled out with Abraham: God chose Abraham (election) so that he would direct his descendants (community) in doing what was right and just (ethics) so that through them God might bless the whole world (mission), as stated in Genesis 18:18–19. This pattern continues in central texts like Exodus 19:4–6; Deuteronomy 4; and 1 Kings 8. It is within this pattern that Peter is writing. It should be noted that there is some fluidity between ethics and community, but what doesn't change is that salvation/election is always first and mission is always last. In between, God's rescued people are to grow in their behavior as well as become the community God intends, so that they can reach the world.[a]

[a] For a more detailed discussion of this pattern and the texts mentioned here, see Wright, *Mission of God*, 358–92.

they may see your good deeds and glorify God on the day he visits us.
This is very similar to Matthew 5:16. By adding the phrase "on the day he
visits us," Peter has shifted the emphasis to Christ's second coming, but the
picture is not of nonbelievers having no choice but to acknowledge God's
glory when Christ returns. Instead, he has in mind non-Christians coming
to faith *now* who will glorify God as believers on the day Christ returns. By
living godly lives amid an unbelieving world, Peter's readers will bring many
to faith in Christ.

2:13 *Submit yourselves for the Lord's sake to every human authority.* While
"God" is used throughout this passage, referring to God the Father (2:12, 15, 16,
17), Peter switches to "Lord" here, which usually refers to Jesus (cf. 3:15). Could
this switch be because Jesus is the one who has submitted himself to authorities, both parental (Luke 2:51) and governmental (Matt. 22:21; John 19:11)?

To "submit" is closely related to "obey," but it is not identical to it. To
submit is to acknowledge the God-given authority of the state and to act in
line with the structures of such a relationship. In the case of the state, that
includes obeying the laws of the state, but it also includes honoring the king
(2:17; NIV: "emperor"), which may or may not be an actual law of the state.
For more on submission and obedience, see the unit on 1 Peter 3:1–7, below.

2:14–15 *sent by him to punish those who do wrong and to commend those
who do right.* In 2:12 Peter said that the nations will accuse Christians of
"doing wrong," and here using the same word he says governors are sent to
punish "those who do wrong." Likewise, governors are entrusted with the task
of commending those "who do right," which is related to the word translated
"by doing good" in 2:15. What Peter seems to have in mind are situations
like that of Daniel 6, where Daniel is accused of evil and thrown into a lions'
den but through his good works bears witness to Darius and silences those
who have accused him. Or more important, there is the example of Jesus.
Accused of doing evil, by evildoers themselves, Jesus was brought before
Pilate, the reigning governmental authority. Although Jesus was put to death,
his resurrection—which was the vindication of his good life—silenced those
who had accused him of doing evil. Doing good, then, has specifically in view
the idea of doing good in relation to governing authorities.

2:16 *Live as free people, but do not use your freedom as a cover-up for evil;
live as God's slaves.* I like the NLT best here: "For you are free, yet you are
God's slaves, so don't use your freedom as an excuse to do evil." In 2:15 Peter
has given the rationale as to why his readers should do good in relation to
governing authorities: because it is God's will. This opens the door to protect
against the constant danger of the doctrine of freedom—that of license to sin.
If Christians are foreigners and aliens and therefore by definition not naturally
under the authority of governments, they are to realize that as Christians who

have submitted to God's rule they must place themselves in submission to these authorities so that God can accomplish his purpose in displaying his glory to the nations. Similar ideas regarding being free and yet being a slave can be found in 1 Corinthians 7:22 and 9:19–23, having the same strong emphasis on willingly submitting one's freedom for the sake of evangelism.

The word for "cover-up" here implies a strategy for concealing something (as in 2 Sam. 17:19). In this case freedom is being used to conceal one's true evil intentions.

2:17 *Show proper respect to everyone, love the family of believers, fear God, honor the emperor.* Of these four parallel phrases, the first and the last use weaker terminology, that of "showing proper respect" and "honoring" (both use the same word in Greek). The middle two phrases use stronger terminology: "love" and "fear." While Christians show proper respect to all humans because every living person is created in the image of God, Christians' responsibility toward other believers is characterized by sacrificial love. This is not to say that Christians are free from loving non-Christians, but it is similar to Paul's command in Galatians 6:10, where Christians do good to everyone, but they are to go above and beyond with others of the household of faith.

Likewise, Peter uses the stronger term of "fear" to describe Christians' responsibility toward God, in contrast to the weaker term of "honor" for his readers' relationship to the governing authorities. (On the fear of God, see the comments on 1 Pet. 1:17.) While it can be said that Christians should fear governmental authorities (Rom. 13:3–5), believers have a stronger obligation, allegiance, and response to God than to the state. This leaves room for the rare occasions of civil disobedience, in which Peter himself engaged (e.g., Acts 4:19; 5:29).

Because "honor" is used for both everyone and the emperor, the idea is to treat those in leadership the way that everyone should be treated: with respect; avoiding slandering, gossiping and being divisive; and treating them as you would want to be treated if you were in a position of leadership.

Theological Insights

A Christian's relationship to the state is a complex issue, but there are some widely accepted essential principles. First, a Christian's allegiance must first and foremost be to God. This is seen in acts of civil disobedience (e.g., Exod. 1:17; Dan. 6:10; Acts 4:19; 5:29), as well as Jesus's command in Matthew 22:21 to give to Caesar what was made in Caesar's image (coins) and to give to God what is made in God's image (our whole self). Second, Christians have a responsibility to pray for secular leaders and those in authority (1 Tim. 2:1–2). Third, Christians have a responsibility to submit to, obey, and honor governmental leaders (Rom. 13:1–7; 1 Pet. 2:13–17). Fourth, Christians are to speak truth to those in positions of power (e.g., Jon. 3; Mark 6:17–18; Acts

25–26). Fifth, many believe that Christians should work with and through the state to promote justice and morality in society, but just how exactly that is to be worked out is highly debated. First Peter 2:11–17 has important explicit contributions to the first and third areas as well as implicit connections to the second and fourth.[1]

Teaching the Text

Verses 11–12 are important programmatic verses for the epistle of 1 Peter and should be given proper attention. What Peter will say about governing authorities, slaves, wives, and general behavior in a non-Christian world will not make any sense without a proper understanding of how election, ethics, community, and mission fit together (see the sidebar). We have become aliens and strangers; now we must avoid sinful desires and live godly lives, so that we can win people to faith in Christ. The teacher may decide that working through the relationship of theology, ethics, and mission is important enough to devote an entire teaching to this connection and deal only with verses 11–12.

When one is teaching 2:13–17, the foremost point to make is that our relationship to the state is determined by our relationship to God. Submission happens "for the Lord's sake." It is "God's will." We do this as "God's slaves" and because we "fear God." It is important for readers to recognize that our interaction with politics and governmental authorities is contingent on our relationship to the lordship of Christ in our lives. For Peter, a Christian's involvement with the political realm can work only when one trusts God, submits to God, obeys God, and fears God above all things. Those who fear the state or trust in the state will not behave properly in relation to the state.

Naturally, each teacher will determine to what extent they want to deal with politics in teaching through this section. However, it should be noted that this particular section of Scripture does not endorse or promote a specific view of political involvement for Christians. Rather, the passage suggests at least three enduring principles: (1) submit to and respect ruling authorities, (2) do good in relation to the state, and (3) keep the state in proper perspective to God. This passage of Scripture is much more concerned with submitting to legislators and new legislation than with how to get different legislators elected or new legislation passed. Sadly, Christians disrespecting governing authorities, refusing to do good to the state, and putting more faith in politics than in God to set things right in this world have pushed non-Christians away from Christ. But doing things Peter's way will instead draw them to faith.

The idea of not using freedom as a cover-up for evil is very prevalent in the interaction of Christians with the state. For example, some Christian workers have opted out of paying social security under the guise of "religious reasons," when it can be simply a cover-up for wanting to retain more of their pay. Likewise, much of the energy expended in the public square in discussions about such issues as health insurance, immigration, taxes, the environment, patriotism, serving in the armed forces, and poverty often is more about our selfish preferences, but we hide this behind the language of Christian freedom.

Illustrating the Text

The church should not feel at home in the world.

Quote: **Karl Schelkle.** New Testament scholar Schelkle comments, "The more the church has sensed its alienation from the world, the more it has been able to influence the world."[2]

Health: In the miracle of birth, the fertilization of an egg is only the first major step in a process that is marked by key points along the way. One of the subsequent major events takes place when the fertilized egg travels down the fallopian tube into the uterus. If the egg connects and develops inside the fallopian tube, this can lead to an ectopic pregnancy, in which case not only the viability of the fertilized egg but the life of the mother is put at grave risk. Similarly, the church is not a community meant for this world. We are meant to be a community of the redeemed on the move, heading for God's ultimate new birth in the new heavens and new earth. When we become too "at home" in the world, our power to witness is compromised.

Understanding the relationship between church and state has long been difficult.

Bible: It is noteworthy that in Matthew 22:15–22, when the Pharisees want to trap Jesus, they choose a question based on the relationship between church and state, about the people of God paying taxes. Nehemiah, Daniel, Joseph, and Esther also provide compelling examples of how to behave in relationship to government authorities who are not believers in God.

The call to fear God trumps the duty to honor the government.

Film: *Chariots of Fire.* In this film we meet Eric Liddell, a Christian preacher and leader who also happens to be an Olympic athlete. When he arrives at the Olympics, however, he learns that his heat is listed for Sunday afternoon. As a strict Sabbatarian, Liddell humbly informs his team that he will not be able to run his race. Panic ensues. He is pressured, cajoled, and finally brought into the presence of England's Prince of Wales, who informs him that running is his duty as an Englishman. Even so, Liddell refuses, willing to turn his back not only on his dreams, but on his deep sense of duty to England. Why? Because he has a deeper duty to his Lord.

Working for God

Big Idea

Workers should be willing to follow Christ's example and suffer injustice and persecution, entrusting themselves to God so that his purposes and sovereignty win out.

Key Themes

- Submit to difficult leaders in the workplace, school, and volunteer organizations.
- Christ willingly suffered in our place.
- Follow the example of Christ's nonretaliation in the face of suffering.

Understanding the Text

The Text in Context

First Peter 2:18–25 applies the general election-ethics-community-mission principle from 2:11–12 to the situation of slaves/workers and masters. Peter also continues to flesh out what he has said in 2:13–17 regarding his readers being slaves of God.

In this section Peter draws on Christ's response to his unjust suffering as an example for the readers. This theological rationale applies not only to slaves who are treated poorly but also to all believers who are persecuted in this world, in which we are strangers. Peter will return to this in 3:8–22.

Peter's comments in 2:25 about Jesus being the Shepherd and Overseer form the theological basis for his exhortations in 5:1–6.

Structure

1. The command to submit to masters, especially those who persecute workers who do good (2:18–20)
2. The theological basis for this command—namely, that Christ endured such ill-treatment to bring us salvation (2:21–25)

Interpretive Insights

2:18 *Slaves.* See the sidebar "Greco-Roman Slavery."

in reverent fear of God submit yourselves to your masters. Although "of God" is not in the Greek, the NIV has correctly identified that "fear" refers to fear of God and is connected to 1:17 as well as 2:17 (see the comments on 1 Pet. 1:17 and "Theological Insights" in that unit). Fear is usually associated with discipline and judgment. Here the idea is that those who are working for masters are actually working for God. The person who is theologically free from earthly masters is still enslaved to a heavenly one. The idea is similar to Ephesians 6:5–8. On submission, see the comments on 1 Peter 2:13 and 3:1–7.

to those who are harsh. The word for "harsh" often means "morally crooked, dishonest, and unjust" (Acts 2:40; Phil. 2:15). It probably includes being unkind and mean-spirited, since it is contrasted with the word "considerate." Therefore, it can refer to those in positions of authority who are seemingly kind but unethical and morally corrupt.

2:19 *pain of unjust suffering.* The suffering must be unjust in order for what Peter is saying to qualify. He does acknowledge that unjust suffering causes grief, so he is not asking his readers to celebrate or enjoy suffering. Instead, there is space to grieve as Jesus did.

because they are conscious of God. Enduring unjust suffering is commendable only if it is done because one is conscious of God, meaning that one puts up with difficult conditions so that God might achieve his missional purposes. Enduring difficult working conditions in an effort to advance one's career or make more money doesn't count.

2:20 *for doing wrong . . . if you suffer.* Two key words in this passage are used: (1) "doing wrong" (often translated "sinning"), which is used in connection with Christ not sinning (2:22) and bearing our sins (2:24) and in connection with the readers in 2:23 and 24; and (2) "suffering," which is used of the readers in 2:19 and 20 and of Christ in 2:21 and 23. Christ suffered for our sins to earn us salvation so that we could be set free from sin. In our freedom from sin we are now able to suffer because of the sins of others and help them find salvation in Christ.

2:21 *To this you were called.* "This" refers to enduring unjust suffering (2:20) and not to submitting to good and considerate masters (2:18).

Christ suffered for you, leaving you an example. Peter doesn't say, "Christ suffered *in order to* leave you an example." The primary purpose for Christ's suffering was to pay for our sins (2:24). A secondary benefit of Christ's atoning work is that it left an example of how Peter's readers should handle unjust suffering. Christ too suffered, not to advance his career or make money, but to accomplish God's missional purposes.

that you should follow in his steps. This is discipleship language. A related form of the verb "follow" is used for Jesus's call to discipleship (Matt. 8:19; 9:9; 19:21; Mark 1:18; 8:34; Luke 5:11; John 1:40, 43). Following in another's footsteps is also used of imitating the example left by others (Rom. 4:12; 2 Cor. 12:18). All of this draws on the Old Testament background of walking in the ways of another (especially prominent in 1–2 Kings and 2 Chronicles, speaking of kings who did or did not follow in the ways of their fathers or in the ways of David).[1]

2:23 *When they hurled their insults at him, he did not retaliate; when he suffered, he made no threats.* This alludes to Isaiah 53:7, where the Suffering Servant is silent like a sheep before its shearers. It corresponds to Jesus's trial. When Jesus was falsely accused of threatening to destroy the temple, he did not respond (Matt. 26:57–63); when on trial before Pilate, he was silent before his accusers (Matt. 27:12–14).

2:24 *"He himself bore our sins" in his body on the cross.* This is the language of substitutionary atonement. Jesus died in our place, as a payment for our sins. The allusion to Deuteronomy 21:23 (the Greek of "his body on the cross/pole" is the same in 1 Peter as in the LXX of Deuteronomy) refers to Jesus becoming cursed to rescue us from the curse our sins earned (cf. Gal. 3:13). This sets up the "glorious exchange" whereby our sins become Christ's so that his righteousness might become ours. Paul uses similar language in Romans 6. This is what it means to die to sins but live for righteousness.

2:25 *now you have returned to the Shepherd and Overseer of your souls.* Peter is recalling the teaching of John 10, where Jesus declares himself to be the Good Shepherd, who watches over and cares for the sheep. Peter will draw on this same imagery in 5:1–6. Given this context, "overseer" probably refers to Jesus watching over his sheep in the sense of providing for them and protecting them rather than being Lord over the sheep. This is a very pastoral way for Peter to end this section. Jesus, the Good Shepherd, is caring for those readers who find themselves in situations similar to his own. As they suffer unjustly, Jesus will watch out for them along the lines of Psalm 23 and Ezekiel 34.

Theological Insights

1. *Christ's suffering and death.* Peter's theology of Christ's suffering and death is thoroughly substitutionary. He died the death that our sins deserved. The punishment that Jesus endured brought us peace. When we suffer for being Christians, we are united with Christ in his sufferings, and his resurrection power radiates through us (Phil. 3:10). Practically speaking, this means that Christ is near to those who are suffering persecution (e.g., Acts 7:54–60) and that others see Christ in us when we suffer as he did.

2. *Slavery.* In addition to this section, 1 Corinthians 7:21–24; Ephesians 6:5–9; Colossians 3:22–4:1; and the book of Philemon all discuss slavery without ever actually condemning the institution. Rather than reject the Bible as ethically immoral, we should realize that a lack of condemnation of a societal institution is not an endorsement. Moreover, it may be that God through the New Testament intended to transform society by transforming

Greco-Roman Slavery

Slavery in the ancient world was different from modern slavery. Bartchy writes,

Central features that distinguish 1st century slavery from that later practiced in the New World are the following: racial factors played no role; education was greatly encouraged (some slaves were better educated than their owners) and enhanced a slave's value; many slaves carried out sensitive and highly responsible social functions; slaves could own property (including other slaves!); their religious and cultural traditions were the same as those of the freeborn; no laws prohibited public assembly of slaves; and (perhaps above all) the majority of urban and domestic slaves could legitimately anticipate being emancipated by the age of 30.[a]

In Peter's day, slaves could hold high-status, high-ranking positions in the government; they could be farmers, doctors, lawyers, nannies, construction workers, writers, accountants, agents, secretaries, and more.[b] It is also important to realize that typical freeborn Roman citizens did not like working as long-term employees for others. This was often left to slaves and ex-slaves.[c] For these reasons, there are more similarities between employment in the modern economy and Greco-Roman slavery than one might initially think, at least for some slaves that Peter would have been addressing.

[a] Bartchy, "Slavery (Greco-Roman)," 66.
[b] Hopkins, *Conquerors and Slaves*, 123, quoted in Bartchy, "Slavery (Greco-Roman)," 69; Bradley, *Slavery and Society at Rome*, 2–3.
[c] Hopkins, *Conquerors and Slaves*, 124.

1 Peter 2:18–25

people and did not directly address any societal institutions—especially since first-century slavery was so radically different from its modern counterparts. (See the sidebar "Greco-Roman Slavery.")

3. *Work*. Work was mandated by God for humans when he created us in his own image and entrusted to us the care of his world (Gen. 1:26–28). Sin added a burdensome aspect to work (Gen. 3:17–19), which severely limits how much that human effort can actually accomplish (Ecclesiastes). But God redeems the concept of work by continuing to do productive work himself (John 5:17), encouraging work (Eph. 4:28; 2 Thess. 3:6–16), and setting limits on work (Exod. 20:8) for our benefit (Mark 2:27). While work, which includes learning and volunteering, is valuable in its own right, 1 Peter 2:18–25 makes a contribution to this theology of work by reminding the worker that enduring suffering and persecution in the workplace can connect us to Christ. Such suffering also points others to Christ since he suffered injustices in winning salvation for us.

Teaching the Text

In explaining 2:18–25, the teacher might need to point out that slavery in the first century had some things in common with modern labor practices—like opportunities for education, advancement, and meaningful work (see the sidebar "Greco-Roman Slavery"). Therefore 2:18–25 can be applied to modern work situations, as long as the teacher keeps in mind that these two situations are not identical. There may be some cases where modern workers should consider opportunities to get out from under abusive bosses, opportunities that were not always available to Peter's readers. However, the overriding principle is applicable: workers should be willing to suffer injustice and persecution in the workplace (or the school or the place where one is volunteering), entrusting themselves to God so that his purposes and sovereignty win out. By doing so they will be following the example Christ set for them.

When one is teaching this text, three areas might prove fruitful to emphasize for those in difficult situations. First is the concept of being "conscious of God" (2:19). Encourage those involved in work, school, or volunteering to ask questions such as, Why did God put me here? What is God trying to accomplish in me through this? What is God wanting to do for others through this? Has God given me any indication that I am not supposed to be in this situation besides the fact that I do not like it? These questions can help someone be conscious of what God is up to in a difficult situation.

Second, it is important to note how much time Peter spends explaining Christ's situation in order to guide his readers. This lengthy engagement with Isaiah 53 in 1 Peter 2:21–25 is a great reminder that encouraging people to

submit to difficult leaders, teachers, or bosses can be done only when someone truly understands what Christ did for us and how his suffering brought
us blessings. In this, it may be important to emphasize how Jesus "entrusted
himself to him who judges justly" (2:23). The only way someone would submit
to a difficult person or situation is if they are assured that God will take care
of them in the midst of the situation.

Third, anyone in a situation like what Peter describes in 2:18–25 will have a
whole host of questions they are struggling with. Do I put up with an abusive
boss no matter what? Do I say something or stay silent? How long should
I stay in this situation if there is a way out? In the face of these questions it
is important to note that the passage ends with Jesus being described as a
shepherd. Shepherds guide their sheep, and it should be reinforced that Jesus
will lead different people through different situations differently by the Spirit.
But he will lead.

It may be necessary to point out that Jesus was not completely silent during his sufferings and trials. Jesus does engage with his accusers, but for the
purpose of helping to bring them to accept the truth of the gospel, not to
defend himself against accusations.

Illustrating the Text

**When we are assured that God is carrying us, we are better able
to endure difficult situations.**

Scenario: A believer is able to treat difficult situations in this world the way a
traveler treats her journey on a train. She might have a seat near the back of
the train. She might have need to walk in the opposite direction of her ultimate destination at times. She might be forced to wait an inordinate amount
of time before receiving her food in the dining car. In short, there might be
all kinds of "setbacks" on the train, but she can handle them. Why? Because
she knows that ultimately, the train is constantly carrying her in the right
direction, always moving toward her destination. Whatever her experience
inside the train cars, the train itself is taking her where she wants to be. In
a similar way, believers can be sustained through many trials by entrusting
ourselves to the Lord, who is carrying us through every circumstance toward
an eternity with him!

Workers endure unjust situations.

Personal Testimony: When I was in college, one of my professors found out
that I was a Christian and would regularly make fun of me in front of the
other two hundred students in the class. The class was such that there was
no opportunity to respond or to defend myself. However, after taking such

abuse on multiple occasions, I formed a connection with the professor that would not have normally happened in a class that size. One day during his office hours, the fact that he had openly ridiculed me and that I had taken it quietly caused him to begin to open up about his struggles with believing in God, and I had a chance to talk about Jesus with him. Share a story from your life where you had to endure something like this, or use a short clip from the movie *God's Not Dead*.

Christians should be more concerned with sharing the gospel than with guarding their rights.

Missions: Through extensive research and fact-finding, Open Doors International has established that, on average, each month 322 Christians face death for their faith, 214 churches and Christian properties are destroyed, and 772 violent acts are committed against Christians.[2] As citizens of a country that values religious freedom and individual rights, and much more as fellow believers, we can feel our blood boil at these statistics. We long to bring an end to this suffering or to rescue believers from such situations. However, one common theme works its way through these persecuted believers: they honestly believe their suffering for the gospel is a profound witness. Many of them, given a choice to leave, would rather stay and point their persecutors to Christ.[3]

Wives and Husbands

Big Idea

Wives are to pursue the inner beauty of a gentle spirit, submitting to their husbands and influencing them for Jesus, and husbands are to treat their wives with consideration and honor.

Key Themes

- Wives are to submit to their husbands, and husbands are to treat their wives with considerate respect.
- The value of inner beauty far exceeds that of outer beauty.

Understanding the Text

The Text in Context

Having applied the election-ethics-community-mission injunction of 2:11–12 to submitting to governing authorities (2:13–17) and slaves and masters (2:18–25), Peter now applies it to wives and husbands. This will prepare the way for 3:8–22, where Peter presents additional evangelistically effective principles for enduring suffering that apply to all three situations of 2:13–3:7.

Structure

1. Two commands to wives (3:1–6)
   a. Submit yourselves to your husbands
   b. Cultivate inner beauty
2. Two commands to husbands (3:7)
   a. Be considerate of your wives
   b. Treat them with honor

Interpretive Insights

3:1 *in the same way.* This does not imply that being a wife is like being a slave, since "in the same way" is used in 3:7 regarding husbands. Rather, Peter is encouraging both wives and husbands to think about their respective positions in terms of the same election-ethics-community-mission framework

149

Submission

"Submission" is situation specific. In general it means "to acknowledge the authority of another and follow their leadership." But a slave submitting to a master looks different from a citizen submitting to governing authorities, which looks different from a wife submitting to a husband.

In the case of husbands and wives, Scripture makes clear that husbands have the responsibility of loving and caring for their wives (Eph. 5:22–33; 1 Pet. 3:7). Wives submitting to their husbands means recognizing that God has given husbands the leadership role in loving and caring for them and supporting their husbands in this assignment. This does involve some level of obedience, as 3:6 makes clear, but obedience as part of submission in a marriage relationship is different from obedience as part of submission in a master-servant relationship.

For example, consider Sarah, whom Peter says submitted to Abraham. Sarah follows Abraham to a new land (Gen. 12) and submits to his misguided schemes to deceive Pharaoh (Gen. 12; cf. Gen. 20). Sarah follows Abraham's leadership in showing hospitality to the Lord (Gen. 18), having the males of her household circumcised (Gen. 17), having her name changed

(Gen. 17), and presumably in allowing her son to be sacrificed (Gen. 22). Yet she also takes the lead at times (Gen. 16; 21), and Abraham is told to listen to her (21:12). Sarah submitting to Abraham is very different from Hagar, who is said to submit to Sarah (16:9). Hagar is a servant who takes orders; Sarah is a marriage partner who allows her husband to lead but who also at times provides leadership.

While some Christians today see the commands for wives to submit to their husbands as a mere condescension to a first-century patriarchal culture,[a] I am not convinced that Peter viewed the Scriptures this way, nor that we should (see 1 Pet. 1:10–12 and 2 Pet. 1:19–21 and the comments for those sections). Likewise, Ephesians 5 roots wives' submission to their husbands within the theological orientation of the church's submission to Jesus.[b] However, even those who adopt such a view acknowledge that mutual submission is a transcultural requirement for all believers (Eph. 5:21). In this mutual submission there are times when a wife is to submit to her husband, even if, as some argue, she is not required to do so on an ongoing basis. During these times of submission, 3:1–6 describes how this should look.

[a] See, e.g., Webb, *Slaves, Women and Homosexuals*; Keener, *Paul, Women, and Wives*.
[b] Schreiner, *1, 2 Peter, Jude*, 148–53.

that slaves (2:18–25) and those under governmental authorities (2:13–17) do—namely, that this is an opportunity to bring others to a place of glorifying God.

if any of them do not believe the word. The general command is for all wives to submit to their husbands (cf. Eph. 5:22), but Peter is emphasizing the more specific case of a wife married to an unbelieving husband. Interestingly, Peter uses a word that means "disobey" (*apeitheō*) when labeling those who do not believe. On one hand, *apeitheō* is used in contexts simply to identify people as nonbelievers (John 3:36; Acts 14:2; 19:9; Rom. 15:31), and Peter has in mind unbelievers since he speaks of them being "won over," a word used in evangelistic contexts (e.g., 1 Cor. 9:19–22). On the other hand, in many contexts *apeitheō* emphasizes the actions of disobedience for the nonbeliever (1 Pet. 2:8; 3:20; 4:17; Rom. 2:8; 10:21; 11:30–32). Given that Peter uses *apeitheō* with this latter shade of meaning (1 Pet. 2:8; 3:20; 4:17) and the fact that it is the wife's *behavior* that wins her husband over—not her compelling intellectual arguments—we should conclude that Peter has the husband's behavior in mind as much as his stated beliefs. This means that while Peter is referring first and foremost to non-Christian husbands, what he says can also apply to situations where a husband claims to be a Christian but is not acting in accordance with that claim.

3:2 *when they see the purity and reverence of your lives.* "See" is used in 2:12 of pagans seeing Christians' good deeds and coming to faith, tying this passage to that one. Here husbands see "the purity and reverence of your lives." This means purity and reverence with regard to a wife's behavior toward both God and her husband. It is toward God, because 3:5a speaks of women who put their hope in God. It is also toward their husbands, because 3:5b–6 speaks of women who submitted themselves to their own husbands. Of the two, the wife's purity and reverence toward her husband flow out of her purity and reverence toward God. This can be seen from the fact that Peter mentions hoping in God first (3:5a) and then submitting to husbands (3:5b–6). It also corresponds to the fact that Peter uses "reverent" (or "in fear") first of the believers' relationship toward God (1:17; cf. 2:17) and then of the relationship of one person to another (2:18).

3:3–4 *beauty should not come from outward adornment.* The theme of outward appearance versus inner heart is articulated most strongly in 1 Samuel 16:7: "The LORD does not look at the things people look at. People look at the outward appearance, but the LORD looks at the heart." This foundational truth forms the background of the Peter-led apostolic search in Acts 1:24 and may have been informed by Peter's own experience as an "unschooled, ordinary man" courageously taking on the Sanhedrin (Acts 4:13).

elaborate hairstyles and the wearing of gold jewelry or fine clothes. "In ancient Rome hair was a major determinant of a woman's physical attractiveness and was thus deemed worthy of considerable exertions to create a flattering appearance. . . . In the Roman world however, hair's erotic potential made it a lightning rod for anxieties about female sexuality and public behavior."[1] Agrippina the Younger (sister of Caligula, wife of Claudius, and mother of Nero) was one such trendsetter in Rome during Peter's time when it came to lavish hairstyles. Peter is not forbidding jewelry or having one's hair done but is discouraging the overzealous pursuit of outward beauty, as does Paul in 1 Timothy 2:9.

unfading beauty. "Unfading" is the same adjective translated "can never perish" in 1:4. A woman's inner character should match the quality of the inheritance she will receive from the Lord. Such character is part of the present realization of that future inheritance. Compare this with 1 Timothy 4:8, where Paul encourages believers to pursue godliness in greater measure than body-sculpting exercise, because godliness has value now and forever.

a gentle and quiet spirit. Gentleness is not weakness. It is strength under control. Jesus is described as gentle (Matt. 11:29; 21:5; 2 Cor. 10:1). Therefore, Peter is not talking about a shy shrinking violet or a quiet wallflower. Rather, when he uses "gentleness" in 3:15, it will be for the person who has something important to say but speaks respectfully and under control. A quiet spirit is a spirit at rest with God because such a woman has cast all her anxiety on God (5:7). It is the wife whose hope is in the Lord, who looks to him for rescue, and who waits for him to come and fix the situation.

which is of great worth in God's sight. This phrase corresponds to the slave who is "conscious of God" (2:19) and acts in ways that are "commendable before God" (2:20) and to Christians who are living as God's slaves (2:16). The wife who acts with a quiet and gentle spirit, submitting to her husband and entrusting the situation to God, has always before her what God thinks—not her neighbors, her family, or her friends. She is acting this way because God has asked her to, not because her husband deserves it.

3:5 *holy women of the past who put their hope in God.* The reason that the NIV has the translation "women" rather than "wives" is because there is a sense in which what Peter has to say applies to women like Ruth who express their hope in God outside the context of a marriage relationship.

3:6 *like Sarah, who obeyed Abraham and called him her lord.* Sarah obeying Abraham probably refers to a general sense of her following his leadership (see the sidebar), while calling him "lord" refers to a specific instance in Genesis 18:12, when God told her that she would give birth to a son. Peter probably chose this example from Genesis 18 because even at this moment of her disbelief—one of her lowest moments—she still chose to acknowledge Abraham's leadership in their marriage and received the blessing of a son as a result. Sarah's example is just that: an example. Wives today are not required to call their husbands "lord," but to follow Sarah's example is to respect their husbands even when they do not agree with them or understand what their husbands are doing.

3:7 *Husbands, in the same way be considerate.* Peter addresses husbands directly, something he didn't do for ruling authorities or masters. "Be considerate" is the idea of paying honor, recognizing that wives are equal inheritors of God's gracious gift of life. It could be translated "live with your wife according to knowledge." In other words, "Husbands, seek to understand the more difficult road your wife has been asked to walk, and recognize what makes her feel loved and valued." The idea here is similar to 1 Corinthians

12:21–26, where members of the church who seem weaker, less honored, and less visible are treated with greater honor and concern, being recognized as indispensable. Husbands are to treat their wives this way.

as the weaker partner. This might mean physically weaker, but more likely it emphasizes the societal disadvantages of being a wife in a patriarchal culture—some of which still linger today; for example, a stay-at-home wife and mother may struggle with getting respect in a society that values ladder-climbing success.

Theological Insights

First Peter 3:1–7 must be understood in relationship to other Scriptures governing husband-and-wife relationships: (1) Ephesians 5:22–33 emphasizes the situation where husband and wife are both believers and living for the Lord, while 1 Peter 3 is more focused on the situation where one spouse is not a believer or not living for the Lord. (2) First Corinthians 7:12–16 deals with divorce and issues of children in a mixed marriage, something Peter does not address. (3) Matthew 18:15–20 is potentially relevant when a husband who claims to be a Christian is sinning against his wife (or vice versa). In Matthew 18:15 the same word translated "won over" in 1 Peter 3:1 is used to speak of returning someone to godly behavior through verbal confrontation. However, a wife may choose not to pursue verbal confrontation and the subsequent pathway toward church discipline but allow her behavior to win over a Christian husband who is living in an ungodly manner. Discerning whether 1 Peter 3 or Matthew 18 is the right passage for a particular situation requires guidance from the Spirit. (4) Second Corinthians 6:14–7:1 protects against the notion that Peter is somehow tacitly approving Christians marrying non-Christians.

Teaching the Text

While the emphasis in Ephesians 5:22–33 is on husbands, here it is on wives. So the teacher should also not be afraid to spend more time on wives when teaching this text, though be aware that the idea of husbands honoring their wives and being considerate is rich with possibilities for elaboration.

When addressing the first six verses on wives, the teacher should understand the different situations in which this passage is applicable, including (1) wives who are married to nonbelieving husbands; (2) wives who are married to husbands who claim to be Christian but are not acting like it (see the comments on 3:1, above); (3) Christian wives who are married to Christian husbands—since Peter uses the example of Sarah and Abraham and both are followers of God; and (4) Christian women who are not married (see the comments on 3:5, above).

It is important to understand the context of this passage, because many women may have heard this passage in the context of how to have a good marriage. It is true that God wants good marriages, and this passage can be a true blessing in that regard, but the scope of this passage is much larger and the implications much grander. Namely, women matter to God, not just in that God cares about women. But women are essential to the plans that he has to rescue the world. If God's kingdom is going to come in this world—if God is going to rescue this world—it depends in a large part on women acting like godly women.

The main message of this passage to women is to pursue the unfading beauty of a quiet and gentle spirit. Peter presents three opportunities to witness a quiet and gentle spirit at work: submission, external beauty, and difficult assignments from God. One of the ways to highlight whether a quiet and gentle spirit or an anxious and fearful heart is at work is to ask what emotions the subjects of submission, external beauty, or difficult assignments engender when women think about them.

With regard to the one verse on husbands, the teacher might want to note that while husbands are not called to submit to their wives outside the mutual submission of Christians to each other in community (Eph. 5:21), husbands can choose the path of allowing their actions without words to win over their wives. It may very well be that the prayers mentioned in 3:7 refer to prayers of a husband for his wife who is not walking with the Lord.

Talking about women as "weaker partners" (3:7) might seem sexist, but the main point is that women are more vulnerable, that this world is more oppressive to them, and that the things that women are more naturally gifted at are less valued in this world under Satan's domination. Women are more likely to be the victims of violent assault; they will struggle more with gaining access to the levers of power in society; even in a Western society that seeks to be egalitarian, women are often objectified by men. Things that women are created to do, like childbearing, for example, are not valued by this world's systems. In many cases there is great pressure for a woman to act like a man in order to succeed in this world. It is important to help people to understand that what Peter means is that women have a tougher path in society.

Illustrating the Text

Awareness of our inheritance should influence our actions.

Television: *Downton Abbey.* On this show, the house itself (and its attendant lands and entailments) is a central character, affecting everyone. It stands as a possible inheritance, influencing people's motivations and actions. And it confers status, influencing people's standing and perception by others. At the same time, the enduring value of the house is seen to stand above the short-term gain or personal interests of its occupants, a theme that weighs heavily and often upon Robert Crawley, the Earl of Grantham, who understands himself to be a steward of a legacy that goes far beyond himself and stretches both backward and forward in time and encompasses far more than the house's occupants alone. Peter reminds us that women will receive a great inheritance. The "unfading beauty" (3:4) of their souls must match the "unfading beauty" of the inheritance.

Submission can be a powerful witness to unbelieving husbands.

Testimony: Rachel Miller Dean, a member of my church, shared the following testimony when I preached through 1 Peter 3:

> My first husband, Peter, was a good man, but not a believer. Add that to the marriage of two strong-willed people, and our home was filled with bickering and strife, and we were growing farther apart. I cried out to the Lord, and graciously, he answered. I did *not* like what I heard! The Lord told me I needed to submit to Peter's leadership. I thought I *had* been. After all, I'd moved 2,500 miles away from family for him, dinner was on the table every night, and I was home with the kids rather than working at a job that would be more fulfilling than picking up Legos and Barbies. I soon learned that submission meant so much more.
>
> It meant putting Peter's needs and desires before my own. It meant not arguing for my own way and for my own rights at every turn. I learned that it was OK to look ahead, make suggestions, and plead my case, but that for peace to reign, I had to let him make the decision and then support him in it . . . even when I *knew* it was going to end up a disaster. I learned that when it *did* end up a disaster, "I told you so" was not the answer the Lord had in mind, and that "How can I help?" was much more effective in building trust. The bickering and fighting stopped, and he learned to trust me with more. Over time, our marriage became rock solid.
>
> In 2001, at the age of 52, the Lord handed Peter something he couldn't control on his own; he was diagnosed with terminal cancer. For the first time, he saw God reaching out to him through his family, through our church family, and through some of his coworkers, Christian men who had been praying for him for years. He accepted the Lord as his Savior in January 2002. The change in him was incredible. The man who had no time for God now couldn't find enough time for him. He was always a man of few words, but once saved, you couldn't shut him up! He had seldom seen the inside of a Bible, but in a very short time he was quoting Scripture like someone who had grown up memorizing God's Word. God used him mightily as he shared his testimony

with everyone. He only had a short time, and God used every minute of it. By the time he went home to be with our Lord, the only regret he had was that he hadn't come to know Jesus sooner. I agree. The man he was as a believer would have been an amazing guy to have been married to for those twenty-two years. But I am more than thankful I got to know him during the nine months we had together as Christians.

Why Do Good People Suffer?

Big Idea

Jesus's death and resurrection provide the basis for why Christians who fear God experience suffering and why they are blessed when they suffer.

Key Themes

- Fear God.
- Christ is Lord.
- Christ's death and resurrection are the basis for understanding blessing in suffering.

Understanding the Text

The Text in Context

In 2:13–3:7 Peter has been exploring the application of the general principle of election-ethics-community-mission to the specific circumstances of governing authorities, work relationships, and husbands and wives. The word "finally" in 3:8 indicates that Peter is drawing to a close this application-specific subsection and is returning to the general discussion of the principle. Now Peter focuses on the question of why those who are following God's plan end up experiencing suffering along the way.

Structure

The flow of Peter's argument in 3:8–22 is very important for understanding what he is saying. He begins with a basic restatement of the election-ethics-community-mission principle in 3:8–9, but with a focus on the aspect that believers who obey God are blessed by God. Peter quotes Psalm 34:12–16 in 3:10–12 to make this point. But the use of Psalm 34 raises an additional question: Why aren't believers who are trusting in God being delivered from persecution and trouble as Psalm 34:7–10 says they will be? This provides Peter with the opportunity to state in 3:13–17 that, paradoxically, those who suffer for doing what is right are blessed. This leads Peter to an explanation in 3:18–22 of how this worked with Christ's death, resurrection, and ascension.

Interpretive Insights

3:9 *On the contrary, repay evil with blessing.* This translation probably overly restricts the sense of what Peter has actually written, which is simply "on the contrary, bless." It is true that this command to bless comes immediately after the injunction to not repay evil for evil or insult for insult in 3:9, and the injunction to repay evil with blessing is quite common (e.g., Matt. 5:43–48; Rom. 12:14; 1 Cor. 4:12). However, the larger context is that believers are to be a blessing to all people at all times whether in response to evil or not. This is the basis of the Abrahamic structure of election-ethics-community-mission, which Peter will discuss in the next phrase.

to this you were called so that you may inherit a blessing. Do believers bless others because they have been blessed by God (e.g., NET, GNT, GW) or so that they can be blessed by God (NIV, NLT, ESV)? It is possible to translate this sentence either way, and both are true, but the NIV has opted for the better

---

1 Peter 3:8–22; Psalm 34; Isaiah 8; and the Fear of the Lord

Underlying everything that Peter writes in 3:8–22 is the concept of the fear of the Lord. Psalm 34:11 (the verse that introduces the section Peter quotes) says, "Come, my children, listen to me; I will teach you *the fear of the Lord*." Isaiah 8:13 (the verse that immediately follows what Peter quotes in 3:14) says, "The Lord Almighty is the one you are to regard as holy, he is the one you are to fear, he is the one you are to dread." Fearing God has been a key theme in this epistle already (1:17; 2:17). Fearing the Lord has multiple aspects to it, but its central idea is focusing on the Lord alone: looking to the Lord alone, being afraid of the Lord alone, trusting in the Lord alone, following the Lord alone, obeying the Lord alone, loving the Lord alone, and so on. One very clear principle from the Old Testament is that things go well for those who fear the Lord. This is explicit not only in Psalm 34:7–10,

the psalm Peter is quoting, but throughout the Old Testament (e.g., 1 Sam. 12:14; 2 Sam. 23:3; 2 Chron. 26:5; Pss. 31:19; 33:18–19; 85:8–9; 112; 128; Prov. 10:27; 19:23). It is not that those who fear the Lord in the Old Testament never suffer. The story of Job was written to prove otherwise (as an aside, notice that the book of Job begins with a discussion about Job's fear of the Lord bringing great material blessings to his life). Rather, in the Old Testament Job is the seeming exception, not the norm. This is why it is so hard for Peter to accept that the Messiah will suffer (Mark 8:31–33). But now that he has grasped the point, Peter realizes that fearing the Lord means fearing Christ, since Christ is Lord (1 Pet. 3:15). If we look at Christ as our example, suffering becomes the norm for the God-fearing Christian, not the exception, and the pathway to blessing.

sense. It is true that Abraham was unconditionally elected by God to receive a blessing and on the basis of this election was called to bless others, so that believers bless others *because* God has blessed us. But it is also true that within the Abrahamic covenant the experience of God's blessings here and now was conditional on obedience to God (Gen. 18:18–19), and the law of Moses was given to explain this aspect of the Abrahamic covenant. From this point of view, believers should obey God and bless others so that we can receive God's blessings now. That is the point of Psalm 34:12–16, which Peter quotes in 3:10–12.

3:10 *Whoever would love life and see good days.* This begins a quote from Psalm 34:12–16. See the sidebar and "Structure" for how this fits into the flow of the argument.

3:14–15 *even if you should suffer for what is right, you are blessed.* Here is the radical concept that Peter himself struggled to understand: suffering for doing right is a sign of blessing. How? The question cannot be answered until 4:13–14. Peter must first establish the foundation for the answer. Christ suffered death but was made alive by the Spirit (3:18) and is now in the position of glory (3:22). This same glory is available to Peter's readers now in the Spirit and will be fully manifested in the future (4:13–14).

"Do not fear their threats; do not be frightened." But in your hearts revere Christ as Lord. Peter's transition to Jesus comes in his citation of Isaiah 8:12, part of a passage he has already connected to Jesus in 2:8. The link is that believers are not to fear what those without God fear (Isa. 8:12), but they are to fear the Lord (Isa. 8:13), who is a stone that causes people to stumble (Isa. 8:14). Since the stone that causes people to stumble is Christ (2:8), and Christ is the stone the builders rejected (2:7), then believers must acknowledge or revere Christ as Lord. To revere Christ as Lord is to realize that the God of the Old Testament who is to be feared is Jesus. Jesus's example of "suffering first, then glory" provides the normative path for all believers in Jesus.

3:17–18 *it is better, if it is God's will, to suffer for doing good than for doing evil. For Christ also suffered once for sins, the righteous for the unrighteous, to bring you to God.* Here the sufferings of the readers are being cast in terms of God's larger plan. Just as Acts 2:23 says Peter taught that Jesus was crucified both because of actions of wicked men *and* as a direct result of God's deliberate plan and foreknowledge, so Peter's readers are suffering because of both the actions of those who speak maliciously against them *and* God's will to cause them to suffer. This follows the pattern of Jesus, who, though righteous, suffered as an unrighteous person in order to bring people to God. So believers in Jesus, though relatively innocent, are suffering as if they were guilty in order to bring people to God.

3:19–21 *those who were disobedient long ago when God waited patiently in the days of Noah.* Most likely this passage refers to angelic/demonic beings engaging in sinful sexual interactions with human women mentioned in Genesis 6:1–8. Further speculation on what happened in Genesis 6:1–8 was prevalent at the time of Peter in the apocryphal work *1 Enoch* (see the comments on 2 Pet. 2:4 and Jude 6). Why does Peter include a reference here to a seemingly obscure event from the Old Testament? First, he sees what happened at the time of Noah to be typologically related to what is happening with believers' salvation (the Greek word *antitypos*—translated "symbolizes"—is used in 3:21). Second, the NIV has not translated a word (*kai*), which could indicate that Peter meant, "After being made alive, he *even* went and made proclamation." "Proclamation" refers not to preaching the gospel—redemption is not available to these angelic beings—but to the proclamation of Christ's lordship. Even these beings, imprisoned and long forgotten by humans, are under Christ's authority, along with angels, authorities, and powers (3:22), making this an important story that affirms Christ's lordship.[1]

saved through water . . . pledge of a clear conscience toward God. It saves you by the resurrection. The parallel that Peter sets up is between Noah being saved "through" (Greek, *dia*) water and believers being saved "by" (Greek, *dia*) Christ's resurrection. For Noah, water was both an agent of destruction that he was saved from and an opportunity for new life without sinful humans who had plagued his existence. For believers, Jesus's resurrection saves us from the destruction of death and gives us an opportunity for new life without being plagued by our sinfulness (cf. 4:1–2) or the sinfulness of others (cf. 4:18). Noah was saved through water and by water; Christians are saved through death and by death. Baptism is the connection—not physical water baptism, the removal of dirt from the body, but baptism by the Spirit (Mark 1:8). Spirit baptism happens when someone places their faith in Jesus and receives the Holy Spirit, who unites them to Christ in his resurrection (e.g., Rom. 6:3–5; 1 Cor. 12:12–13; Gal. 3:26–28). The fact that this Spirit baptism is symbolized through water baptism strengthens the symbolic connection between Noah and believers even further.

The "pledge of a clear conscience toward God" represents the decision that a person makes to submit to the lordship of Christ in salvation. This commitment, which is connected to Spirit baptism, is afterward commemorated in water baptism.

Teaching the Text

This passage is talking about the blessings of being a righteous sufferer. One way to set up the passage is to take a cue from the book of Psalms, which identifies different ways of experiencing blessings: In Psalm 1 blessings come through keeping the law. In Psalm 32 blessings come to those who break the law and confess. In Psalm 34 blessings come to those who are righteous sufferers. It may be helpful to point out that in many ways, some of the greatest blessings of God are reserved for those who are asked by God to suffer because of their righteousness. (On Abraham as an example, see "Illustrating the Text.")

How do blessings come to righteous sufferers? According to this passage, these blessings come in two ways: (1) God pays special attention to righteous sufferers and is near them to help them (3:12). (2) Righteous sufferers are blessed in having the opportunity to see people drawn to God through their suffering (3:15). When a righteous person suffers for being righteous, it will inevitably cause people to ask questions, which will allow them to hear about Jesus.

When one is teaching this passage, helping people see the transitions will be important, since Peter doesn't make them explicit. When one moves from 3:10–12 to 3:13–14, it is necessary to realize that Peter is interacting with Psalm 34 and the questions it raises about why Christians who are obeying God still end up suffering and how it is that they are blessed. Likewise, the move from this question to the rest of the passage makes sense only if the teacher points out that Peter is consciously identifying the "Lord" from Isaiah 8:12–14 with Christ so that "revere Christ as Lord" (3:15) means to fear Christ, which in turn means to look to Christ alone for how things are supposed to work. The rest of the passage is an explanation for how suffering was central to the blessing Christ is now experiencing.

Another challenge to the teacher is handling 3:18–22. Peter's point is relatively simple. Jesus is Lord over every power and authority, and believers will ultimately be victorious through his resurrection. However, the references to angels sinning, Noah, and baptism may be more obscure and raise ancillary questions. The parallel with Noah being saved by and through water is really powerful when connected to Christians being saved by and through death, especially since this is what the rite of water baptism symbolizes. However, since 3:21 says that this "baptism . . . now saves you," it is important to help people realize that the primary referent is *Spirit* baptism, not water baptism.

Finally, it is worth noting that the Greek word for "answer" in 3:15 is *apologia*, from which we get the modern theological word "apologetics." This verse is often used as a rationale for doing apologetics as evangelism, that is, offering intellectual arguments in defense of creation, the Bible, Christ's resurrection, the existence of God, and so on. What Peter has in mind here is much broader. The focus of 1 Peter is not on preparing believers to present philosophical, historical, or scientific arguments. It is on living the gospel in community in such a way that it testifies to the reality of the risen Christ.

Illustrating the Text

God gives different kinds of blessings.

Bible: Psalms 1; 32; and 34 provide a framework for understanding the different ways in which we experience God's blessings. Abraham experienced the Psalm 1 blessings of being a lawkeeper when he acted kindly toward his nephew Lot and offered him his choice of land in which to settle. Abraham experienced the Psalm 32 blessings of being a forgiven lawbreaker when he lied to Abimelek about Sarah being his wife and ended up still being blessed by God after his sin had been acknowledged. But the greatest blessings of God came when Abraham was living Psalm 34 and experiencing righteous suffering in being asked to sacrifice his son Isaac. The blessings that God provided in Genesis 22 include God having his eyes on the righteous who are suffering in his presence and helping Isaac come to see God in a new way and worship him.

God blesses the one who suffers in righteousness.

News Story: A woman named Sarah Farkas felt compelled to give one of her kidneys to a man named Duke Guy from her church, whom she barely knew. God asked Sarah to suffer not because she had done anything wrong but because she had done everything right. God blessed her first with a tangible sense of his presence and second by the fact that she ministered to this man and testified to the love of Jesus to thousands of people through this story.[2]

Always be prepared to give an answer for the hope that is in you.

Personal Testimony: The first person I led to faith in Jesus was my next-door neighbor in college. We began talking about Jesus because one night she was feeling especially miserable about how life was going. As we were out walking, she wanted to know why it was that she was doing many of the sinful things that the world says make you happy yet she was miserable, while I was avoiding many of the sinful things that the world says make you happy yet I was full of joy and life. I was not as well prepared to give an answer as Peter tells us to be, but I was able to tell her that the hope and joy that I had came not from circumstances or from the world but from Jesus's love for me.

Armed with the Right Attitude

Big Idea

Arm yourself with the attitude that submitting to God's will and following the path of suffering lead to glory.

Key Themes

- Choose to follow Christ's path of suffering in obedience to God's will as opposed to living for yourself.
- Jesus is the Judge of all people.
- The gospel brings life through death.

Understanding the Text

The Text in Context

Having moved from election (1:3–12) to ethics (1:13–2:3) to community (2:4–10) to mission (2:11–3:7), Peter is now answering the question, what role does suffering play in all of this? Having begun with the argument that because Christ was blessed through suffering, believers are blessed in suffering (3:8–22), Peter now turns to focus on the need to adopt this same attitude about suffering that Jesus had, specifically in relation to our ethical orientation, and the results from adopting this attitude.

Two aspects of this section prepare the way for what is next. First, those who choose suffering are choosing to live for God's will (4:2), and 4:7–11 will give more instruction on what living for God's will looks like in community. Second, choosing suffering now is necessary in light of judgment day (4:5–6), and 4:12–19 will explain this further.

Structure

There is one command in this section: "Arm yourselves" (4:1). This command is not to do an activity as much as it is to reorient one's thinking around the pattern of Christ's suffering. The structure of this passage flows out of

Peter's argument for adopting this attitude. (1) Having Christ's attitude about suffering sets one on the different path of doing God's will (4:1–2). (2) This is a better path—even though the world doesn't realize it—because of the judgment of God (4:3–6).

Interpretive Insights

4:1 *since Christ suffered in his body, arm yourselves also with the same attitude.* The word for "arm" is often used in the sense of military preparation for battle. It is ironic to *arm* oneself for *nonretaliation* in the face of suffering. However, since the battle is with an enemy whose tactics are lies, intimidation, and deceit, readers do need to be armed. The best preparation for battle with Satan is to be armed with Christ's attitude.

To understand the attitude that Peter wants believers to have, notice that five of the six times Peter uses "body" (*sarx*) are in this section (3:18, 21; 4:1, 2, 6; cf. 1:24). In particular there is the juxtaposition between body and Spirit explicit in 3:18 and 4:6, like the juxtaposition of baptism with water and Spirit in 3:21 (see the comments on 1 Pet. 3:19–21). Peter's point is that Christ experienced death in his body because of the sins of others but was made alive by the Spirit. His resurrection power in the Spirit and lordship over all things came not by avoiding sin and death but by embracing the will of God for him to suffer (1:11) and entrusting himself to the one who judges justly (2:23). The attitude Jesus exemplified is that life comes through death, and glory comes through suffering. Believers are commanded to adopt this same attitude.

because whoever suffers in the body is done with sin. This doesn't mean that whoever suffers in the body no longer sins. Otherwise there would be no need to encourage godly behavior in this letter. Rather, those who embrace suffering in the body because of the sins of others are choosing the pathway that Jesus himself established and exemplified. God has willed us to walk the path of suffering and death to get to glory and life. To embrace such an attitude sets one free from the lie that joy and glory come from following our own desires and the desires of the world.

4:2 *they do not live the rest of their earthly lives for evil human desires, but rather for the will of God.* "Earthly lives" means life in these physical bodies (Greek, *en sarki,* "in the flesh"). Again, the point is not that Peter's readers will never have another evil desire if they embrace the attitude that glory comes through suffering. To embrace suffering as a pathway to glory represents a fundamental shift in ideology. One can choose either God's will or one's own will as the determinative compass for life. Those who have embraced suffering are embracing the attitude of Jesus that God's will is the compass by which they navigate their lives.

4:3 *you have spent enough time in the past doing what pagans choose to do.* In other words, "You have spent enough time being on that other path—the path where the world's and your own evil desires drive your actions." The word for "choose to do" (*boulēma*) can also be translated "will" (as in Rom. 9:19). It is not the same word as "will" in 4:2 (*thelēma*), but it does set up the contrast for readers between whose will one is going to choose to follow: God's will or the pagan world's will.

living in debauchery, lust, drunkenness, orgies, carousing and detestable idolatry. "Living in" emphasizes a lifestyle choice. The list that Peter has chosen has parallels other places in Scripture (e.g., Rom. 13:13; Gal. 5:19–21; Eph. 5:3–5), but the emphasis here is on behaviors in which the lack of self-restraint is more obvious and the pleasure factor is higher, such as alcoholism, partying, pornography, or obsessive addictions to food or money. Anger, laziness, and bitterness are just as bad but don't conjure up the same sense of "reckless, wild living" (4:4).

4:4 *They are surprised that you do not join them.* "Surprised" has the sense of "shocked, dumbfounded, and astonished." To not participate in excessive drinking, rampant sexual activity, or the pursuit of happiness at all costs is shocking to people who have made these their life goals. Such a radically different orientation to life has great value in drawing the attention of unbelievers. For example, most secular college students are astounded when they come upon someone who has chosen not to participate in sex outside of marriage. Most Wall Street barons (or, in fact, most people in general) are stunned to find out that there are people who care very little how much money they have.

they heap abuse on you. This is one of the reasons why choosing God's will inevitably results in suffering. Darkness hates the light (John 3:19). Those who are not living for God feel convicted by those who are and respond with verbal abuse. Such verbal abuse contributes to the feelings of estrangement and isolation associated with being a foreigner or outsider.

4:5 *they will have to give account to him who is ready to judge the living and the dead.* People can submit to God's will or that of the world now, but this choice will disappear in the future. Everyone will have to give an account to God, the one who will judge the living and the dead, and this Judge is Jesus (Acts 10:42). This adds more poignancy to following the path Jesus blazed of suffering and then glory, since all people will stand before Jesus to give an account of their lives. The fact that God is ready means that he has already made plans to judge all things. He is simply waiting to enact those plans. Judgment is inescapable, no matter how much people may want to deny its reality.

4:6 *For this is the reason the gospel was preached even to those who are now dead.* This does not refer to Jesus proclaiming his lordship to the imprisoned spirits in 3:19. "Preach the gospel" is used here; "proclaim" is used there. Those are imprisoned spirits; these are dead humans.

"For this is the reason" connects what Peter is saying here to the fact that Jesus is the Judge of the living and the dead, something Peter considers an essential part of the message of the gospel (cf. Acts 10:42). Because Jesus is the one who judges the living and the dead, the gospel was preached to people before they died, so that now that they have died, they are made alive with Jesus according to the power of the Spirit. This ties back not to 3:19 but to 3:18. Jesus was put to death in the body but made alive by the Spirit. Likewise, those who died having believed the gospel have been made alive by the Spirit.

Therefore, while alive—and even after dying—believers in Jesus will be judged by the world's standards with regard to outward appearance. They will be declared to be prudish or narrow-minded or denounced as having wasted their life on following God or judged to have missed out on truly living. But while these judgments can be damaging and hurtful, they are effective only during life in the body. But regardless of what humanity says about a believer, God has already rendered his judgment over the one who has died in Christ in that he has made them alive by the Spirit.

This is like Jesus's point about not fearing those who have power in this life only but fearing the one who has power not only to kill but to condemn to hell (Matt. 10:28). Peter is essentially saying, "Do not fear and follow those whose only power is to judge you by heaping verbal abuse on you in this life; fear and follow him who in his power to judge can raise you to life again."[1]

Theological Insights

Having the attitude of Christ. What Peter says here, about arming oneself with the same attitude that Christ had in regard to suffering, fits well with Philippians 2:5–11, where Paul highlights that Jesus chose to obey God's will and become a servant, suffering death, and as a result he is glorified above all names. Hebrews 12:2–3 is similar: Jesus endured the cross because of the possibility of joy that was in front of him. In this way believers are to fix their eyes on him so as not to lose heart when enduring suffering. The narrative account in Mark 8:31–9:1 of Jesus's teaching on his suffering demonstrates this attitude toward suffering in action. Jesus's command to rejoice in the face of persecution in Matthew 5:11–12 has this same attitude at its core.

Teaching the Text

This is an important text in 1 Peter to get right because having the right attitude about suffering is so essential for being able to endure it. The reason

Peter says "arm yourselves" (4:1) with this attitude is because he knows that in spiritual warfare, having the right attitude about suffering is absolutely essential to enduring it. The genius of Peter's argument may take more time to unfold because of its unfamiliarity to many who will be listening. While many will be familiar with the idea that suffering brings maturity, Peter's point is that suffering is part of a binary choice that humans must make, between orienting one's life under the will of God and orienting one's life under the will of the world. To choose God's will is to choose to suffer abuse. Perhaps the description of Moses in Hebrews 11:25 sums up what Peter is trying to get across: "He chose to be mistreated along with the people of God rather than to enjoy the fleeting pleasures of sin." All must choose to be mistreated along with Jesus or to enjoy the pleasures of sin for a short time. Those are the only two choices.

In teaching this material, the teacher may find it useful to strongly emphasize that there are only two choices, not three. Many Christians desire a middle way between being pagans and suffering for God. They would like the ability to have a comfortable life now and then a good experience on judgment day. No such third path exists.

The teacher of this text will do well to employ the implicit and explicit arguments that Peter uses. The implicit argument is that the pleasures of sin do not satisfy in this life because of the wild, reckless, out-of-control way of life they offer. The more explicit argument is that all human beings will stand before Jesus, the Judge of the living and the dead, and he is the only one who has the power to give life.

Inherent within this dichotomy that Peter presents is the idea that one cannot please God and humans (especially non-Christians) at the same time (cf. Gal. 1:10). If the world celebrates how you've chosen to live your life, God probably does not. If God approves of your lifestyle choices, the world likely will not. This contrast between the two is growing stronger as our culture becomes more and more post-Christian. Even those Christians deemed successful in the world's eyes in relation to money, sports, accomplishments, and so on will often be considered narrow-minded, puritanical, unenlightened, or foolish if they are truly following Jesus. Having listeners think through to what extent they experience or desire approval from the world can be a useful window into this topic.

It should also be pointed out that Peter's primary emphasis is positive: suffering for being a believer is a sign that believers are on the path of following God's will, not the path of being ruled by sin. This is part of Peter's point from 3:14 about being blessed for suffering. One of the blessings is that it affirms one's status as a follower of Jesus.

Illustrating the Text

Do not long for the life of the ungodly.

Bible: **Psalm 73.** This is a powerful psalm for putting into words the attitudes that many of us feel as we long for a way to live out our faith without all the sufferings of life. Like this passage in 1 Peter, it illustrates that when viewed from the present, the path of the wicked looks like the better choice. But all of that changes when viewed from God's eternal perspective. Most Christians don't want the wickedness of the wicked, but they wouldn't mind having their easier life.

Arm yourself with the attitude of Jesus.

Personal Testimony: I remember that my father, near the end of his life, occasionally would get discouraged at financial struggles he regularly dealt with. He would look back on a series of sacrifices that God asked him to make for the sake of his family and for the kingdom and at times wonder—wasn't there some way to do this whole Christian thing without those sacrifices? Many of his non-Christian contemporaries had money to spare, and he would ask aloud, "What if I made a mistake, and there was a way to have a comfortable life without all the financial struggle and still accomplish the things God wanted me to accomplish?" He never would have given up his Christianity, but maybe there was a way to have an easier life here and eternal life too. In his discouragement and doubt, I could see the attacks of Satan. As my father armed himself with the same attitude that Jesus had—that there were only two paths and he had chosen the right one—and as he focused on the blessings that had come through his sacrifices, he would experience relief from Satan's attacks.

Suffering is tolerable when we focus on the joy to come.

Human Experience: Mothers endure a lot. With pregnancy, many experience morning sickness for at least the first trimester. Just when those difficulties pass, they watch as their body is radically transformed. Aches. Pains. And finally, birth, the biggest struggle of all. If there were no baby at the end of the journey, the process would be nothing but torture. But because there is new life at the end of it all, and little signals of that life along the way in the form of kicks and flips and ultrasounds, the struggle is worth it all!

Community Evangelism

Big Idea

Living out God's will in community involves being united in love, exercising hospitality, and serving one another with spiritual gifts, resulting in others coming to faith.

Key Themes

- Be united through love.
- Exercise hospitality.
- Serve others with spiritual gifts.

Understanding the Text

The Text in Context

Having established that those who are willing to suffer have chosen the pathway of God's will as opposed to their own will or the will of the world (4:1–6), Peter proceeds to speak more about living out God's will in the community of faith. In many ways this draws to a close the section that began in 2:11 by filling out the more general commands of 3:8–9 regarding how to behave in relation to other believers in community so that the community of faith wins over people who do not believe. Just like citizens and governing authorities (2:13–17), slaves and masters (2:18–25), and husbands and wives (3:1–7), the community of faith is another social location where Peter's election-ethics-community-mission framework must be lived out.

Structure

Verse 7 functions as the transition from 4:1–6. After this transition, Peter gives three primary ways in which a community can glorify God in the midst of suffering. The key phrase "each other / one another," which appears three times in 4:8–10, is the structural marker. The three ways a community can glorify God are (1) loving one another (4:8), (2) offering hospitality to one another (4:9), and (3) serving one another with the spiritual gifts God has provided (4:10–11). The final phrase of the section ties back to 2:12 and brings some closure to 2:11–4:7.

Interpretive Insights

4:7 *The end of all things is near.* In 4:5–6 Peter was speaking about judgment, and now to transition to this next section he reminds his readers that God's judgment is always imminent because the end of all things is near. This draws on the Old Testament language that "the day of the LORD is near" (Isa. 13:6; Ezek. 30:3; Joel 1:15; 3:14; Obad. 15; Zeph. 1:7, 14). While it is true that when these prophetic passages were written the day of the Lord was far off chronologically, "near" represented "close at hand" more than "close in time." Israel and the nations did experience some level of day-of-the-Lord judgment from God as they waited for the final day of the Lord. So too Peter was not wrong in saying the end of all things was near. For his original readers, who have all died, functionally speaking the end has come. So too for believers today, while Christ's second coming may yet be far off chronologically, it is always "near at hand," not only because it can come at any instant, but because God's judgment is occurring in the present (1:17). Moreover, death is always near at hand. (See also the comments on James 5:8.)

be alert and of sober mind so that you can pray. While the clause can mean "be alert and of sober mind with respect to prayer," the NIV translation is probably right. Choosing to follow the will of the world results in wild, reckless living. Those who choose God's will are choosing alertness and sobriety. The purpose of alertness and sobriety is prayer. By this Peter most likely has in mind praying for God's will to be done on earth as it is in heaven, just as Jesus taught him to pray (Matt. 6:10). If one is going to live according to God's will, one must pray for guidance to understand God's will and strength to carry it out. In the next three verses Peter will give three primary commands so his readers can understand important aspects of God's will.

4:8 *love each other deeply, because love covers over a multitude of sins.* Here Peter alludes to Proverbs 10:12 and/or 17:9, both of which heighten the sense that Peter is talking about relationships in community. Proverbs 10 pairs the statement on love with "hatred stirs up conflict," and Proverbs 17 pairs it with "whoever repeats the matter separates close friends." Unity is the goal (see the sidebar). Love refuses to allow relational shortcomings to overcome unity. It also creates unity through acts of hospitality (4:9) and serving one another (4:10).

4:9 *Offer hospitality to one another without grumbling.* The basic idea of hospitality is welcoming strangers into your life—especially the disadvantaged—not on the basis of what they can provide to you, but on the basis of how you can serve them (Matt. 25:35, 43). The essential form of hospitality is sharing a meal together with no thoughts of repayment (Luke 14:12–14). The word for "hospitality" is a compound adjective (*philoxenos*), which could be translated, "loving strangers." It is a fitting word in a letter in which the

1 Peter 4:7–11 and John 13–17

Surely the Thursday before Good Friday was a memorable one for Peter. What Jesus taught, did, and prayed that night was etched into his memory and most likely formed his thoughts on how believers were to relate to one another in community. That evening especially, as recorded in John 13–17, seems to stand behind what Peter is writing here. First, the major themes Peter has recently been speaking about in 3:8–4:6 were all brought up in that teaching: Jesus's suffering and the suffering of his followers at the hands of the world (John 15:18–16:4), the world's wrong judgment (16:20), suffering followed by joy (16:20–22), the Spirit (14:15–17, 25–26; 15:26–27; 16:12–15), and the fact that Jesus's followers would live because he lived (14:19). Now Peter tells his readers that above all else they are to love one another (1 Pet. 4:8). The command to love is the primary command Jesus taught his disciples on that night (John 13:34; 15:12, 17; cf. 13:1) and correlates to John 13:31–38. Second, Peter instructs his readers to show hospitality (1 Pet. 4:9), which correlates to John 13:18–30, where Jesus is extending hospitality to the disciples (including Judas) by sharing the Last Supper with them. Third, Peter commands believers to serve one another, and John 13:1–17 records Jesus teaching and modeling servanthood in washing the disciples' feet. Significantly, in John's account Peter is named in all three portions of John 13—that is, the Upper Room Discourse, the Last Supper, and the footwashing.

All of this leads to John 17, where Jesus prays for all believers, including Peter's readers. Specifically, he prays for unity so that the world may believe and so that Jesus and God the Father might be glorified. Here Peter is addressing the issues of prayer (4:7) and of Jesus and God the Father being glorified (4:11). What this means is that 4:7–11 has unity as its goal and witness to the world as a fundamental aspect of these commands.

purpose is to address those who were now strangers in society because of their faith in Christ. Hospitality within the Christian community was absolutely essential in fostering family ties among these new believers and reshaping their identities now as Christians.[1] Interestingly, this same word for "hospitality" is used two other times in the New Testament (1 Tim. 3:2; Titus 1:8), both in contexts of requirements for elders (a subject 1 Pet. 5:2–3 is about to address) and in connection with being "alert" and "of sober mind," as here in 4:7. Therefore, we can say that hospitality is a hallmark of spiritual maturity. It is the opposite of reckless, wild living, which is the hallmark of spiritual immaturity. Instead of us viewing people as objects to be used sexually and using raucous parties as opportunities to pursue selfish pleasure, hospitality is the intentional decision of mature Christians to take the initiative to invite people in to bless them, not out of obligation, lest there be grumbling, but out of an understanding of the truth of the gospel. In this way hospitality is a visual representation of the gospel, drawing nonbelievers toward faith as they see it practiced.

4:10 *use whatever gift you have received to serve others, as faithful stewards of God's grace.* Peter's third command is for his readers to use the spiritual gifts they have received to serve one another. On spiritual gifts, see "Theological Insights," below.

4:11 *as one who speaks the very words of God.* What makes a spiritual gift powerful is that it is not a natural ability but a means by which God manifests his grace-filled presence through the gifted believer to others. Those who are exercising gifts of speaking, like teaching, preaching, words of encouragement, and evangelism, should realize that they are speaking words from God. It is noteworthy that Peter does not reuse his previously employed terms for "Scripture" (*graphē*; as in 2:6) or "word of God" (either the term from 1:23; 2:8; 3:1 [*logos*] or the one from 1:25 [*rhēma*]), Greek words that he uses to refer to the Bible and the gospel (cf. 2 Pet. 1:19, 20; 3:2, 16). By using a different word here, Peter is distancing these "words of God" from the once-for-all, inerrant revelation of God contained in the Bible and the gospel. In other words, the Scriptures and the gospel contained in them are the Word of God, while someone using a spiritual gift of preaching is sharing words from God.[2] But it shouldn't be missed that this is still a message from the Lord. After all, living for God's will (4:2) requires hearing messages from others in the community through which God speaks about his will.

so that in all things God may be praised through Jesus Christ. The connection to 2:12 is not obvious in this translation: Peter writes there that believers should live such good lives that those who do not believe might "glorify" God; here he says that the believing community should love one another, exercise hospitality, and serve one another so that God might be "glorified/praised." As in 2:12, then, this verse has in mind reaching the lost, but the language of "all things" probably expands the scope to include the fact that God is glorified in the good done in the community, whether or not others come to faith.

Theological Insights

Spiritual gifts. First Peter 4:10–11 fits theologically with Romans 12:3–8; 1 Corinthians 12–14; and Ephesians 4:11–16. Like Romans 12, 1 Peter speaks of spiritual gifts in terms of apportionments of "grace," a related word ("gift," *charisma*; "grace," *charis*). By correlating this with 1 Corinthians 12:6–7, where spiritual gifts are manifestations of the Spirit, we can see that Peter thinks of God being present in and through the use of spiritual gifts, which is why he talks of people serving in God's strength and speaking words from God. This is the reason why the exercise of spiritual gifts within the community can result in people coming to faith, as Paul describes in 1 Corinthians 14:23–25.

Whereas Paul lists various examples of spiritual gifts, Peter subsumes them all under two categories: speaking and serving. But both Peter and Paul speak about God's grace coming through a variety of ways and means, with Paul spelling this out more fully using the analogy of the body.

Teaching the Text

One of the opportunities afforded by this passage of Scripture is the chance to teach on the much misunderstood and neglected theme of hospitality. Too many people today either think of hospitality as entertaining one's friends or don't think about hospitality at all. It might be helpful to explore the power of hospitality, especially for those who are suffering. The contrast between partying and wild living in the previous section of 1 Peter can be helpful because hospitality is the opposite of partying. Partying uses others selfishly; hospitality serves others. As a result hospitality counteracts the message of this world to people and reminds them that they are created in the image of God and worthy of being served by others; it counteracts the loneliness that suffering brings; it counteracts the identity crisis that suffering brings on by communicating to the person who is being changed through suffering that you are interested in getting to know this new person who is emerging. Hospitality is also a blessing for those who offer it (see examples in "Illustrating the Text," below).

Encouraging believers in communities of faith to house Christians in need of lodging, to invite brothers and sisters in Christ over to share a meal, and to actively seek out new people and help them become involved can have a powerful effect on both the community of faith and those who are watching.

A second opportunity afforded by this passage is the chance to teach people about spiritual gifts. While Peter does not provide the same level of detailed description that Paul does, this passage opens the door for a very helpful outline of teaching on spiritual gifts, namely, (1) each person has a gift; (2) they were given to us by God, and accepting this and using them is part of submitting to his will; (3) they were given to us to serve others, not for our own personal pleasure; (4) when we use them we are distributing God's grace in a variety of ways; (5) when each person uses their speaking or serving gifts, God is present, working through those gifts; and (6) God is the one who provides the strength to use the gifts.

Whether one focuses on loving one another, hospitality, spiritual gifts, or all three, it is important to tie these to evangelism. Evangelism is not the only reason for love, hospitality, and service, but in the context of Peter's letter, evangelism is certainly in the mix. Showing listeners that 4:7–11 is still part of the "mission" section introduced in 2:11–12 and drawing the connection between 4:11 and 2:12 can help make this explicit. Additional support can be found in the connection to John 13–16 and Jesus's prayer in John 17 (see the sidebar). Just as citizens, workers, and husbands and wives can bring people to believe in Jesus, so can the community of faith. This happens both as non-Christians come to church and observe and experience God's grace in the loving, hospitable, and serving community and as Christians who have experienced this love, hospitality, and service go into the world and testify to the reality that Jesus is Lord.

Illustrating the Text

Hospitality facilitates gospel mission and blesses those who offer it.

Bible: Peter's own experience in Acts 10–11 with hospitality is a beautiful illustration of the value of hospitality for gospel work. There God uses the hospitality offered by Cornelius and accepted by Peter as an illustration of the gospel truth that all ethnicities are loved and accepted by God. Other examples of hospitality occur throughout Scripture. Abraham offers hospitality to the Lord and receives the promise of a son (Gen. 18). Lot offers hospitality to the angels in Sodom and ends up having his life saved (Gen. 19). Boaz offers hospitality to Ruth and ends up with a wife (Ruth 2–3). The widow offers hospitality to Elijah and receives a miraculous provision of food (1 Kings 17). The Shunammite woman offers hospitality to Elisha and gets her son back from the dead (2 Kings 4). Zacchaeus invites Jesus to his house and receives salvation (Luke 19). Hebrews says that some people have offered hospitality to strangers, and these strangers have turned out to be angels (Heb. 13:2).

Testimony: Many churches have international student ministries, where congregational members take in exchange students or show hospitality to college students visiting from other countries. These host families feed the students, teach them about the culture, transport them, and provide a home away from home. Many students have become Christians through this hospitality. Ask a person who has participated in something like this to share their story.

Be a faithful steward of God's grace in various forms.

Scenario: Imagine a wealthy billionaire philanthropist who wants to give generously. He enlists you to help him do this. He begins by giving you $100 to buy flowers for someone, take them to lunch, buy them gas for their car, pay for housecleaning, or whatever you can think of to bless someone who needs encouragement. When you are done spending the $100, he will give you $200, and when you spend the $200 he will give you $300 dollars to spend, and so on. He is anxious for you to prove yourself faithful in this so that you can reach the point where he is able to entrust to you enough money to help a family to go to camp, make a major contribution to someone's college expenses, or even provide a vehicle for someone in need. Would you be interested in a job like this? Our spiritual gifts allow us to administer God's infinite supply of grace in various forms, of which financial generosity is one.

Why Suffering Christians Are Blessed

Big Idea

God's will is for believers to suffer so that we can experience the presence of the Spirit in unique ways now and glory when Christ returns. Therefore, trust God and keep doing good.

Key Themes

- The Holy Spirit is uniquely present with those who are suffering.
- Suffering leads to glory.

Understanding the Text

The Text in Context

In 3:14 Peter raised the issue of suffering believers being blessed. After digressing to explain the connection between Christ's sufferings and his glory (3:8–22), how sufferings establish which path in life we are on (4:1–6), and how the community can bear witness for Christ in the midst of suffering (4:7–11), Peter now returns to explain how it is that believers are blessed in the midst of suffering. This final theological section will wrap up many of the issues that Peter has been addressing with regard to suffering. There is an especially close tie to 1:3–12.

Structure

This section is oriented around one primary theological affirmation and one primary command.

1. Primary theological affirmation: believers are blessed through suffering because of the presence of the Holy Spirit (4:12–14)
2. Primary command: God is working everything out according to his plan, so when he places you in the midst of suffering, trust him and keep doing good (4:15–19)

Interpretive Insights

4:12 *do not be surprised at the fiery ordeal that has come on you to test you.* The imagery of fire and trials recalls 1:6–7, where Peter introduced the refining fire of grief-inducing suffering. Interestingly, although Peter focuses on being foreigners, he does not use the noun for "stranger" in his epistle, but here he uses the verb ("do not be surprised" = do not think it strange) and adjective ("strange"). Those who are strangers and foreigners in this world should not think of suffering in this world as something strange or foreign.

4:13 *rejoice . . . overjoyed.* "Rejoice" and "overjoyed" are translations of the same Greek word (*chairō*). The NIV has helpfully intensified the word "overjoyed" because Peter not only uses "rejoice" again but adds another word meaning "rejoice" that he used in 1:6 and 1:8 to intensify this feeling (*agalliaō*). It is as if he is saying that believers rejoice now in suffering, but when Christ comes the rejoicing will be way over the top.

participate in the sufferings of Christ. In Philippians 3:10, Paul uses the same type of language to speak about believers participating in Christ's suffering (cf. Rom. 8:17; 2 Cor. 1:5–7).[1] The idea of participation that Peter expresses here (using the Greek verb *koinōneō*, a cognate of *koinōnia* = "fellowship/participation") is stronger than what we generally think of in English when we think of "participation." Believers do not just suffer *with* or *alongside of Christ.* We participate *in* his sufferings. This suffuses "participate" with powerful overtones. To suffer for the sake of being a Christian is to be connected to Christ in a unique and powerful way. This connection between suffering believers and the suffering Messiah is essential because it is the basis for believers sharing in Christ's glory when he returns (cf. 5:1).

4:14 *you are blessed, for the Spirit of glory and of God rests on you.* This is the key verse in this section. In 3:14 Peter made the statement that believers who suffer now are blessed. This verse explains why: the "Spirit of glory and of God rests on you."

The language of the Holy Spirit "resting" on believers recalls the events of Acts 2, where Peter and the other apostles experienced the Holy Spirit being poured out on them, symbolized by tongues of fire coming to "rest" on them (Acts 2:3). It may also recall the Spirit descending and alighting upon Jesus at his baptism (Matt. 3:16) since the Spirit is predicted to "rest" on the Messiah (Isa. 11:2 LXX, same word), something that is actualized at Jesus's baptism.

The presence of the Holy Spirit at Jesus's baptism and especially at Pentecost in Acts 2 is the sign that the plan of God to save humankind is now being enacted. Therefore, in Acts 2 Peter ends his citation of Joel with "everyone who calls on the name of the Lord will be saved" (Acts 2:21).

He then urges his listeners to realize that the Spirit's presence affirms that God has made Jesus both Lord and Christ (Acts 2:36) so that they too can receive the Holy Spirit (Acts 2:38). For the suffering Christian, the Holy Spirit is the sign first and foremost that what happened to Jesus in being made alive in the Spirit after death (3:18) is what will happen to them. Second, the presence of the Holy Spirit means that God is present with them now to teach them, empower them, guide them, and enable them to do greater things than Jesus did, just as Jesus taught in John 14–16. Third, the Spirit's presence means that all the Old Testament prophecies about the Spirit of God—that he will cleanse believers, give them a new heart, move them to follow God's commands, no longer hide his face from them, shower them with blessings, give them rest (Isa. 32:15–20; 44:3; 63:11–14; Ezek. 36:25–28; 39:29)—all these are now the inheritance of those who suffer with Jesus.

But isn't this true of all believers? Yes. But by using the term "rests on you" Peter is saying that God is present with the suffering believer in a unique and powerful way: affirming, empowering, guiding, transforming, and so on. Just as the Spirit was present at Pentecost and at Jesus's baptism in unusually powerful ways, the Spirit will be present with suffering Christians in unusually powerful ways. Perhaps Peter has in mind his own experiences of miraculously being set free from prison (Acts 12) or of being given just the right words to say in times of persecution (Acts 4:8–20). He may have in mind Stephen's experience at his martyrdom (Acts 7:54–60) or an overwhelming sense of peace in the midst of trouble (John 14:26–27). Whatever form it might take, the suffering Christian is blessed because the Spirit of glory and of God is with them in a unique and powerful way in the midst of suffering. (See "Theological Insights," below.)

4:16 *if you suffer as a Christian, do not be ashamed.* The term "Christian" is used only three times in the New Testament (here and Acts 11:26; 26:28). Since it may have begun as a derogatory term, Peter may be drawing on that background to emphasize the nature of suffering.[2] To embrace the name Christian is to embrace not only Christ but the public scorn that comes from embracing Christ.

4:17 *it is time for judgment to begin with God's household.* Are the sufferings and persecutions that believers experience somehow part of the punishment of God for sin? While "judgment" usually entails punishment, and when God was angry he often began his punishment with Israel first (e.g., Jer. 25:29; Ezek. 9:6), that doesn't seem to be the idea here. The same word for "judgment" is used in John 9:39, where the focus is on differentiating between good and evil, as opposed to punishment: "For judgment I have come into this world, so that the blind will see and those who see will become blind."

This is an important parallel, because in John 9 the man is blind not because of sin but so that God can be glorified, and the man suffered persecution for his faith in Jesus. Additionally, suffering brings refinement and transformation (as in 1:6–7). This in turn leads to better discernment of the realities of good and evil.

what will the outcome be for those who do not obey the gospel of God? If those who are part of the household of God have to be refined, what will happen to those who are not part of the household of God? In other words, if suffering is required simply to distinguish between good and evil, the actual punishment of evil will be far worse.

4:19 *those who suffer according to God's will should commit themselves to their faithful Creator.* Here again Peter affirms that suffering happens as part of God's plan, but he adds the encouraging tag that God is their faithful Creator. This means he is trustworthy ("faithful") and knows best, since he is Creator of all things. Being assured of God's faithfulness in the midst of trials is absolutely essential (cf. 1 Cor. 10:13) because it can seem at times as if God has abandoned the believer.

To "commit" oneself is to entrust oneself to God in the midst of suffering, as Jesus did (2:23). This draws on the fear-of-the-Lord motif running throughout Peter's first epistle. To "fear" God is to trust him and wait for him and not take matters into one's own hands. There is the temptation to abandon the pathway of good in order to alleviate the suffering, and Peter encourages his readers not to do that.

Theological Insights

Unusually powerful activity of the Spirit. All believers are indwelt by the Holy Spirit (1:2), but the Spirit also "rests" in a unique way on those believers who are suffering for doing the right thing. This is part of a larger theme throughout the Scriptures that the Spirit both is active in all believers and "comes upon," "rests on," or "fills" some in unique ways at distinct times. This often was the sign of someone being called and empowered by God for unique service or to deliver a message from the Lord.[3] Peter's contribution is to apply this unique calling and empowering to suffering so that the person suffering persecution should think of themselves as being set apart and empowered in a unique way for work that God is calling them to.

Furthermore, being filled with the Spirit has the sense of being led, controlled, and ministered to by the Spirit, so that Paul can command believers who already have the Spirit (Eph. 1:13–14) to be filled with the Spirit (Eph. 5:18), and Matthew can speak of the Spirit coming on Jesus at his baptism and then leading Jesus through his temptation and ministering to him after it was over (Matt. 3:16–4:11). Peter's contribution is that Christians who are suffering for doing good can be sure that God will be with them in a unique way, providing comfort, guidance, and strength.

Teaching the Text

The most important affirmation in this section is that the Holy Spirit rests on those who are experiencing suffering for being Christians. It can be a challenge to help people understand that while every believer has the Holy Spirit, those who are in the midst of suffering for being Christians experience the Holy Spirit's power and presence in unique ways. It may be helpful to go through different ways that the Holy Spirit manifests his presence during times of suffering. As discussed above, the Spirit may be present with miraculous signs and wonders, like Peter escaping from prison; or the Spirit may be present in more subtle ways, such as giving believers incredibly rich times of prayer during periods of suffering, providing an inexplicable sense of peace, showing more clearly how God is using this suffering to accomplish his will, or showing up with a word of encouragement at just the right time.

It also may help to explain the Spirit's unique presence during suffering in terms of related concepts, like God's power being more present in our weaknesses (which in 2 Cor. 12:7–10 includes persecutions and hardship), God being close to the brokenhearted (Ps. 34:18), or Jesus being uniquely connected to the disadvantaged (Matt. 25:31–46). All these are the same theme: God is especially near to his people in difficult times.

Teaching through the primary theological application also opens the door to teach through the primary injunction: trust God and keep doing the right thing. If God gives his Spirit in a special way to those who are suffering, it is to encourage them that they are on the right path and to keep going. Difficult struggles are remarkably discouraging. This passage offers the teacher the opportunity to encourage suffering Christians by affirming that this is all part of God's plan. It is not something strange or unusual. They are not being picked on. God has planned this situation for them and sent his Spirit to guide them through it. God is not tempting them (cf. James 1:13), because he will work faithfully to ensure that the suffering becomes a blessing and not a stumbling block. The teacher should be eager to encourage listeners that the greatest comfort in the midst of suffering is that God is faithful.

It is too easy in the midst of suffering to try to find a way out, whether denying the faith in more dramatic cases of suffering, backing down from true Christian commitment in more subtle cases, or embracing ungodly solutions to the problem. Encouraging people to trust God and keep doing the right thing cannot be stressed enough.

Finally, the inclusion of 4:15 in this passage might be a prompt to the teacher to continually differentiate between suffering for doing good and suffering for doing wrong. The fact that Peter continues to repeat this point means that it is a point we should continue to repeat. These teachings about suffering apply to those who are suffering in obedience to God's will.

Illustrating the Text

God is near to his people during times of suffering.

Bible: Many biblical examples could be marshalled to highlight this point. These include Shadrach, Meshach, and Abednego in the furnace (Dan. 3); Daniel in the lions' den (Dan. 6); Elijah being persecuted by Jezebel (1 Kings 19); and Paul and Silas in prison (Acts 16).

Testimony: As a pastor or teacher, share a time in your own life when you felt God's closeness in the midst of struggle. You could also have a church member share an experience of God's gracious presence during a very difficult time (reading a testimony or sharing it on video).

God has a purpose for our suffering.

Church History: Pastor Josef Tson suffered greatly as a pastor in communist Romania in the 1970s. Arrested, threatened, and tortured, he was warned again and again to stop preaching the gospel. Yet Pastor Tson remained firm in his conviction. Recalling one particular instance, Pastor Tson comments:

> I told the interrogator, "You should know your supreme weapon is killing. My supreme weapon is dying. . . . Now here is how it works, sir: You know that my sermons are on tape all over the country. When you shoot me or crush me, whichever way you choose, [you] only sprinkle my sermons with my blood. Everybody who has a tape of one of my sermons will pick it up and say, 'I had better listen again. This man died for what he preached.' Sir, my sermons will speak 10 times louder after you kill me and because you kill me. In fact, I will conquer this country for God because you killed me. Go on and do it."[4]

In the midst of suffering a follower of Jesus can be assured that God has a purpose!

God is faithful in the midst of suffering.

Personal Testimony: One of the hardest parts of my job as a pastor is preaching. Preaching is a constant source of stress for me. But I wouldn't trade it for anything in the world, because every week I feel God's Spirit resting on me. Not one week in ten years has God failed to show up. It has always been in different ways and at different times, but every week he is with me. He has explained passages to me that I never would have understood on my own, given me illustrations, showed me where I was going wrong about things, provided strength for preaching, let me see him at work, and brought me encouragement. I feel his presence with me. Never once has he abandoned me. Even when I mess up and sin against him, he is so faithful to forgive me in his grace and mercy and be with me. This is how I am learning that God is faithful—through the suffering of a difficult assignment from God. What is your challenging assignment? Don't quit—press on.

Instructions for Those Suffering

Big Idea

Humbly submitting to God and to each other and being alert in the face of spiritual warfare are the keys to enduring the sufferings that all Christians experience.

Key Themes

- Care for others in the community.
- Submit to leadership in the local church.
- Have humility toward all.

Understanding the Text

The Text in Context

Peter closes his letter with instructions to his readers about how to endure sufferings and difficulties. Having argued in his letter for the theological place of community (2:4–10) and how the community can proclaim the gospel while living in the midst of suffering (4:7–11), Peter returns to give instructions to the community on how to interact with each other as well as to give general practical instructions for all believers to endure sufferings.

The section on elders and those under their authority recalls earlier sections on citizens (2:13–17), slaves (2:18–25), and husbands and wives (3:1–7), although the focus is on not mission but endurance. The pervasive theme of fearing God makes an appearance in 5:5–7, and there are strong ties between 5:1 and 4:13.

Structure

1. Relationships within the community (5:1–5b)
   a. Elders to people (5:1–4)
   b. People to elders (5:5a)
   c. Everyone to one another (5:5b)

2. Relationship to God (5:5c–7)
3. Relationship to Satan (5:8–9a)
4. Relationship to the wider Christian church (5:9b)

Interpretive Insights

5:1 *To the elders among you, I appeal as a fellow elder.* Peter begins chapter 5 by appealing as a fellow elder to the elders in the local church communities. Although Peter holds a position higher than elder—that of apostle (1:1)—he chooses to identify himself as an elder, a role he presumably functioned in for the church in Jerusalem. Therefore, Peter is writing from his own experience of presiding over a community of strangers-in-this-world who experienced suffering for their beliefs as well as from his continued role of being an apostle for all believers.

a witness of Christ's sufferings who also will share in the glory to be revealed. Peter mentions two more qualifications out of which he is writing. The first is that he witnessed Christ's sufferings himself. This is part of his qualification as an apostle (Acts 1:21–22) and, practically speaking, makes him able to instruct his readers about how best to endure suffering, having witnessed what Jesus did. The second qualification is that Peter himself is one who has suffered persecution, although he refers to his suffering using the positive language of being one "who also will share in the glory to be revealed." This is an allusion to 4:13, which uses the same or cognate words for "suffering," "glory," and "revealed" and two closely related words for "participate/share." Peter is offering advice as a fellow leader of a suffering community and one who has suffered himself.

5:2 *Be shepherds of God's flock that is under your care.* Ezekiel 34 gives a fuller sense of what it means to be a shepherd caring for his sheep (see the sidebar).[1]

not because you must, but because you are willing. This is the first of three opposites that are to characterize the elders. They should serve (1) not out of obligation, but willingly; (2) not for the money, but out of an eager desire to serve God and help others; (3) not ruling over people dictatorially, but being examples for them to follow.

5:4 *you will receive the crown of glory that will never fade away.* This word "crown" is metaphorical, as it is in 1 Thessalonians 2:19, where the Thessalonians are not literally a crown but represent what a crown represents—a source of honor and recognition. Those who serve as elders have taken on a task uniquely aligned with Jesus's ministry as Chief Shepherd. When Jesus returns, he will acknowledge and honor those who served him in this way. (Cf. 1 Tim. 3:1 on the "nobility" of being an elder.)

1 Peter 5:1–9 and Ezekiel 34

In Jeremiah 3:15 God promises that he will provide "shepherds after [his] own heart" to care for his people. To the reader of the Old Testament, such a promise brings to mind Ezekiel 34, the most extensive discussion in the Old Testament on the requirements of being a shepherd to God's people. As Jeremiah 3:15 is being fulfilled in Peter's audience, it is not surprising that Peter would draw on the background of Ezekiel 34 when he discusses shepherding God's flock. Six elements from Ezekiel 34 are present in 1 Peter 5:1–9.

1. In Ezekiel 34:4–6 God's sheep need someone to strengthen the weak, heal the sick, bind up the injured, bring back the strays, and search for the lost. Without good shepherds God's people will be scattered and become "food for all the wild animals." In 1 Peter 5:2, elders are to care for those who are suffering.
2. In Ezekiel 34:3 God condemns the shepherds who profit materially from their role as shepherd without caring for the flock. First Peter 5:2 urges elders not to serve for financial gain.
3. In Ezekiel 34:4 God condemns shepherds who rule harshly and brutally. First Peter 5:3 commands elders not to lord their authority over those entrusted to them.
4. Ezekiel 34:16–20 promises judgment on the sheep of the flock who have grown sleek, strong, and fat at the expense of others. Peter promises that God will fight against the proud and urges the sheep to embrace humility (1 Pet. 5:5–6).
5. In Ezekiel 34:23–24 God promises to send David's descendant to be their shepherd and a prince among them. First Peter 5:4 calls Jesus the Chief Shepherd of the flock and of the elders, who are shepherds.
6. In Ezekiel 34:25, 28 God promises to protect his sheep from savage beasts that try to devour them. First Peter 5:7–9 speaks of the devil wanting to devour believers and of God's ability to care for them in the midst of this.

5:5–6 *In the same way, you who are younger, submit yourselves to your elders.* The NIV translation here is a little vague. While this sentence could mean that younger people submit to older people (so the NIV 1984), in the context it means those who are younger (or newer in the faith) submit to the elders of the church (so ESV, NLT, NET, HCSB).

The use of "in the same way" and "submit" draws the readers' attention back to 2:13–3:7. As was argued there (see especially the comments on 3:1), submission means to follow the established rules of the relationship, which will look different in the contexts of marriage, business, and civic life. So too, submission in the church context has its own unique look. While obedience is part of this (cf. Heb. 13:17), the focus here is more on following the example that the elders set for the church, which is the last instruction Peter mentioned to the elders in 5:3. As elders model serving voluntarily, eagerly, and in an exemplary way, those who are younger in the faith are instructed to follow their examples. This is akin to the discipleship/imitation language that is used throughout the Scriptures (e.g., John 13:14–15; 1 Cor. 4:14–17; 11:1; Phil. 3:17; Heb. 13:7).

God opposes the proud but shows favor to the humble. This is a quote from Proverbs 3:34, used also in James 4:6. Here it is combined with an allusion to Matthew 23:12, also alluded to in James 4:10 ("Humble yourselves before the Lord, and he will lift you up"). "Opposes" was a military term for fighting against, and it sets up three contrasts: proud versus humble, God fighting against someone versus God showing favor, and God's mighty hand bringing someone low versus God's mighty hand lifting someone up. Peter has repeatedly stressed that if his readers are going to suffer, they should suffer for doing good as opposed to doing evil. To be proud and unsubmissive is to invite suffering at the hands of God. To embrace humility is to invite help from God. The choice is either to suffer at the hands of the world or to suffer at God's hands.

The reason that humility toward others in the community, especially elders, is so important is because this is an expression of humility toward God. God has placed believers into the community of faith under the authority of the elders to help them endure suffering. To arrogantly reject this is to pick a fight with God.

5:7 *Cast all your anxiety on him.* The language of "casting" cares comes from Psalm 55:22. Although the Greek word for "cast" is used only one other time in the New Testament, for literally casting nets when fishing (Luke 19:35), the Hebrew word from Psalm 55:22 is more common in the Old Testament and has the idea of "abandon," and Peter likely intends that meaning here. To cast your anxieties on God is to abandon your worries to him.

because he cares for you. The verb "care" is used in Mark 4:38 and Luke 10:40 in accusations that people make against Jesus, accusing him of not caring. Peter is affirming the exact opposite. God cares about everything that we are going through.

5:8 *Your enemy the devil prowls around like a roaring lion.* Always lurking in the background of the idea of suffering has been the concept of spiritual warfare—that believers are going through difficult times because their enemy is seeking to destroy them. Peter now makes this explicit. It is no accident that, having spoken about pride and anxiety, Peter transitions to speaking directly about Satan, because these are Satan's tools. Satan stands behind Job's sufferings, and Satan was the source of Peter's great trial in having to stand up for his faith (Luke 22:31–32). Peter knows what it is like not to be self-controlled and alert heading into a confrontation with Satan, having fallen asleep instead of obeying Jesus's injunction to pray that he might not fall into temptation (Luke 22:39–46). Likewise, Peter was neither alert to Satan's influence nor self-controlled in Matthew 16:22–23 when he took Jesus aside to rebuke him for teaching that the Messiah had to suffer. Having learned his lesson, Peter is strengthening his brothers and sisters in Christ by advising them to be alert to the reality of spiritual warfare and to be self-controlled in the face of Satan's deceptions and attacks.

5:9 *the family of believers throughout the world is undergoing the same kind of sufferings.* As in 4:12 an important component of enduring suffering is the realization that it is normal for a Christian to suffer. Suffering is an integral part of what it means to be a follower of Christ—no matter where one lives in the world. It is easy to think that other people in other places have it better than we do, but all believers in Jesus suffer for their faith. The universality of suffering unites believers together.

Theological Insights

For more on spiritual warfare, see "Theological Insights" in the unit on James 4:1–10.

Elders. In the Old Testament elders had a number of responsibilities, including praying and inquiring of God (e.g., Josh. 7:6; Ezek. 20:1–3; Joel 1:14), being resident historians (e.g., Judg. 2:7; Jer. 26:16–19; Joel 1:2), providing wise counsel (e.g., 2 Chron. 10:6–8; Job 12:20; Ps. 119:100; Ezek. 7:26), judging and exercising authority (e.g., Deut. 21:13–19; Josh. 20:4; Ruth 4:4; 1 Chron. 11:3; Ezra 5:9), and providing leadership for the people of Israel (e.g., Num. 11:16–17). In many cases the elders represented the people of Israel (e.g., Lev. 4:15; Deut. 21:6–9) and functioned as witnesses of God's divine power and communication (e.g., Exod. 17:5; Deut. 31:28).

In the New Testament elders first appear in the church in Acts 11:30. In Acts 15 they appear to be exercising authority alongside of the twelve apostles. By Acts 21:18 authority in the church appears to have transitioned from the apostles to the elders. Qualifications for elders are given in 1 Timothy 3 and Titus 1, the overriding characteristic being that elders should be "above reproach." Acts 20:28–35; 1 Timothy 5:17–20; and James 5:14 are important passages for elders and should be read alongside of 1 Peter 5.[2]

Teaching the Text

First of all, one should decide what to do with 5:10–11. This commentary has set them off with 5:12–14 to provide a separate teaching with which to close the whole book. They could also be taught as the close of this section.

The "Structure" section above provides a useful outline for teaching through the material. Three relationships are explicitly mentioned: relationships with those in the community, with God, and with Satan—and a fourth is implied in verse 9: believers' relationships with others in the wider Christian church.

One way to talk about the responsibility of elders to the church is to break down Peter's teaching and the background of Ezekiel 34 into four actions and four attitudes. Shepherding elders are responsible for (1) healing the sick, strengthening the weak, and binding up the injured; (2) searching for the lost and bringing back strays; (3) protecting; and (4) guiding. They should demonstrate the following attitudes: (1) remembering these are God's sheep; (2) serving willingly; (3) being eager to serve and not pursuing dishonest gain; and (4) not lording it over others but being an example. It may be worth noting how important it is for those who are suffering to have the right kind of leaders available to care for them.

Because most people being taught this passage will not be elders, it is fair to apply these attitudes and actions to all Christian leaders, and really all Christians, since elders are to be an example to the flock. Only one phrase addresses the behavior of people toward their elders. This provides the opportunity to discuss again the need for submission.

The one character trait that ties together what Peter has to say about relationships in community as well as our relationship with God is humility. While suffering for being a Christian is often humbling, it is interesting to note that it can also lead to pride. Instead of looking to community and waiting for God, suffering Christians can look to themselves, become defensive, refuse to forgive others, or try to hide their pain. That's why the encouraging picture of God caring for us in 5:7 is so essential.

With regard to the relationship with Satan, there are always two dangers: overemphasizing Satan's involvement and underemphasizing Satan's involvement. Although Peter mentions him only here, the wider witness of the Scriptures gives Satan a prominent place in the sufferings we experience, and so the teacher should take this opportunity to speak explicitly about Satan's role.

Finally, some might want to add the fourth relationship addressed in this teaching, the relationship to the wider Christian community. Verse 9 provides the opportunity to expand on the idea that Christians around the world are suffering for following Jesus and that we are one with them in part through the common sufferings that we share.

Illustrating the Text

Pride can be a danger for people who have endured suffering.

Television: *Big Bang Theory.* As opposed to many television shows that chronicle the lives of the beautiful or popular, this show portrays the lives of social outcasts. In the episode "The Cooper-Hofstadter Polarization" (season 1, episode 9), we see that it's not only the privileged who are in danger of pride. Whereas one might think that all the suffering associated with being a social outcast would have resulted in humility, this episode shows that it is just as likely to create pride.

Cast your cares on God.

Bible: **Genesis 21.** The story of Hagar and Ishmael provides a literal example of what it means to abandon your cares to God. The first time the Hebrew word for "cast" appears is in 21:15, where Hagar casts Ishmael under a tree to die. She thinks that she is abandoning him to death, but in reality she is abandoning him to God. God hears the boy crying and shows that he cares for Ishmael beyond what Hagar does. She merely wants him to survive, but God has plans to cause him to thrive.

Despite differences, suffering Christians are all united.

Cultural Institution: When we celebrate Veterans Day in America, we do not draw a distinction between those who served in hostile combat situations and those who did not. A veteran is a veteran, and this is recognition that every veteran made a sacrifice and a contribution to our freedom. Likewise, some Christians are serving in more openly hostile situations and others are not, but every Christian who suffers for God is making a sacrifice and contribution to God's kingdom.

Closing Summary

Big Idea

The sovereign and gracious God has purposed to save humans and have them experience his glory forever through being united with Christ in his sufferings.

Key Themes

- God's grace saves and sustains.
- God is sovereign over all things.
- Believers are united with Christ.
- Suffering is followed by glory.
- Suffering in Christ purifies and transforms.

Understanding the Text

The Text in Context

In 5:10–14 Peter provides his closing statements, attempting to do for his readers what he commanded them to do in 1:13: set their hope fully on the grace to be given to them when Jesus Christ is revealed. He does this by focusing on the future and reemphasizing the sovereignty of God in their suffering.

Structure

1. Closing theological statement summarizing the major teachings of the letter (5:10–11)
2. Closing greetings (5:12–14)

Interpretive Insights

5:10 *the God of all grace.* Grace is the first theme that Peter summarizes in this closing statement. Grace represents anything that comes from God to humans. On one level, it represents the salvation given to believers (1:10), which comes in its fullness when Christ returns (1:13). This is what we might call "saving grace." On another level, grace stands for the blessings that come when believers exercise their spiritual gifts (4:10) and the favor God bestows on the humble (5:5). This is what we might call "sustaining grace." By referring to God as "the God of all grace," Peter is referencing both God's saving grace and his sustaining grace; everything that a believer needs now and forever is found in God.

who called you. A second theme present in this closing is the theme of God's sovereignty. This comes out in the use of the word "called" (and the related word "chosen"), which Peter has used throughout his epistle to represent the fact that God has a plan that he is carrying to completion and he has chosen believers to participate in this plan. Everything that is happening, including believers' suffering, is part of God's plan for achieving the salvation that he has designed.

to his eternal glory. The third major theme Peter mentions in his closing is glory. "Glory/glorify" is used fourteen times in this epistle. Just as "all grace" summarizes all the different ways that God blesses humans, "eternal glory" sums up all of the honor, praise, and worship that is God's now and forever. God has taken the initiative to call believers to participate in this glory. This also incorporates Peter's emphasis on evangelism, as noted in 2:12. God is glorified when people come to believe that Jesus is Lord, and so the glory that God has called believers to participate in is a glory that demands to be shared with others so that they can participate as well.

in Christ. A fourth theme is that of union with Christ, which speaks of believers' connection both with Jesus and with the community of faith. Scholars long ago noted that for Paul the language of "in Christ" is corporate in nature, meaning that union with Christ unites believers individually not only to Jesus but to one another. Although Peter uses "in Christ" language less often than Paul and doesn't use "body of Christ," Peter's conception of union with Christ is similar to Paul's.[1] Christ, the living Stone, is the cornerstone of the building. Believers are living stones united with this cornerstone to form a single temple for the Lord (2:4–7). Therefore, Peter speaks of believers doing good deeds "in Christ" (3:16), participating in the sufferings of Christ (4:13), and being raised with Christ (1:3; 3:21). In 5:10, God's plan to include believers in his glory happens through their union with Christ and as they follow the example of Christ.

after you have suffered a little while. A fifth major theme is that glory follows suffering. Because believers are strangers in this world and belong to God, they experience suffering as a result of being Christians. This is an inescapable part of God's plan. It doesn't say, "if you suffer," but "after you have suffered." Because Christ suffered, believers in Christ must suffer in order to share in his glory.

will himself restore you. Most major translations give a meaning of "restore" for the Greek word *katartizō*—in other words, fix something that is broken and put it back to its original condition. This is usually based on the fact that it is used of fishermen "repairing" their nets (Matt. 4:21; Mark 1:19) and of spiritual believers restoring a fallen brother or sister (Gal. 6:1). However, the much more common use of this verb (and related terms) in the New Testament has the idea of "equip, prepare, make complete" (see Luke 6:40; Rom. 9:22; 2 Cor. 9:5; Eph. 4:12; 1 Thess. 3:10; 2 Tim. 3:17; Heb. 13:21; cf. 1 Cor. 1:10; 2 Cor. 13:9). Since Peter is concerned with how suffering brings about purification and demonstrates the genuineness of faith (1:7), it is more likely that *katartizō* here represents the fact that God does not just repair the damage caused by suffering but uses suffering as part of the process of purification and verification necessary so that in the end all believers will be complete, strong, firm, and steadfast.

strong, firm and steadfast. These final four words reveal a sixth theme from Peter's letter: God's plan to create a holy people, strong and established, and the fact that he uses suffering as part of that process.

5:11 *To him be the power for ever and ever.* While many doxologies like this use the word "glory," Peter has chosen "power" to emphasize God's sovereignty over all things. The only way for God to accomplish everything that he has planned is if he possesses infinite power. This is a reassurance for those who are struggling through life as strangers in the midst of suffering. The last affirmation before the official close is that God is in control of all things.

5:12 *With the help of Silas.* What role Silas played in the formulation of the letter of 1 Peter is not clear. While he may have been Peter's amanuensis or scribe for this letter, it seems most likely that he is the one who delivered the letter to the various churches to whom Peter is writing.[2] This Silas is probably the same person who accompanied Paul on his journeys (Acts 15:40), which shows the level of continuity in the early church among the leadership. The same is true for Mark mentioned in 5:13. Ironically, it was because of Paul's difficulty with Mark that Silas ended up replacing Barnabas as Paul's missionary partner. Yet near the end of the time of the New Testament, both Silas and Mark are closely connected to Peter (as seen here) and Paul (on Paul's restored relationship with Mark, see Col. 4:10; Philem. 24; 2 Tim. 4:11).

encouraging you and testifying that this is the true grace of God. Peter reveals the two things that people in the midst of suffering need most: encouragement and confidence that God has a plan. "Encouraging" includes urging people toward correct behavior (as in 2:11 and 5:1, where the word is translated as "urge" and "appeal"), as well as comforting them in the midst of their struggles (as it is used, e.g., in Col. 2:2; 4:8). Peter's readers also need to know that God has a plan for all that is happening. This is what he means when he testifies that this is the true grace of God. Everything that is happening is happening as part of God's gift of salvation to his people (on "grace," see the comments on 5:10, above).

5:13 *She who is in Babylon . . . sends you her greetings.* Babylon is most likely a metaphorical reference to the city of Rome, from which Peter is writing. The "she" who sends her greetings is probably the church in Rome. Second John 1 and 13 use the language of a single female to refer to the church as well. Church tradition relates that Peter experienced martyrdom in the city of Rome around AD 64, which adds poignancy to this letter about suffering that the original audience wouldn't have understood but that subsequent readers will have gotten.[3]

While it may be that Peter does not want to identify Rome by name because he fears persecution, it is more likely that by referring to Rome as Babylon, Peter is highlighting two related things. First, beginning with the tower of Babel on through to the destruction of "Babylon" in Revelation 17–18, Babylon represents the city that is against God. In this sense, Babylon represents for Peter a place where he and his fellow Christians are going to experience suffering for being Christians as well as the place where people most desperately need to hear the gospel. Second, Babylon represented the place of exile for Judah, where they were strangers in another land for seventy years. Peter living in Rome would have felt a connection to Israel living as strangers in exile, a major theme of his letter.

so does my son Mark. Peter would have known Mark from the earliest days of the church, since Mark is Barnabas's cousin, and the believers met in the home of his mother (Acts 12:12). To describe Mark as his "son" indicates that Peter was a mentor to Mark (just as Paul describes Timothy in 1 Cor. 4:17). Traditionally, the second Gospel is thought to be authored by this Mark and is believed to be based on Peter's recollection of his years with Jesus.[4]

5:14 *Greet one another with a kiss of love.* A nonerotic kiss was a standard way of greeting fellow believers and is comparable to what Paul called a "holy kiss" (Rom. 16:16; 1 Cor. 16:20; 2 Cor. 13:12; 1 Thess. 5:26). Peter calls it the "kiss of love," emphasizing the idea of love for one another that he has urged for his readers (1:22; 3:8; 4:8).

Peace to all of you who are in Christ. Peace would have had an extra measure of meaning as a closing to those who were suffering and experiencing turmoil as strangers in this world. Peter ends with "in Christ," reminding them that peace comes not "in this world" but "in Christ." This may also recall Jesus's statement in John 14:27: "Peace I leave with you; my peace I give you. I do not give to you as the world gives. Do not let your hearts be troubled and do not be afraid."

Theological Insights

Babylon. The city of Babylon is both a historical city and a theological image used throughout the Scriptures. The heightened language in Isaiah

13–14 makes clear that what Isaiah is attacking is not so much the historical city of Babylon but that which Babylon represents: pride and self-reliance. From the first reference to Babylon (= Babel) in Genesis 11 to the last reference to Babylon in Revelation 17–18, the theological imagery of Babylon is that of humanity's attempts to live life apart from God. Babylon stands "more generally for world power in opposition to God."[5] In this context, because Babylon was the place of the exile for Judah, it comes to represent theologically the exile that God's people experience in this world. Acts 7:43 (Stephen's quotation of Amos); 1 Peter 5:13; and Revelation 17–18 draw on and extend this imagery. While some have argued that Babylon is only to be associated with the destruction of the temple, since this was explicit in post-70 Jewish sources,[6] for New Testament Christians Babylon is more naturally connected with the exile, as can be seen in Matthew 1:1, 12, 17; Acts 7:43; and 1 Peter 5:13.

Teaching the Text

The teacher may decide that 5:10–11 belongs best with 5:1–9, as in many translations. Or you may want to pull it out to use as a summary of the teachings of Peter, as is done here. If it is used in this way, the six major themes from 5:10 make for an excellent review of material. These are (1) salvation / God's grace; (2) God's sovereignty; (3) God's glory, including the evangelistic emphasis Peter gives to the notion of God's glory in his epistle; (4) union with Christ and following the example of Christ; (5) the necessity of suffering, and the fact that suffering precedes glory; (6) God creating a holy people. While these six themes do not cover everything from 1 Peter, they do provide a nice framework to review and summarize the major teachings of the epistle.

While many people skip over the final greetings of an epistle, 5:12–14 provides some great opportunities for teaching these truths. First, there is Peter himself, who will experience persecution in the city of Rome, from which he is writing. His own personal experience of being an outsider in the godless city of Rome is characterized by his description of Rome as "Babylon," highlighting its godlessness and that it is a place of exile for him. This means that Peter is writing out of his own personal experience, understanding the need to live his life as a stranger in this world in reverent fear (1:17) and live such a godly life among the pagans that they would see his good deeds and come to faith (2:12).

Second, the mention of Mark brings up the story of someone who most likely deserted serving God because the suffering was too great (Acts 15:38) but who had been restored to a position of usefulness. Whatever he was before, by the time of the writing of 1 Peter, Mark is now strong, firm, and established, a

1 Peter 5:10–14

testimony of God's ability to use suffering—and even failure—in the life of a believer to bring about the purification that Peter speaks of in 5:10 and 1:6–7.

Finally, 5:12–14 leaves clues that the teacher of the text can pick up on for how to help people in the midst of suffering. Encouraging and testifying about the plan of God are vitally important (5:12). The fact that Peter urges his readers to "stand fast in it" means that reviewing again the plan of a sovereign and gracious God to use suffering to accomplish salvation is useful as a final teaching. The community of love—represented by the "kiss of love" in 5:14—is vitally important because it is the place where one is not a stranger. And finally, the notion of God's peace coming to those who are in Christ, which is what suffering Christians long to experience, is mentioned as well. These closing remarks can provide good opportunities for teaching that help summarize and hammer home the message of 1 Peter.

Illustrating the Text

God's grace not only brings salvation but also sustains us through life.

Human Experience: Do you remember being taught to ride a bicycle? Or perhaps you remember teaching a child to ride. Usually, the parent puts the child on the seat, guides them as they get going, and keeps running with them until the child can pedal on their own. Then, the child takes over and rides on their own. Grace is not like this. God *never* takes his hand off the seat! We are always dependent on his amazing grace.

God is sovereign over all things.

History: It was said, "The sun never sets on the British Empire." This greatest of human empires was formed in the age of exploration and reached its zenith immediately following the First World War. By the end of the Second World War, however, Britain was already breaking apart. For perhaps a century, this great empire had stamped its culture on the globe, but within a few decades, its power to define had dissipated. The great leader Winston Churchill ironically led the greatest victory in history, only to see his victorious nation diminish on the world stage. Even the greatest human attempts to exert sovereignty can last but a few years. God, the sovereign Lord of history, has ruled over every electron in creation from the moment he spoke it into existence. His rule and reign cannot be threatened and will have no end.

Believers are united with Christ.

Scenario: Imagine for a moment you are on a trip to Washington, DC. You approach the gate outside the White House and ask to visit the president. How far do you think you would get? Now, imagine you have had a chance to meet one of the president's children. She takes you by the hand and brings you to the gatehouse, past the guards, through the front door, and into the Oval Office (with a few guards for company, of course). Access is granted because you are with the president's own daughter. Because Jesus has taken us by the hand, we are brought through life and into heaven at his side.

Suffering for Christ purifies our faith.

Science: When we look at a piece of gold with the naked eye, we see something beautiful and brilliant. However, gold can almost always be refined. It contains impurities that can be extracted only when the gold is placed over the fire. As the gold melts down and is liquefied, the impurities rise to the top, becoming visible. Like gold, our faith is purified and proven authentic through suffering.

Introduction to 2 Peter

The purpose of 2 Peter is to encourage believers to grow in their godliness through reminding them of the opportunity to participate in God's divine nature (1:3–11), the value of true prophecy (1:12–21), the danger of false teachers and immoral behavior (2:1–22), and the truth of Christ's return (3:1–18).

Importance of 2 Peter

Although often overlooked and undervalued, 2 Peter contains some of the most important teachings on the subjects it addresses. One of most impactful sermons that I remember from my childhood was one preached on 1:5–7. I remembered it because for the first time I began to understand what it meant to grow in my faith, because Peter presented the process of spiritual growth so plainly and clearly.

Likewise, 1:12–21 provides one of the most important discussions on the value of Scripture and the relationship between Scripture and personal experience. Today there is a great deal of confusion about the Bible as the Word of God and how we are to evaluate our personal experiences in light of the testimony of Scripture.

While there is much overlap between 2 Peter 2 and Jude, Peter's second chapter focuses on the reality of false teachers and God's ability to protect the righteous, especially with regard to false teaching about sexual ethics. My observations of America and contemporary Western culture as well as the growing fear Christians are feeling in the face of a society that has embraced false teaching and false teachers means that 2 Peter will grow in value and importance for the church.

Finally, the way Peter frames the delay of Christ's return with reference to God's timing, patience, and desire for all to be saved is unique and immensely helpful.

Author, Setting, and Date

The letter of 2 Peter claims to be written by Simon Peter (1:1). While the authorship of 2 Peter is among the most disputed of all the books in the New Testament, the evidence for Peter as author is stronger than the significant doubts about it.[1]

Given that Peter says this is his second letter that he has written "to you" (3:1), it may very well be that this epistle is coming from Peter in Rome to the same churches mentioned in 1 Peter 1:1. While some have argued that 1 and 2 Peter can't be written to the same churches because they deal with different issues, the fact of the matter is that anyone who has ministered in a church over a period of time knows that the issues addressed in 1 Peter (sufferings and persecutions that arise from being elect exiles in this world) are not antithetical to the issues addressed in 2 Peter (the dangers of false teachers within the congregation who are influenced by the world's values). In fact, theologically, the two epistles complement each other quite well.

Second Peter was probably written in the early to mid 60s AD. Church tradition reports Peter was martyred under Nero, who himself died in AD 68.

On the relationship between 2 Peter and Jude, see the introduction to Jude, below.

Theological Themes and Suggestions for Teaching

Theologically, 1 and 2 Peter fit well together, and the teacher may want to consider teaching them together. Many of the themes that were emphasized in 1 Peter, such as evangelism, fearing God, and holiness, are in the background of 2 Peter. Many of the theological themes that are emphasized in 2 Peter are present in a less developed form in 1 Peter. These include the following:

1. *Scripture and prophecy*. Peter engages with the Old Testament somewhat differently in 2 Peter than he did in 1 Peter. Second Peter has fewer direct quotes and more allusions. But Peter's message is still firmly grounded in the Old Testament Scriptures (e.g., Noah, Lot, Balaam, the fallen angels of Genesis, the day of the Lord, a day being like a thousand years, etc.). The prophetic message, which can also now be found in the writings of Paul and the teachings of the apostles, is where the authoritative truth from God is found. The confidence that Peter expresses and expects his readers to have is something that modern readers need to be encouraged toward as well.

2. *Christ's return.* The idea of Christ's return is present in 1 Peter (1:5–7; 2:12; 4:5–7; 5:4) but is given more prominence in 2 Peter. The certainty, timing, and result of Christ's return are all discussed. But in 2 Peter, as in 1 Peter, the purpose of discussing the future is to change present behavior and attitudes.

3. *Sanctification.* Again, what was discussed briefly in 1 Peter 2:1–3 is now given much more prominence in 2 Peter. Believers are to give every effort to grow in godliness. Growing in godliness is how they will be assured of their salvation and reap the blessings of participating in the divine nature.

Participating in the Divine Nature

Big Idea

God has graciously allowed believers to participate in his divine nature, and therefore we must work diligently to grow into this reality and thereby be assured of our calling by God.

Key Themes

- Know God by becoming like him.
- Growing in seven key virtues provides assurance that we are saved.

Understanding the Text

The Text in Context

Second Peter 1:1–2 introduces the author, readers, and God. By positioning the readers as sharing a common faith with the apostolic author, Peter is foreshadowing the themes of apostolic integrity and prophetic continuity (1:12–21) over against false prophets and teachers (2:1–22). The fact that the readers' faith is precious and God is righteous provides the foundation for the instructions on godly living in light of the reality that God will keep his promises regarding the end of time (3:1–18).

After the introduction, Peter begins his epistle in 1:3–11, spelling out the precious nature of the faith that his readers have received and why it is essential that they diligently labor to grow in it. The preciousness of the faith that readers have been given is the central focus of 1:3–11. Peter will return to these issues in chapter 3.

Structure

1. Introducing Peter, the readers, and God (1:1–2)
2. The goal of the process of spiritual growth: participating in the divine nature (1:3–4)
3. The process and the exhortation: make every effort (1:5–7)

4. The rationale for engaging in the process: becoming like God and being assured of one's salvation (1:8–11)

Interpretive Insights

1:1 *Simon Peter, a servant and apostle of Jesus Christ.* There are two differences between the apostle's introduction in 1 Peter and this introduction: (1) he calls himself Simon Peter, which reflects a more personal feel as he pleads with his readers to avoid false teachers; and (2) he adds the term "servant," which contrasts with the false teachers who want to greedily exploit the readers (2:3) in their bold, arrogant insubordination (2:10).

through the righteousness of our God and Savior Jesus Christ have received a faith as precious. The readers are described not as elect exiles, as in 1 Peter, but as the recipients of a precious faith through the righteousness of God. This introduces the theme of faith that must be grown into and guarded, as well as the contrast between unrighteous false teachers and a righteous God. "Our God and Savior Jesus Christ" is one of the strongest affirmations of the deity of Jesus Christ in all of Scripture. Peter uses one article in Greek, indicating that "God and Savior" refer to the same person, Jesus.[1] Verse 2 refers to the Father and the Son separately.

1:3 *everything we need for a godly life through our knowledge of him.* The key to godly life is the intimate relational "knowledge" (*epignōsis*; see the sidebar) that believers are able to have of God because he is powerful enough to make such a relationship happen and possesses gloriously exceptional goodness. God's power and his loving character are the basis and guarantee of the promises that God has made to believers.

Relational Knowledge versus Knowledge of Truths

Peter uses two related words for knowledge, *gnōsis* and *epignōsis*, both translated by the NIV as "knowledge." While these words can be synonymous, it is likely that, given the way they are used in 1:1–11, Peter is here using *epignōsis* to refer to a deeper, relational understanding and experience of God and *gnōsis* to refer to the truths of the faith. It is the difference between knowing one's spouse and knowing truths about one's spouse. This is why "knowledge" (*epignōsis*, 1:3) is the goal

of the process of spiritual growth while "knowledge" (*gnōsis*, 1:5) is one aspect of the process. Knowing truths about God is part of the process of knowing God, but so are self-control, brotherly kindness, and love. In 2 Peter "knowledge" (*epignōsis*) is used three times in this section (1:2, 3, 8), plus it is used in 2:20; the related verb is used twice in 2:21. "Knowledge" (*gnōsis*) is used in 1:5, 6, and 3:18, and the related verb is used in 1:20 and 3:3.

1:4 *participate in the divine nature.* In shockingly strong language, Peter says that believers are able to partake of or participate in God's divine nature. This doesn't mean that believers somehow become God. It means that believers' natures are transformed so that we are like God. This is the essence of the process of growth for Peter. Every promise that believers have been given is for the purpose of causing us to escape from the corruption of this world and make us like God. (On divinization, see "Theological Insights," below.)

1:5-7 *For this very reason, make every effort.* Because participation in God's divine nature is possible, believers are to "make every effort." This is the first imperative command in the epistle and the central command of this section. Believers are to work diligently with earnest zeal and passion, bringing to bear whatever energy, time, resources, and opportunities are at their disposal, for one purpose: seeing the possibility of participating in God's nature actually realized here and now in their lives. Peter's point is that since it is possible to become like God, it is worth every effort to see that actually happen.

add to your faith. Faith is not one of the virtues that believers are to add to their lives. It is the solid foundation upon which all the rest are built. "Your faith" is the fundamental belief in Jesus that makes one a Christian. Without this foundation, all attempts to add moral goodness to one's life will fail.

goodness, knowledge . . . self-control, perseverance . . . godliness, mutual affection . . . love. These seven virtues provide a sense of completeness. While it is unlikely that each represents a discrete stage that readers pass through, there is a logical order to them. Love would be impossible without some level of knowledge, self-control, affection for others, and so on.

"Goodness" is the same word used of God in 1:3 and represents excellence of character. Here at the beginning of the list, the emphasis is on moral behavior. Those who want to participate in God's nature must turn away from sinful choices. "Knowledge" (*gnōsis*) is an understanding of the truths of the faith. It is not the full relational knowledge (*epignōsis*) referred to in 1:2–3. "Self-control" is the discipline to be able to restrain one's desires and follow through on doing what is right, even when it is difficult. "Perseverance" is the ability to continue moving forward or standing one's ground despite suffering and opposition. This is often a virtue that is produced through enduring suffering (e.g., Rom. 5:3–4; James 1:3–4). "Godliness" is doing good deeds toward others and acts of piety toward God. "Mutual affection" is kindness toward others—namely, brotherly love. All of these virtues are building toward the final and greatest virtue: sacrificial, unconditional love.

1:8 *if you possess these qualities in increasing measure.* Here it becomes clear that Peter's list is not "the seven stages of discipleship" but a cyclical process where each virtue must continue to grow. God may provide a season where the emphasis is on growing in the knowledge of Christian truths, followed by a time of suffering designed to increase perseverance; but this time of suffering will also include opportunities for continued growth in knowledge. To be stagnant in any of these areas for too long is a problem.

1:9 *whoever does not have them.* The use of the impersonal and distant "whoever" here, as opposed to the personal "you" in 1:8, indicates that Peter is addressing more of a hypothetical situation rather than an actual one his readers are currently experiencing (something similar can be found in Heb. 6:4–9).

forgetting that they have been cleansed. Peter does not say, "they are no longer cleansed." For those Christians who stumble at times during the process of growing to be like God, the result is not that they lose their forgiveness but that their experience and memory of it become clouded.

1:10 *make every effort to confirm your calling and election.* The command to be diligent in growing in these virtues is restated here. Growing in these virtues does not cause one to be called and elected, but it gives evidence that one has been called and elected by God for salvation.

1:11 *you will receive a rich welcome into the eternal kingdom.* Peter seems to be implying that some people's welcome into the eternal kingdom will not be as rich as others, an idea supported by other New Testament passages (e.g., Matt. 6:19–21; 25:14–30; 1 Cor. 3:10–15; Heb. 11:35).

Theological Insights

1. *Divinization or theosis.* Second-century theologian Irenaeus famously stated that Jesus Christ "because of his immeasurable love became what we are in order to make us what he is."[2] This refers to a process of divinization whereby believers become like God. In Paul, the language is "being conformed to the image of Christ" (e.g., Rom. 8:29; 12:1–2; 1 Cor. 15:49; 2 Cor. 3:18; Gal. 4:19). For John it means becoming like Christ (1 John 3:2). Because of the process of divinization, believers are moving to a higher level of existence through union with Christ. They are not returning to the state in which they were in the garden of Eden. This is why the order in the first creation is God-angels-humans (see Heb. 2:5–8), but in the new creation it is God-humans-angels (as evidenced by the fact that believers will judge angels; 1 Cor. 6:3). The strength of Peter's articulation of "participating in the divine nature" makes a unique contribution to the idea of divinization in the New Testament.[3]

2. *Assurance of salvation.* Assurance of salvation is often confused with the related doctrine of eternal security, but they address two different things. Eternal security is the belief that if someone is a believer they cannot lose their salvation (e.g., John 10:28–30; Rom. 8:31–39; 2 Tim. 2:11–13). Assurance of salvation is the belief that those who are Christians can know that they are. This is a subject that the entire epistle of 1 John is taken up with (see

1 John 5:13). Second Peter 1:1–11 addresses assurance, not eternal security. If the seven virtues of 1:5–7 are present in increasing measure in the life of a believer, a person can be sure that they have been called and elected by God to salvation. This emphasis on good works and godly character providing assurance of salvation is consistent with other sections of Scripture (e.g., Matt. 7:15–20; Gal. 5:19–24; James 2:14–26). This means of assurance is complemented by the inner witness of the Holy Spirit, who testifies as to the reality of one's faith in Jesus (e.g., Rom. 8:16), and by persevering until the end (e.g., Heb. 3:12–14).

Teaching the Text

Second Peter 1:1–11 is one of the great scriptural passages on the process of spiritual growth because it contains the goal of the process (becoming like God through our relationship with him), the steps to achieving this goal (making every effort to add the seven virtues), and the reasons to diligently pursue spiritual growth (assurance of salvation here and a rich welcome in heaven).

When the process is being taught, most listeners in the Protestant tradition, especially those well schooled in Enlightenment thinking, will have a hard time wrapping their minds around the concept that we can become partakers in the divine nature. While there is some mystery to what this means, this is not metaphorical language. Some actual transformation is happening. The teacher may find it helpful to supplement how Peter says this with how it is said in other Scriptures (see above), especially if Paul's or John's language is more familiar. The following objections will probably be common: (1) Does this mean I am being absorbed into God and losing my identity? (No. Jesus retains his unique identity though he is one with the Father, so we retain our identities as we become one with Jesus.) (2) If this is happening, why do I continue to struggle with temptation? (Because while our nature is being transformed, we still have sinful flesh that we struggle against, and even Jesus was tempted to sin despite his fully divine nature.)

When teaching through the process of spiritual growth, the teacher should be wary of allowing this to be seen as a mechanical process. Somehow it should be communicated that there is a balance between the more linear order of the seven virtues and the more circular nature of growing in all of them at the same time. Whether listeners are encouraged to evaluate and work through one at a time or all at once depends on the situation and the listener. One useful tool when teaching through this list is to ask listeners which of these seven virtues God seems to be working on currently in their lives.

When one is teaching through the motivations for engaging in this process, it is worth noting that these are pretty substantial motivations: (1) you will become like God and know God; (2) if you don't make progress, you will forget that you are a believer and descend into confusion; (3) if you do these, you will know for sure that you are called and elected by God for salvation; and (4) if you continue to grow into your salvation, you will receive a rich welcome into the kingdom of heaven. With regard to someone forgetting that they are a believer, my personal experience is that this passage is extremely helpful for explaining to people why it is that friends and family who once claimed to be Christians and showed real fruit have walked away from God. It can also bring comfort to them to know that it is possible (though unknowable with any certainty) that their loved one has been forgiven of their sins, even though they have forgotten about being forgiven.

Illustrating the Text

There is a difference between knowing about Jesus
and actually knowing Jesus.

Bible: The Bible is filled with examples of people who knew about Jesus but didn't know Jesus. Judas tops the list (Matt. 7:21–23).

Participate in the divine nature and escape the corruption in the world.

Literature: *East of Eden,* by John Steinbeck. In Steinbeck's novel on the story of Cain and Abel, characters in succeeding generations live out the roles of those who came before them. Charles and Caleb both play the role of Cain (over against Adam and Aron, who play the role of Abel). The thematic center of the book is around "Timshel," the Hebrew word from Genesis 4 that is meant to encourage Caleb not to live into the character of Charles (and Cain). Here Peter is offering to all who are reliving the mistakes of previous generations the opportunity to become participants in the divine nature. Rather than live out the role of anger and hatred (or anxiety, negativity, selfishness, etc.) handed down to them, believers can live out God's nature.

People forget that they have been cleansed from past sins.

Personal Testimony: One summer I came home from college and was eager to hang out with old friends from high school. When I was in college, my relationship with Jesus had really begun to flourish, and I was looking forward to sharing this with old friends whom I should have talked to about Jesus in high school. One night I was hanging out with a friend, and I began to talk about all the amazing ways that God had shown up for me in the past year. She listened, and I thought when we got to the end she would ask me how she could become a Christian. Instead she got angry with me. She told me how in high school she had accepted Jesus and how she had begun on the journey of faith. She also told me about some terrible things that she went through and how she prayed and prayed but God never answered or helped her. She had decided that the things she had believed were fairy tales and I was being misled by false beliefs. Yet as she recounted what had happened to her, it was clear that she had not given every effort to embrace goodness, the first quality listed in this passage. The part of her life in which she experienced the most difficulty was one in which she was engaging in sin despite God's commands not to. As a result she had become nearsighted and blind, forgetting what God had done for her.

We know God more clearly when we watch people who live and love like Jesus.

Testimony: Have someone share a story about growing up with a very godly grandparent or parent. You might want to show a picture of these two people together. Have them describe how the grandparent or parent lived, loved, and followed the Savior and tell about how this example impacted their life. Explain that we can know God better by watching people who look a lot like Jesus. Then challenge your listeners to think about who is watching them, and ask them to reflect about how Jesus is being revealed to the next generation through them.

True Prophecy

Big Idea

Understanding reliable truths from God will stir us to action.

Key Themes

- It is important to remember and be reminded.
- Scripture is true prophecy.

Understanding the Text

The Text in Context

Second Peter 1:12–21 serves a pivotal role in the letter. It provides the purpose, incentive, and reliability for what Peter is writing in this epistle and deals with the theme of true prophecy. It is strongly connected to 3:1–2, where Peter repeats the reminder to his readers that truth comes through the prophets and apostles. The theme of the Scriptures will also reappear in 3:15–16. This section on true prophecy is necessary because Peter must warn his readers against false teachers who are introducing destructive heresies (2:1–22), as well as provide the foundation for why they should believe the promises of God (1:3–4 and 3:4–10) and live in light of these promises (1:5–11 and 3:11–18).

Structure

1. Peter's purpose in writing this letter: to stir his readers to action by reminding them of truths they have been taught from God's Word (1:12–15)
2. The incentive for writing: the reality of the truthfulness of who Jesus is, combined with Peter's own imminent death (1:16–18)
3. The reliability of what Peter is writing and what they have been taught: these truths are ultimately from God, even though they are communicated through humans (1:19–21)

Interpretive Insights

1:12 *So I will always remind you of these things.* Reminding/remembering is key. Words for "remember/remind" are found in 1:12, 13, and 14, and then the act of remembering happens in Peter's recollection of the transfiguration in 1:16–18.

To remember is not simply an intellectual exercise. The call to remember is the call to obey (e.g., "remember the Sabbath," Exod. 20:8; see also Num. 15:39; Deut. 4:23; 2 Kings 17:38–39; Ps. 103:17–18). It is also the call to continue to meditate on the promises, actions, and character of God. Doing so will bring things said or done in the past into the present. This can be seen most clearly with the celebration of communion, where the regular remembrance of Jesus is a proclamation of his death until he comes (1 Cor. 11:23–26).[1]

Peter is calling them both to meditate on these things and to obey them. "These things" that they are being reminded of are the great and precious promises that make participation in the divine nature possible. By remembering the story of the transfiguration, Peter is affirming the lordship of Christ to the readers of this epistle. By reminding them of these truths even though they already know them, Peter is stirring the readers to obey and to make every effort to grow in their faith. This is the purpose for the writing of this letter, to remind them of these truths that they already know so as to motivate them to live in light of these things.

1:13 *to refresh your memory.* A better translation is "to arouse by way of remembrance."

1:14 *I know that I will soon put it aside, as our Lord Jesus Christ has made clear to me.* Peter's own experience with prophecy and memory is informing what he is saying to his readers. Jesus prophesied to Peter the kind of death he would die when he was older (see John 21:18–19, and perhaps John 13:36). Although the prophecy was made many years earlier, Peter has been reminded of this prophecy recently. This may have happened through another, recent revelation where Jesus told Peter that the prophecy was to come to pass soon. Or through the Spirit, Peter has reasoned that since he is old, that prophecy must be coming true soon. In either case, remembering Jesus's prophecy from John 21 has motivated Peter to write this letter. This is exactly what Peter wants to have happen with his readers, that God would speak to them through this reminder and motivate them to be busy about making their calling and election sure.

1:16–18 *we did not follow cleverly devised stories . . . when we were with him on the sacred mountain.* Verses 16–18 refer to the transfiguration. Peter has chosen this event because it validates the Christian faith and the message of Jesus. The resurrection usually plays that role, and Peter references his personal experience of Jesus's resurrection in contexts where he is sharing the gospel (e.g., Acts 2:32; 3:15; 10:40–41). Here Peter is affirming the truthfulness of Christ's second coming—that is, the "coming of our Lord Jesus Christ *in power*" (1:16). It is the return of Christ that the false teachers are denying in 3:4. So Peter relates to them his personal experience of the transfiguration because it was the preview of Christ's second coming. We know this because the transfiguration was the fulfillment of Jesus's prophecy that some standing there would not taste death until they saw the Son of Man coming into his kingdom (Matt. 16:28). At the transfiguration, Peter, James, and John saw Jesus coming into his kingdom. This is why they asked Jesus, "Why then do the teachers of the law say that Elijah must come first?" (Matt. 17:10, referring to Mal. 4:5–6).

1:19 *We also have the prophetic message as something completely reliable.* Given that the Greek form of "completely reliable" (*bebaioteron*) is usually used for comparisons, there are three interpretive options: (1) translating the comparative as emphatic, "completely reliable," as the NIV has done (also NET); (2) translating the comparative as "more reliable," meaning that the written prophecies of Scripture are more reliable than Peter's personal experiences at the transfiguration; and (3) translating the comparative as "more fully confirmed," meaning that Peter's transfiguration experience brings additional confirmation to the prophecies of the Scriptures (so ESV, HCSB, NLT). The first option is grammatically possible. But it ignores the connection Peter is making between his experience at the transfiguration and what is written in the Scriptures. It also fails to do justice to the use of the comparative form. The second option is unlikely. How can God speaking during the transfiguration be more reliable than God speaking through the prophets? Both the Old Testament prophets and Peter received revelations from God and wrote them down as Scripture. For anyone reading 2 Peter then or now, Peter's experiences and the experiences of the Old Testament prophets were both coming to them in the same form, the written word. (On the fact that Peter understood current writings to be Scripture, see 3:16.) The third option is preferred. The related verb "to confirm" (*bebaioō*) is used in Romans 15:8, where what God is doing in Jesus confirms the promises made to the patriarchs. Also in 1 Corinthians 1:6 spiritual gifts "confirm" (*bebaioō*) the apostolic proclamation about Jesus (cf. Mark 16:20). What Peter experienced on the Mount of Transfiguration makes the prophecies in the Old Testament more confirmed than they were before.

until the day dawns and the morning star rises in your hearts. The theme of "morning star" comes from a messianic prophecy in Numbers 24:17. Although Revelation is most likely written after 2 Peter, its interpretation of Numbers 24:17 is illuminating of seeing how Peter is reading this Old Testament prophecy. In Revelation 22:16 the "morning star" *is* Jesus in his kingdom. In

Revelation 2:28 the "morning star" is *given by* Jesus to believers in his kingdom. If we put these two together, when Jesus comes as the Morning Star we will be part of that new day dawning because we will be "morning stars" with him. Peter is emphasizing the aspect of Numbers 24:17 highlighted in Revelation 2:28. When Jesus comes in his kingdom, we will be full participants in the divine nature (2 Pet. 1:3–4). This happens "in your hearts" because the promise of participating in the divine nature comes through deep relational knowledge of God, which is linked to the heart in the new covenant (Jer. 31:33–34; Ezek. 36:26–29).

1:20 *no prophecy of Scripture.* "Prophecy" refers to any truth revealed by God, not just things about the future. It can be messages from God used for strengthening and encouraging believers (Acts 15:32), knowing something unknowable from the past (Matt. 26:67–68), exposing sin (Lam. 2:14; Luke 7:39), interpreting history (1 Chron. 29:29), or delivering God's warnings or moral instructions (2 Kings 17:13). This means that Peter is referring to all of Scripture with this phrase, and not just books that are considered "the Prophets" or those sections that are predicting the future.

1:21 *prophecy never had its origin in the human will, but . . . spoke from God.* This is one of the great verses in the Bible on how the Scriptures were inspired. According to Peter, the Scriptures have their origin in God's desire to communicate to his people. They are the product of both human activity and divine inspiration. Jesus reflects just such a view in Matthew 22:43 when he says, "How is it then that David [human author], speaking by the Spirit [divine author], calls him 'Lord'?" We see something similar in Matthew 24:15, when Jesus talks of the prophecy that was spoken "through the prophet Daniel" instead of speaking of a prophecy spoken "by or from the prophet Daniel." This way of speaking shows that Daniel is not the source of the prophecy. Likewise, Jesus taught Peter that during times of persecution, "just say whatever is given you at the time, for it is not you speaking, but the Holy Spirit" (Mark 13:11). In Acts 4:25 Peter himself uses this kind of language.

as they were carried along by the Holy Spirit. The verb "be carried along" is used in Acts 27:15, 17 of a ship being carried along by the wind and waves in a storm. In Acts 2:2 it is used for the wind itself. The word is important for this section of 2 Peter, appearing in verses 17 ("*came* to him"), 18 ("that *came*"), and the beginning of this verse ("*had its origin*"). All three indicate that God is the source of what was said by those who spoke as prophets.

Theological Insights

Second Peter 1:12–21 makes an important contribution to a biblical theology of prophecy and Scripture. Other important passages include Exodus 7:1–2; Deuteronomy 18:14–22; Matthew 22:29–32; Luke 24:25–32; 1 Corinthians

2:6–16; Ephesians 3:1–5; and 2 Timothy 3:15–17. In the Bible, prophecy is a wider category than Scripture. Many who prophesied communicated messages from God that were not recorded as Scripture. But some prophets in the Old Testament and some apostles in the New Testament communicated messages from God that were to be written down and viewed as authoritative for all believers everywhere. These are what Peter refers to as the prophecies of Scripture. These are simultaneously the product of human authors and divine inspiration and, as Peter shows here, they are the most important (but not the only) way that God continues to speak to his people today.

Teaching the Text

For the teacher of 2 Peter, 1:12–21 presents an important opportunity to teach through the purpose, authority, and reliability of the message of 2 Peter.

With regard to the purpose, Peter says that he is writing to remind them of truths that they already know. Teachers and preachers easily fall into the related traps of teaching simply to transfer information and desiring to always have something new to say. Both dangers are rooted in the pride of knowledge versus the love of building others up (cf. 1 Cor. 8:1). Peter encourages a different approach, reminding listeners of things they already know in order to stir them to action. This text provides an opportunity for teachers to remind themselves that while already-known things can be said in a fresh way, the desire to constantly be sharing something new and revolutionary is not faithful teaching. Nor is faithful Christian teaching simply transferring information. If the goal of Christian teaching were transferring information, there would be no need to remind people of what they already know. The desire to teach never-before-heard things or to be satisfied with transferring information can be a strong pull that many listeners can relate to.

With regard to authority, 1:12–21 provides a great chance to explain that the Scriptures are God's Word mediated through the prophets and apostles. The purpose of teaching this would be to stir people to action—that is, embracing, loving, listening, meditating, obeying, and living out God's Word. To know that the Scriptures are the Word of God means to "pay attention to" them (1:19). In the context of 2 Peter, the Scriptures are the safeguard against false prophets and false teachings. They are central for accomplishing the purpose of this letter, which is becoming partakers of the divine nature.

With regard to reliability, 1:12–21 provides an opportunity to discuss the relationship between personal experience and the written Scriptures, although this must be done carefully. From the readers' point of view, Peter's experience on the Mount of Transfiguration is not their personal experience. And it is coming to them as written Scripture from an apostle. But from Peter's point of view, what happened on the Mount of Transfiguration confirmed what the Old Testament said about the Messiah. Therefore, personal experiences (ours or others') can confirm the reliability and truthfulness of Scripture. Those who share testimonies of God's power and love confirm what we know from the Scriptures, which is that God is powerful and loving. I have found it important to help Christians understand the interplay between personal experience and Scripture.

Illustrating the Text

The transfiguration is a preview pointing toward Christ's second coming.

Human Experience: The transfiguration is like watching a trailer for a long-rumored and anticipated movie. People may say, "They are not going to be making any more *Star Wars* movies," but if you have seen the trailer for the latest movie, your response would be, "But I have already seen the trailer." In most circumstances, Hollywood doesn't make a trailer if they aren't coming out with the movie. The transfiguration is the trailer—the sneak peak—for Christ's second coming.

Experiences can confirm the truthfulness of Scripture.

Human Experience: Scripture is like the press release for a new movie. If the studio announces in writing that they are going to make a new movie, this announcement is confirmed when someone actually sees a trailer for the new movie. The written announcement reveals their plans, but the trailer confirms the validity of the written announcement. Similarly, Scripture reveals God's truth, but our experiences confirm the truthfulness of what God has revealed.

Props: Hold up a map and talk about its power to provide direction. However, the trustworthiness of the map is proven as you actually use it to navigate your way from point A to point B. Furthermore, the more you use the map to travel, the more proficient you become at recognizing the connections between the lines on the page and the path before you. So, too, when we experience what God has promised in his Word, this confirms the validity of what was said, since the test of true prophecy is that it comes true (Deut. 18:22).

Scriptural authors were carried along by the Holy Spirit.

Object Lesson: Imagine a sailboat being carried along by the wind. When the wind is blowing, it catches the sail and the boat moves forward. If the boat doesn't have a sail, it won't catch the wind and move forward. So you need both the sail and the wind to make the boat move forward, but the wind is where the power for movement comes from. In this analogy, the Holy Spirit is the wind, and humans are the sails. People who, like the apostle Peter, were prophets were moved to write the Bible as God carried them along, so that what you have in your hands is exactly what God wanted written. Although Peter authored the letter, God is the power, inspiration, and source behind it, and therefore it is God speaking to us.

Avoid False Teachers

Big Idea

Do not follow false teachers, because the Lord will protect the godly and bring destructive judgment on the unrighteous.

Key Themes

- Beware of false teachers.
- God is able to protect the righteous while punishing the wicked.

Understanding the Text

The Text in Context

In order to stir his readers to action (1:12–21), Peter must warn them about the ever-present danger of false teachers who so easily entice some to follow after them. Peter knows that such false teachers can deceive his readers and cause others to feel fearful as they see the world's values invade the community of faith. Peter writes this section to warn them about false teachers and to reassure them that God knows how to protect the righteous and punish the wicked. While the previous section focused on the value of true prophecy, this section focuses on the dangers of false prophets/teachers. The section that follows this one, 2:10–22, will focus more specifically on the characteristics of the false teachers and their destiny.

Structure

1. The reality of false teachers (2:1–3)
2. God's demonstrated ability to preserve the righteous and punish the wicked (2:4–9)

Interpretive Insights

2:1–3 *false prophets among the people . . . false teachers among you.* Having discussed the great blessing of prophecy, Peter goes on to warn of the great danger of false prophets. Both Jesus and the Old Testament frequently mentioned false prophets (e.g., Deut. 13; 1 Kings 22; Jer. 23; Ezek. 13;

215

Matt. 7:15; 24:11, 24; Luke 6:26). These false prophets were motivated by greed (1 Kings 13:7; 2 Kings 5:16, 22; Jer. 6:13; Mic. 3:11), associated with abuses of power (Isa. 9:15–16; Jer. 5:31; 23:10), and prone to whitewash sin and proclaim only peace (Lam. 2:14; Ezek. 22:28; Mic. 2:11; 3:6–8). They prophesied out of their own selfish desires (Ezek. 13; Mic. 3:6–8) and as a result of demonic deception (1 Kings 22:22). False prophets were identified when their prophecies didn't come true (Isa. 44:25), when what they urged counteracted God's revealed truth (Deut. 13; 1 Kings 13), or when they were powerless to stop God's punishment from happening (Jer. 27–28). God's response to false prophets was to prophesy truth to counteract their lies (e.g., Ezek. 13:17) and to punish them (Jer. 28:15–17; 29:29–32; Ezek. 14:9–10). By shifting from "false prophets" to "false teachers," Peter is still connecting what is happening in their day to what happened in the past, but he is allowing for some differences in the way it was happening in the church. For example, false teaching can come from someone in the church who doesn't have a formal position or a gift of prophecy, since "teacher" is less formal than "prophet."[1]

They will secretly introduce destructive heresies. Peter has in mind doctrinal heresies, like denying Christ's return, but he is particularly concerned about the fact that they produce immoral behavior. In 2:2 Peter says, "Many will follow their depraved conduct," putting the focus more on the behavior the false teaching inspires. This is consistent with Revelation 2:20, where the false prophet is connected to sexual immorality and eating food sacrificed to idols. This also agrees with the Old Testament, where false prophets were more frequently encouraging the people to engage in immoral behavior than to believe incorrectly about God.

denying the sovereign Lord who bought them. As to whether these false teachers are Christians, see the sidebar "Are or Were the False Teachers Saved?" in the unit on 2 Peter 2:10–22. Based on the conceptual parallels between 2 Peter 2 and 1 John 2, I do not believe that they are. Both 2 Peter 2 and 1 John 2 use this word "deny" to speak of the attitudes of those whose eternal standing is in question. Likewise, 1 John 2:2 identifies Jesus as "the atoning sacrifice for our sins, and not only for ours but also for the sins of the whole world." This indicates that Jesus did die in some way for everyone in the world, although his sacrifice provides forgiveness of sins only to those who accept it. So too, when Peter says that the Lord "bought" the false teachers, he is indicating that Jesus's death paid the price necessary for the purchase of false teachers, but the Lord has not been able to take ownership of these false teachers, because they have rejected his claim on their lives.[2]

"Deny" is also used of Peter's rejection of Jesus in all four Gospels (Matt. 26:70, 72; Mark 14:68, 70; Luke 22:57; John 18:25, 27; cf. John 13:38), the difference being that Peter denied Jesus during one event in his life (albeit three times), repented bitterly, and was restored. Here Peter uses the present tense for the verb "deny" to stress that the false teachers' denial is ongoing with no end in sight.

bringing swift destruction . . . condemnation has long been hanging over them. "Swift" means "imminent" or "near," not necessarily happening quickly or over a short span of time. Like the sword of Damocles, destruction is hanging over the heads of these false teachers, ready to fall at any moment with no warning. Compare this to 1:14, where Peter's death is also described as being "imminent" or "near" (NIV: "soon"; same word as the word "swift" in this verse). But Jesus has warned Peter that it is coming, and it is described as a departure, not a destruction.

2:4 *God did not spare angels when they sinned, but sent them to hell.* This is the first of three examples Peter cites to make the point that God knows how to punish the wicked and protect the righteous. Unlike the following two, there is no explicit mention of protecting the righteous with this example. Peter is most likely referring to the sin of sexual immorality between angelic beings and human women alluded to in Genesis 6:1–4. For more on this, see the comments on Jude 6, below.

2:5-6 *brought the flood . . . condemned the cities of Sodom and Gomorrah.* In Luke 17:22–37, Jesus pairs Noah and the flood with Lot and Sodom in talking about the swift judgment and rescue that will come for the ungodly and the righteous. Such a pairing was common in Peter's time,[3] and most likely Jesus's teaching in Luke 17 influences the choice of these examples. In Luke, the emphasis is on the swiftness of the judgment and the unsuspecting nature of those who experienced it.

2:7-8 *distressed by the depraved conduct of the lawless . . . that righteous man . . . was tormented.* Three questions arise from these verses: (1) How can Lot be considered righteous? (2) What was the conduct that Lot was distressed by in Sodom? (3) What does it mean that he was distressed and tormented by it?

First, Lot settling in Sodom, offering his daughters for rape, and fleeing Sodom in fear rather than faith are not the behaviors and attitudes of the righteous (Gen. 13; 19). But neither is Abraham abandoning Sarah to Pharaoh and Abimelek (Gen. 12:10–20; 20:1–18), nor the whole situation with Hagar and Ishmael (Gen. 16). But righteousness is not the absence of sin and failure; it is the result of faith in God, which Lot clearly had. He demonstrated this faith in God by offering hospitality to his angelic guests, recognizing and hating the immoral behavior of those around him, and, most important, believing God that destruction was coming. Furthermore, the implication from Abraham's negotiation with God in Genesis 18 is that Lot must have been considered righteous by God to have been rescued.

Second, Peter discusses the sins of Sodom using the word "depraved." This word means a complete lack of self-control and is especially associated with sexual misbehavior (Rom. 13:13; 2 Cor. 12:21; Gal. 5:19; 1 Pet. 4:3). Combine that with (1) the reference to the sexual sin of Genesis 6:1–4; (2) the use of "desire" (*epithymia*) of the flesh in 2 Peter 2:10 and 2:18; (3) the association of Sodom with the sexual sins of the false prophets in Jeremiah 23:13–14; and (4) Jude's reference to Sodom's sexual immorality and perversion (Jude 7). These additional four observations confirm that sexual misconduct is an integral part of what Peter is talking about here. Given that Genesis 19 presents the men of Sodom earnestly pursuing sex with other men, it is hard not to think that homosexual activity is included in the depraved conduct being touted by the false teachers. The fact that Ezekiel 16:49 identifies Sodom's sins as including more (but not less) than sexual sins and the attitudes exhibited by the people of Sodom in Genesis 19 means that pride, greed, selfishness, and oppression of the poor and the stranger are also in mind.

Third, the words "tormented" and "distressed" usually indicate some level of physical or societal oppression that brings about emotional suffering. Therefore, it is fair to say that Lot experienced what Peter wrote about in his first epistle, which is being an "elect exile" in Sodom. This would have included physical, social, and emotional suffering as Lot tried to live righteously amid the people.

2:9 *for punishment on the day of judgment.* "The day of judgment" is a reference to the final judgment (see 3:7). For Peter there is both imminent judgment for false teachers that will happen here and now (2:2–3, 11) and a final judgment for them in the future (2:17; 3:7). That God is reserving the wicked for final judgment does not mean that they do not experience some aspects of the wrath of God here and now.

Theological Insights

Second Peter 2:1–9 is applicable to the Bible's theology of homosexuality. While other sins were present at Sodom (as stated in Ezek. 16:49), Peter's mention of Sodom and Gomorrah within a context that includes sexual misconduct reaffirms that illicit sexual activity was part of the issue at Sodom. Likewise, the illicit sexual activity is probably not limited to non-consensual homosexual sex, since Peter describes Lot as being tormented by what he saw and heard day after day, not just on the day the angels visited in Genesis 19. Peter's commentary on Sodom should be added to Genesis 19; Leviticus 20:13; Judges 19; Romans 1:24–27; 1 Corinthians 6:9; 1 Timothy 1:10; and Jude 7 in understanding what God has to say about homosexual activity.

The purpose of this section is twofold: to convince readers of the reality of false teachers today and to assure them that God has everything under control, despite the presence of false teachers in the church. When teaching this text, the teacher may need to give prominence to one or both aspects, depending on the situation.

When one is thinking through the applicability of this passage to particular individuals or certain situations, it is necessary to think carefully about what constitutes a false teacher. Great damage has been done by those who have applied Peter's warnings to teachers who differ with regard to more debatable doctrinal issues, such as the details of Christ's return, sign gifts, women in ministry, and how to interpret certain passages. Peter's focus is much more on those who are introducing beliefs that lead to immoral behavior. Also, when teaching this, one must be careful to differentiate between those who are maliciously introducing destructive heresies and those who are confused by them. For example, teachers today who attempt through their teaching in the church to normalize illicit sexual activity, such as adultery, premarital sex, and homosexual sex, are in mind; those who are deceived by these teachers and confused by these issues and are trying to figure out what God is saying are not.

With regard to the second point, Peter's use of Noah and Lot can be especially helpful. Both men lived in societies that had rejected God and his authority. Neither man was called on to execute judgment on the society in which he lived. This was left up to God to do. Likewise, this passage is not a call to arms to reform society, or even to attempt to stop false teachers in society from teaching what they are teaching. It is a call to trust in God, who knows how to rescue the righteous and punish the wicked, even when the righteous are sorely outnumbered and are being abused by those around them for adhering to righteousness. As far as pointing out the character of the false teachers, that is an important application from the text, but perhaps best left for the next section.

The use of the angels, Noah, and Lot can encourage the teacher of this text to include other examples from both current times and modern history to demonstrate God's ability to rescue the righteous and punish the wicked. (See "Illustrating the Text," below.) Connecting this notion of false teachers to history is important because Peter does it and because it brings some sense of assurance that this is not some strange thing that is happening.

Overall, my experience with false teachers is that they create great fear, fear that everything is falling apart and that the righteous will be swept away. This passage is meant to bring assurance that God is in control and that he knows what he is doing. To teach this passage as a way to assuage fear in those who are listening, rather than to rail on false teachers (see the next unit), can be a very kind and loving thing to do.

Illustrating the Text

We should beware of false teachers.

Science: As humans increasingly gain knowledge and control of nature, we have learned to manipulate our food supply at the genetic level. This has brought a great fear to many who are concerned with where the stuff in our produce aisle got its start. So we have seen a rise in the level of discomfort for the wedding of technology and food sources. For instance, the world is increasingly questioning the rush toward genetically modified crops. Why the worry? Many people recognize that when we make changes at the most fundamental level of our food source, the implications are vast. When DNA is altered, everything that springs from it and everything it touches can be altered. The teaching of the church is like seed. It goes out and produces fruit. False teaching is so dangerous because it represents humans modifying the seed of truth that God has given to the church. The only result will be fruit that harms rather than gives life.

We should compassionately instruct people whom false teachers have misled.

Scenario: If a doctor encountered a patient on the verge of death, one of the first things he would do is control the most extreme symptoms, and then he would look for a cause. Suppose he discovered the person had been dutifully following the instructions of an incompetent physician. Would the doctor be harsh with the patient? Hopefully not. In the same way, we must show compassion with those who have been given false information.

God rescues the righteous and judges the wicked.

Bible: While there are lots of examples of God rescuing the righteous (Joseph from his brothers, Daniel in Babylon, Paul from being shipwrecked, etc.), it is harder to find examples where God rescued the righteous and brought judgment on the wicked at the same time. God protecting David from Saul in the wilderness and keeping David out of battle with Israel while using the battle to bring down Saul is a good example. So too, Peter being set free after Herod imprisoned him and Herod being killed in the theater, both in Acts 12, is another.

Testimony: Invite a church member to share their own story about how God protected them when someone else was wrongly accusing or attacking them. Have them also talk about how God vindicated them and made things right.

False Teachers Described and Denounced

Big Idea

False teachers are wolves in sheep's clothing, and their destruction is assured.

Key Themes

- False teachers have identifiable character traits.
- False teachers engage in outward sinful acts.
- Sin has an enslaving power.

Understanding the Text

The Text in Context

Having just warned his readers about the possibility of false teachers among them and having assured them that God knows how to punish the wicked and protect the righteous, Peter moves on to describe and denounce these false teachers. To do this he picks up some of the ideas he used when he introduced the false teachers in 2:1–3. This current section of 2:10–22 is also connected to 1:1–11 in that some of the opposite characteristics from that section are highlighted here. The encouragement is to pursue the qualities of 1:5–7 rather than those exhibited by the false teachers. After Peter describes and denounces the false teachers, the way is open for him to return to his stated theme of stirring up his readers to godly living and spiritual maturity. In chapter 3 Peter will also address a specific heresy introduced by false teachers that has led to immoral behavior.

Structure

The entire section is one long diatribe that intertwines the false teachers' character flaws, outward sinful actions, and promised future destruction.

Are or Were the False Teachers Saved?

Second Peter 2 describes false teachers as those whom the sovereign Lord bought (2:1), who were once on the straight way (2:15) and "have escaped the corruption of the world by knowing our Lord and Savior Jesus Christ" (2:20). But he also describes these false teachers as condemned (2:3), on the verge of destruction (2:3, 12), and destined for punishment (2:9). They never stop sinning (2:14), are slaves of depravity (2:19), and have turned their backs on the sacred command passed on to them (2:21). Most chillingly, Peter claims, "blackest darkness is reserved for them" (2:17).

Are these false teachers believers? No. First John 2 provides the best parallel text to what is going on with these false teachers, since John is writing about those who try to lead people astray (1 John 2:26). John says that such people who "deny" Jesus do not have the Father (1 John 2:22–23). The word John uses for "deny" is the same word in 2 Peter 2:1 to speak of false teachers. By saying that they do not have the Father, John is saying that they are antichrists, not believers, and do not have eternal life.

The more difficult question, and one which there is significant dissent with regard to 2 Peter 2 is, were such false teachers ever believers? First John 2:19 says, "They went out from us, but they did not really belong to us. For if they had belonged to us, they would have remained with us; but their going showed that none of them belonged to us." Although from outward appearance such teachers looked to be part of the community of faith, their willingness to abandon Jesus and lead his people astray indicates that they were never really believers in Jesus in the first place. The same type of thinking is behind Peter's statements in 2 Peter 2. The positive statements reflect the fact that at an earlier time these false teachers appeared to be part of the community of faith, but their current actions and attitudes demonstrate that they were never believers in Jesus. (See the comments on 2 Pet. 2:1–3; 2:20; and 2:22.)[a]

Whether or not one takes these false teachers as having been Christians once and no longer, or understands them as never having truly been redeemed by Jesus, the main thrust of the passage is a warning to stay away from such people now and to avoid falling into their errors.

[a] See also Schreiner's comments in 1, 2 Peter, Jude, 331, 364–65.

Interpretive Insights

2:10–11 *Bold and arrogant.* The first and primary characteristic of these false teachers is their pride, mentioned again in 2:18. Pride is the basis for the false teachers' despising of authority; it is the basis for their lack of fear in heaping abuse on angels; it is the reason they are willing to deny the Lord, who bought them (2:1). Pride provides the audacity to introduce heresies (2:1) and fabricate stories (2:3). Pride is connected to the other great evil motive mentioned throughout this chapter, which is greed. Both pride and greed were the root sins at Sodom, according to Ezekiel 16:49. The results of pride and greed were illicit sexual behavior and oppression of the poor and weak. The same is true for these false teachers. Their corrupt behavior is driven by pride and greed. (Pride furnishes greed with the rationale for always wanting more—because I deserve it and because I need it to hide my insecurities—while greed fuels pride in that the more that I get, the more I think I deserve.)

heap abuse on celestial beings; yet even angels . . . do not heap abuse on such beings. While some believe that "celestial beings" refer to demons, it is more likely that this refers to holy angels. First, why would false teachers be slandering demons? Demons engaged in the kinds of behavior—like sexual immorality—espoused by these false teachers, while angels were unwilling speak abusively of others. Second, disrespect for holy angels features prominently in the story of Sodom (one can only imagine what was said about the angels after they struck the men of Sodom with blindness). Third, Jude 8 is also talking about holy angels.

If this is correct, then the point of 2:11 is that even angels, who are stronger and more powerful than false teachers, do not slander the false teachers when they deliver judgment from God. For example, at Sodom the angels did not engage in verbal taunting or boastful, demeaning slander when they brought judgment from the Lord.[1]

2:15 *Balaam son of Bezer, who loved the wages of wickedness.* Numbers 22–24 recounts the story of Balaam, a prophet whose desire for money led him from the right path. While Numbers does not say explicitly why God was mad at Balaam, Peter reveals that it was his love of money, a point easily inferred from the story. So too, these false teachers may have once given some evidence of being teachers who spoke for God, but now they have been seduced in part by the love of money. These false teachers are worse than Balaam, since he was at least restrained in his madness by God speaking through his donkey. Interestingly, angels and animals figure prominently in Peter's discussion of false teachers and in the Balaam story. The Balaam story is also fitting because, although Balaam wants to take money to curse Israel, he is not able to pronounce a curse, because God won't let him. Instead, he ends up blessing Israel and cursing Moab. This further reinforces Peter's point that God knows how to protect the righteous, even when they do not know they are in danger of being cursed.

2:17 *Blackest darkness is reserved for them.* This verse is connected to 2:4, where Peter uses "darkness" and "held/reserved" to speak of the fate of fallen angels in hell. Jesus also speaks of "darkness" in connection to judgment in Matthew 8:12; 22:13; and 25:30. Jude 13 uses the same language, except it adds "forever." This is the very sobering language of eternal damnation. (On eternal punishment, see "Theological Insights" in the unit on Jude 1–7.)

2:18 *appealing to the lustful desires of the flesh, they entice people.* Those who are new to the faith are most susceptible to false teachers. False teachers lure those who are young in the faith by appealing to the desires of the flesh. Given the context and the words used here, this refers especially to illicit sexual desires.

2:20 *escaped the corruption of the world by knowing our Lord and Savior Jesus Christ . . . they are worse off at the end than they were at the beginning.* While most commentators point to this verse as evidence that the false teachers (or their followers) were at one point Christians who have walked away from the faith, that is not the view here. The phrase "they are worse off at the end than they were at the beginning" is virtually a quote from Luke 11:26. In Luke 11 a person experiences freedom from demonic power, presumably through Jesus's power, but does not experience genuine conversion. Later on in Luke's Gospel there is another story of ten lepers who receive an experience of God's power through Jesus, but only one of them actually experiences salvation (17:11–19).[2] Likewise in 2 Peter, the false teachers have experienced something of God's power and blessing through Jesus but have not experienced genuine conversion.

Now admittedly, "knowing" is the same word used in 1:3 (*epignōsis*), and Peter does connect this with the notion of escaping corruption, both of which could point to the false teachers having been Christians. However, the most that is said about the false teachers is that they escaped corruption, which can mean—like the man in Luke 11 who was set free from demonic power but never actually saved—that these false teachers experienced some level of escape from darkness. The positive aspects of 1:3–9 are never attributed to these false teachers. In other words, their nature is never actually changed (see commentary at 2:22).[3]

It is also noteworthy that Peter calls Jesus "our Lord and Savior," meaning that he is not their Lord and Savior.

2:21 *It would have been better for them not to have known the way of righteousness.* The same principle appears in Matthew 11:21–24; 12:44–45; and John 15:22, where those who have heard the truth or experienced the miraculous power of God are more liable for guilt when they reject it than those who have never had such an opportunity.

2:22 *"A dog returns to its vomit," and, "A sow that is washed returns to her wallowing in the mud."* The proverb about the dog is from Proverbs 26:11. The proverb about the pig is not from the Old Testament, though its meaning is clear enough, and the imagery of pigs and mud is common enough. In both cases, while the animals have been cleaned up on the outside, there has been no change in their nature. As Jesus said of false prophets in Matthew 7:15, they are wolves in sheep's clothing, rather than wolves that became sheep and are now transformed back into wolves again.

Theological Insights

The presence of non-Christians among genuine believers. In Matthew 13:24–30 Jesus tells a parable describing the kingdom of heaven as having weeds planted by Satan growing alongside the wheat. Paul identifies the same thing in Romans 9:6–8 with regard to not all of Israel being true Israel and in Romans 11:1–10 with the theme of a remnant. This same reality is present among the Twelve, which included Judas (see Jesus's comments in John 13:10–11). Letters such as Hebrews, with its warning passages, seem to assume that some in the target audience are not believers, even though they claim to be.[4] The same thing is seen in 2 Corinthians 13:5.

More specifically, 2 Peter 2 fits within the theological theme that among those identifying themselves as Christians will be those specifically there to bring destruction. Matthew 7:15; Acts 20:29–30; 2 Corinthians 11:13–15; and 1 John 2:18–19 are among those passages that form this theological trajectory.

Teaching the Text

There is nothing in this text addressed specifically to the readers. Rather, it is all about describing the character and destiny of the false teachers. While some false teachers or potential false teachers might be in your audience, since they are "among you" and feast "with you" (2:1, 13), the vast majority of listeners both then and now are not false teachers. Even still, there are natural inferences that any listener would take away from hearing this material, and these provide ways for the teacher to teach this material in a relevant way.

1. Beware of the enslaving and destructive power of sin, especially pride and greed (i.e., selfishness). In teaching this point, one may find it useful to differentiate between outward expressions of sin and the inner character traits that drive them. This passage lists slander (2:10–12), the absence of self-control (2:13–14), a love of money (2:15–16), and sexual immorality (2:14, 18) as outward expressions of sinful behavior. Each of these can be enslaving in its own way, but the root causes of these behaviors are pride and greed. Failing to address these root causes will render futile any efforts with these outward expressions of sin.

2. Continue to make every effort to participate in the divine nature and so demonstrate the genuine nature of your faith and avoid the fate of these false teachers. Whether one takes the false teachers as wolves in sheep's clothing (as I have) or Christians who have lost their salvation, the warning is still the same, to make every effort to display the qualities of the divine nature (1:3–11) so as to make one's salvation sure.

2 Peter 2:10–22

3. Recognize character traits and qualities of false teachers so that the false teachers can be identified and avoided. One identifies false teachers on the basis that what they are saying contradicts what God has said in his Word. But recognizing character traits of pride and greed as well as the outward expressions of sin listed in point 1 above can also help in identifying false teachers. Helping people who are confused by what a teacher is saying to look at the life they are living can be helpful.

4. Recognize ways in which genuine, well-meaning Christians can be enticed by false teachers and therefore cause unknowing harm to others. Christians in positions of leadership, especially, who by their lifestyle or teachings encourage people to slander other Christian leaders, to make light of God's teaching on sexual immorality, or to greedily pursue money may not be actual false teachers, but having been enticed by false teachers are unwittingly propogating things that cause others to stumble. For example, a small group leader may spend time listening to a media personality who claims to be a Christian but engages in vicious slandering of others who don't agree with him or her. That small group leader, who is genuinely a Christian, may then begin to heap abuse on others because that is what he is hearing modeled for him. That small group leader is not a false teacher, but if God is furious with false teachers who lead others astray, he will not be pleased with genuine Christians who may be unintentionally causing others to stumble in these things either.

One overall objection some listeners may have is this: isn't Peter hypocritically heaping abuse on false teachers with what he says here? Given the culture we live in, correction and rebuke like this sound abusive to many. But there are two differences between rebuke and slander. One, rebuke is true, while slander is false. What Peter says about false teachers is hard but accurate; what the false teachers were saying about celestial beings was not accurate. Two, Peter is rebuking false teachers with the authority given him by God; false teachers were slandering celestial beings on their own authority.

Illustrating the Text

Sin always carries the power to make slaves.

Literature: Most science fiction is built around humanity's relationship with technology. In many instances, a fear that the machines might one day take over lies at the backdrop of this interaction between human beings and the machines they make. Futurists have coined a term for this: "technological singularity." This term indicates the moment when machines have an intelligence of their own, capable of self-improvement and replication. In that moment, humanity may become obsolete, banished to extinction. At least, that's the way the story is told. And yet, the most brilliant humans are still working hard to usher in artificial intelligence. Likewise, when sin is let in the door, it has the capacity to take over. For a time, it is something we do. If left unchecked, it becomes something that does us and then undoes us.

Our continued growth in Christlikeness provides evidence our faith is real.

Nature: Imagine walking through an old, abandoned homestead. As you make your way along, you come across several trees that appear to be fruit trees. You're not sure what kind of trees these may be, but in time, you can find out. You don't have to be an expert arborist to know. Just keep checking back until you see what kind of fruit they produce! True Christians will produce a certain kind of fruit. We need to watch our own lives with honest humility. As we see fruit grow (good or bad), we will have a sense of how closely we are following Jesus.

Pride and greed are two clear marks of false teachers.

Medicine: Modern medicine has produced many marvels. One of the best gifts it has given is the ability to diagnose disease. With an incredible level of specificity, medical professionals are able to perform certain tests to discover what may be wrong with a body. For instance, in a blood test, we are able to determine whether key blood levels are within the normal range. If one or more of these are outside an acceptable average, then it become clear that something is amiss. Because we have built enough knowledge, not only are we able to establish what constitutes an acceptable, healthy range for these key markers, but we are also able to tell, in many instances, precisely what diagnosis is indicated by these abnormal levels. In the same way, when we are diagnosing whether a soul is healthy, pride and greed are two key markers. If they are overinflated, we can be sure there is sickness present.

Remembering Christ's Coming

Big Idea

False teachers spread deception that Christ is not returning, but believers must remember that God is patient and that Christ will return.

Key Themes

- Pay attention to true prophecy.
- Jesus will return and bring judgment.
- God is patient with and loves the lost.

Understanding the Text

The Text in Context

With 3:1–10, Peter returns to the purpose of his letter, which is to stir his readers to action by reminding them of truth. Having turned his attention in chapter 2 to false teachers, Peter now turns his focus to one of the false teachings that has been circulating, that Christ will not return. Correcting this false teaching with the truth will allow Peter to remind his readers what kind of people they need to be in light of this truth (3:11–18).

Structure

1. Reiteration of and return to the main theme (3:1–2)
2. False teaching about Christ's coming and refutation (3:3–7)
3. The reason for the delay of Christ's coming and explanation of how that coming will happen (3:8–10)

Interpretive Insights

3:1 *I have written both of them as reminders to stimulate you to wholesome thinking.* The Greek words the NIV has translated "as reminders to stimulate you" are the same words in 1:13 translated "to refresh your memory." Peter is now restating his purpose for this letter, which is to remind his readers of the words spoken to them by the prophets and apostles in order to stir them to action. In chapter 1, it was Peter's imminent death that stirred him to write. Here, it is the imminent nature of Christ's return that is supposed to stir readers to right actions. Peter is experiencing personally what he is urging them to do: being motivated today about the end that is soon coming.

3:2 *and the command given by our Lord and Savior through your apostles.* Why is "command" singular? It probably is collective for all the commands Jesus gave, which can often be summarized as one command (as in John 15:10–17). If not, it may be foreshadowing the "one thing" Peter wants them to remember in 3:8. This would be a reference to Jesus's main command with regard to his second coming, which is to keep watch and not be deceived (see Matt. 24–25).

3:3 *in the last days scoffers will come, scoffing and following their own evil desires.* In Peter's sermon at Pentecost in Acts 2, he quotes Joel 2, which begins, "In the last days." The coming of the Holy Spirit at Pentecost signaled that the "last days" prophesied in the Old Testament had in some sense begun. Therefore, "the last days" signifies "now" (cf. Heb. 1:2; James 5:3), but with an emphasis on the eschatological nature of the event. This means that the appearance of scoffers is a sign that the end is indeed coming. By saying scoffers "will come," Peter means that it is a present possibility for his readers. It is also a prediction for all future generations. The irony of those who mock the reality of the coming of Jesus is that their very activity affirms this apostolic prophecy and the truthfulness of the return of Jesus.

"Scoffers" is another way to speak of the false teachers of chapter 2. To scoff means "to mock," but what they are scoffing about is the coming of the Lord. This is more like "blasphemy," the word used for heaping abuse and slandering in 2:10–12. The related verb "to scoff/mock" appears most in connection with Jesus's crucifixion (Matt. 20:19; 27:29, 31, 41; Mark 10:34; 15:20, 31; Luke 18:32; 22:63; 23:11, 36). Additionally, the scoffers follow "their own evil desires," which is similar to the description of the false teachers in 2:10. And pride, the underlying character flaw of the false teachers, often manifests itself in "scoffing" in the Old Testament (e.g., Pss. 73:8; 119:51; Prov. 21:24; Zeph. 2:10).

3:5 *they deliberately forget that long ago by God's word.* Words of remembering/reminding (3:1–2) and forgetting (3:5, 8) are key ideas in this section. On remembering as stirring to action, see the comments on 2 Peter 1:12. Here, remembering is contrasted with forgetting. Just as "remembering" is not simply cognitive recall, "forgetting" is not simply memory lapse. The word itself carries the idea of a deliberate choice, a nuance that is made explicit when Peter adds the word "deliberately." Romans 1:18–32 is similar in that

Peter and Noah's Flood

Second Peter 3:6 is the third time in his two epistles that Peter mentions Noah's flood (cf. 1 Pet. 3:20; 2 Pet. 2:5). By comparison, the only other times Noah or the flood are mentioned in the New Testament are once by Jesus (Matt. 24:38–39 // Luke 17:26–27) and once in Hebrews (11:7). Clearly this event is important for Peter. In this third reference, various themes of Noah's story come together to inform this whole section.

1. *The relationship of judgment by water to judgment by fire.* In 3:5–7 Peter ties together creation, flood, and the final day of judgment. The current earth was created "out of water and by water," so the waters of the flood were essentially God hitting "reset" on the current earth. However, at the day of judgment it will be fire, not water, that will destroy the elemental substance of this creation (3:10, 12). This is not a "reset" but a new heaven and a new earth, where righteousness dwells (3:13).

2. *The concept of God's patience and salvation.* First Peter 3:20 speaks of God patiently waiting while Noah built the ark, and 2 Peter 3:9 speaks of God's "patience" (related word) in delaying Christ's coming. Both times patience has to do with rescue and salvation—God rescuing Noah and his family and God rescuing people today. Though Noah wasn't an itinerant preacher, he was a preacher of righteousness (2:5), meaning that through Noah's life and story God was proclaiming righteousness to his and subsequent generations. God is still patiently preaching righteousness in the hopes of bringing salvation to many today.

3. *The day of the Lord coming like a thief.* When Jesus speaks of his return and the day of judgment in Matthew 24, he says it will be like the days of Noah (vv. 38–39) and come like a thief (v. 43). Peter, influenced by Jesus's teaching, relates the day of the Lord coming like a thief (3:10) and sees the flood as the prototype of this.

the wicked know God through creation but choose to suppress and refuse to retain that knowledge. This is an active forgetting.

the earth was formed out of water and by water. "Out of water" refers most likely to Genesis 1:2, where the Spirit is hovering over the primordial waters, ready to begin the work of creation. "By water" refers most likely to Genesis 1:6–10, where land is created as God separates the waters, causing dry ground to appear.

3:8 *do not forget.* This is the one imperative in this section, and 3:8–9 constitutes the central teaching. Judgment is still coming, but God is waiting so that as many as possible might be saved.

a day is like a thousand years, and a thousand years are like a day. The actual comparison of a thousand years being like a day (the second half of the phrase) comes from Psalm 90:4. Here, like there, it emphasizes that human years last but a moment to God. But Peter has added the corollary, which is that a day is like a thousand years (the first half of the phrase). This may be an allusion to Psalm 84:10 (even though the comparison there is one day to a thousand days) and possibly introduces a more positive notion into timelessness with God. If judgment has taken a long time from a human point of view, so will the bliss of eternal life when Christ appears. In either case the point is that the human perspective on time is not the determining perspective.

3:9 *patient with you, not wanting anyone to perish, but everyone to come to repentance.* This is a beautiful verse reminding readers of God's love for the whole world (so also John 3:16; 1 Tim. 2:4; Ezek. 18:32). Despite Peter's harsh language about false teachers in chapter 2, God does not want even them to perish: he wants *everyone* to come to repentance. This is why we don't understand the timing of Christ's return. We are viewing his return from our point of view—how everything will be great. God is viewing Christ's return from the point of view that when Jesus returns there will be some left out. Unfortunately, the fact that God does not "want" people to perish is balanced against the sad truth that some do perish and are held for punishment on the day of judgment (as is clear from 2:9). So 3:9 expresses God's desire, not a unilateral decree that all will be saved, since God doesn't force salvation on anyone.

It is noteworthy that Peter says God is patient with "you" as opposed to patient with "them." It is a reminder that God's patience is the reason why those who are believers have been saved. This same patience will be the reason why others will come in as well. It may also be that God's patience with the readers is allowing them to develop the kind of godly character that will enable them to be "productive and effective" in their knowledge of Jesus (cf. 1:8), which of course will result in helping others come to salvation.

Theological Insights

The patience of God. One of the often-overlooked attributes of God is his patience, yet this is an important theme in the Scriptures. The primary description of God in the Old Testament calls him "slow to anger" (Exod. 34:6; cf. Num. 14:18; Pss. 86:15; 103:8; 145:8). The usual expression of God's patience is in regard to sin (e.g., 1 Pet. 3:20; Neh. 9:30), as he waits for people to come to repentance (2 Pet. 3:9, 15; Rom. 2:4; 1 Tim. 1:16). But God also demonstrates his patience in carrying out his plans, whether bearing with patience the objects of his wrath (Rom. 9:22) or enduring the conduct of the Israelites in the wilderness (Acts 13:18).

The downside to God's patience is that the wicked seem to go unpunished (Ps. 73; Hab. 1–2), and God sometimes seems slow to help (as in the oft-repeated

"How long?" of the Psalms). As a result, God's people must show patience as we wait for God to act (e.g., Pss. 37:7; 40:1; Hab. 3:16; Rom. 8:25; 12:12; Heb. 6:15; James 5:7–8).

Teaching the Text

There are multiple ways to approach the preaching and teaching of this passage. First, the one injunction in the passage—"Do not forget this one thing, dear friends" (3:8)—makes teaching the passage as a way to remind Christians of Christ's return absolutely vital. In teaching the passage in this way, the teacher should emphasize the patience of God and the purpose for the delay in Christ's coming, which is so that many can be saved. The fact that Christ's return will be like a thief in the night is also an important aspect of this teaching. But Peter has not reproduced the earlier portion of Matthew 24 with its discussion of the signs of Jesus's coming. Instead, he has highlighted that Jesus's coming will be like a thief. Therefore, this passage is not about teaching end-time chronology or trying to predict when Jesus will come. One of the main reasons why people who study prophecy (a good thing) will never be able to accurately predict when Jesus is coming is that they are approaching Jesus's coming from the point of view of how it will bless them (which it will). God is approaching Jesus's coming from how it will mean that some are left out of the kingdom. Because we do not have God's heart for the lost, we will not be able to figure out when Jesus is coming.

Second, this passage can be taught evangelistically. Verse 9 shows the very heart of God. His patience flows out of his mercy and love. The fact that God is willing to wait and endure all the sin in this world is because he loves the whole world and doesn't want anyone to perish. Sometimes discussions of Christ's coming can focus our attention on ourselves: "I will be vindicated." "I will not have to put up with sin and suffering anymore." "I will be rewarded." But this passage is about God's love for others who do not yet know him.

Third, as a corollary, this passage can be used to teach the patience of God and his delay in "coming" in smaller-scale situations. By these I mean, for example, when God "delays" coming to rescue us from a vicious neighbor, and it turns out that God wanted to use us to help bring that neighbor to faith. Or when God allows a cruel and bitter person to live a long life, it can be because he wants to give them every chance to repent. Helping people understand how God shows patience in these smaller situations can help confirm that this is how he is operating on the grand scale of Christ's return.

One other comment: scoffers today may not express their skepticism using the same words as in 3:4. More likely the argument about the coming of Christ in 3:4 will come in the form of doubting God's existence because of suffering (i.e., if there were a God, he would "come" and do something about all the evil in the world) or doubting that there will be judgment and punishment for unrighteousness in this life.[1]

Illustrating the Text

Compare God's patience with our impatience regarding Christ's return.

Sports: Imagine a soccer game between two high school rivals. On the one side, the star center midfielder has scored two goals to give his team a 2–0 lead over the heavily favored opposition team. But the opposing team continues to have opportunities to score. As they get further and further into the second half, the midfielder keeps asking the ref how much time is left. For him the minutes can't move fast enough. He's exhausted and ready for the game to be done, to seal the victory. Why do the minutes keep dragging on? How long until this game is done?

However, rooting for the opposing team is a set of parents whose child is on the team but hasn't been in the game yet. They can see from where they are how disappointed their son is that he hasn't had a chance to play. They are hoping and praying that the coach will look down the bench and give their son a chance to get into the game. For them the minutes are flying by, going way too quickly. Every second that goes by is a missed opportunity for their child to get into the game.

We view Christ's second coming more impatiently than God because for us it means the end to all our problems, while for God it means that he has some whom he loves who will not make it into heaven.

God's patience leads people to salvation.

Bible: One example of God's patience is in the life of the apostle Paul, whom Peter will reference in 3:15 in the context of God's patience resulting in salvation. Paul describes himself as a blasphemer who is an example of God's immense patience leading to salvation (1 Tim. 1:13–16).

God loves his lost children.

Applying the Text: If we are going to become people who reach out and witness to our lost friends and neighbors, we need to have God's heart for lost people. The best way to align our heart with God's is through prayer. The time spent with him leads us to become more like him. Challenge your congregation to spend an intentional season of prayer for people they love who do not yet know Jesus (or, better yet, for people they *don't* like!). One easy tool is simply to set an alert on your cell phone or watch for the same time every day. You commit to pausing whenever the alarm goes off, no matter what you're doing, and praying for at least one lost friend. Some people have done a 1–1–1 prayer, where they pray for one person at 1:00 each day for one minute. The prayer is for this person to come to faith in Jesus and for God to use us in any way he sees fit.

What Kind of People We Ought to Be

Big Idea

Because Jesus is coming to judge and remake the world, Christians should commit themselves to living righteously for the sake of evangelism and to growing in their faith.

Key Themes

- False teachers distort true Scripture and prophecy.
- Look forward to the new heavens and new earth.
- Holy living leads to evangelism.
- Give every effort to grow in spiritual maturity.

Understanding the Text

The Text in Context

In this section Peter draws out the ethical implications of his teaching on the return of Christ from 3:1–10. He also closes the epistle, circling back to his major themes of true prophecy/Scripture (1:12–21), the danger of false teachers (2:1–22), and the need for growing in the faith (1:1–11).

Structure

1. Statement of the question of ethical implications of the teaching of Christ's return (3:11)
2. A reminder of what will happen when Christ returns (3:12–13)
3. The answer to the question of verse 11 (3:14–18)
   a. Give every effort to grow in the faith (3:14)
   b. Beware false teaching and teachers (3:15–17)
   c. Give every effort to grow in the faith (3:18)

Interpretive Insights

3:11 *Since everything will be destroyed in this way . . . live holy and godly lives.* "Godly/godliness" links this instruction back to the beginning of the epistle, where the word was used three times (1:3, 6, 7). Peter is making the same point about growing in maturity, but now he has added a new dimension. There is an urgent need for godliness, since everything will be destroyed. This not only means to pursue character traits that will last for eternity, but by saying that these godly lives are "holy," Peter is signaling that there is an evangelistic purpose to such maturity as well. The phrase *"live holy"* contains one of Peter's favorite words (*anastrophē*, "way of life") when talking about evangelism (e.g., 1 Pet. 1:15; 2:12; 3:1–2, 16). The Lord does not want anyone to perish, and a major way that people come to faith is when they see the holy and godly lives of believers living in light of the truth of Christ's return. It is noteworthy that one of the first imperatives in 1 Peter is, "Be holy [*hagios*] in all you do [*anastrophē*]" (1:15), and one of the last imperative-like[1] statements in 2 Peter is, "Live holy [*hagios*] and godly lives [*anastrophē*]" (3:11). In this way, the themes of 1 and 2 Peter come together.

3:12 *as you look forward to the day of God and speed its coming.* As regards "speed its coming," the NIV footnote contains an alternate reading, "as you wait eagerly for the day of God to come" (cf. HCSB). The word *speudō*, translated "speed its coming," can mean "eagerly desire" and is used this way in classical Greek with a direct object, as it is here. However, in the New Testament the word appears only in Luke-Acts and there always means "speed" or "hasten." Likewise, this is the more common meaning in nonbiblical Jewish literature about the end times, which is why many translations opt for that meaning here.[2]

If it does mean "speed its coming," then through evangelism and righteousness believers can hurry along the coming of Christ. However, the context of 2 Peter seems to suggest the alternate NIV reading. If Peter's corrective to false teachers is to remind his readers of God's patience (3:10, 15), why would he turn around and urge believers to try to hurry God up? So too, Peter's statement in Acts 3:21 seems to be shutting down any inference from Acts 3:19–20 that mass human repentance will bring Christ's return more quickly. And Jesus's statement in Matthew 24:36 seems to imply that the day of Christ's coming is fixed. The response of believers is to keep watch and be ready (Matt. 24:42, 44; 25:13). There are no instructions to try to speed up the process in that foundational teaching for Peter on Christ's return.

Finally, the word "look forward to" appears in 3:12, 13, and 14 (also Matt. 24:50). In 3:14 it appears with the word *spoudazō* ("make every effort"), a word that is semantically related to *speudō* ("eagerly/speed") from 3:12. Thus the dominant idea of how believers are to relate to Christ is to "look forward to his coming," and this is supplemented by the notion of "eagerly waiting" and "making every effort."

3:13 *a new heaven and a new earth.* See "Theological Insights," below.

3:15 *Paul also wrote you with the wisdom that God gave him.* Given Paul's rebuke of Peter in Galatians 2, this affirmation of Paul is an example of Peter's humility over against the arrogance of the false teachers. Having been rebuked by Paul for his hypocritical actions, Peter accepted the rebuke and refused to harden his heart. He demonstrated the same quality in the multiple times he was rebuked by Jesus.

3:16 *some things that are hard to understand, which ignorant and unstable people distort.* The issues most likely to have been difficult to Paul's first readers, including Peter, are the things that are still difficult for many today. Peter's refreshing acknowledgment that it can be difficult to understand all of what Paul says (which also applies to other portions of the New Testament) was probably just as encouraging to his original audience as it is to those of us today who read these words. As to what exactly Peter is referring to, one can safely conclude that Paul's teaching on the law was easily misunderstood and easily distorted. This is evident from Galatians 2 and Acts 15, as well as a number of other places where Paul addresses this issue. Some think that James 2:13–26 may also be written in response to misunderstandings about Paul's teaching on faith and works. The same may even be true of Jude (see Jude 4). Another possible distortion may concern the return of Christ. Second Thessalonians 2:2 reports false teaching allegedly from Paul asserting that the day of the Lord had already happened, something similar to what Peter is trying to refute in this chapter.

as they do the other Scriptures. The word for "Scriptures" is used at least fifty times in the New Testament and always refers (at least) to the Old Testament. In places such as 1 Timothy 5:18; 2 Timothy 3:16; 2 Peter 1:20; and here, the meaning seems to be broadening to include writings like Paul's that are to be viewed on a par with the Old Testament as God's authoritative revelation. Such a declaration by Peter counters the popular view among some today that the authoritative writings of the New Testament were not recognized as such until the fourth century.

Given Peter's comments about Paul's writing, his authoritative tone in this letter, his stature as an apostle, and his comments in 1:12–21, it is safe to assume that he also believed that this epistle was to be viewed as having the authority of Scripture.

3:17 *carried away by the error of the lawless and fall from your secure position.* This phrase can also be translated, "led astray by the deception of the lawless and drift away from your steadfast commitment." One way to look at Peter's language here is from the perspective of a journey. The danger of false teachers is that they will lead Peter's readers off the path and cause them to stumble. This would fit with 1:10, where Peter is worried that if they do not continue to grow in godliness they will stumble on their faith journey. To speak of falling from one's secure position might indicate that if you fall, you are lost forever. More likely, Peter is saying that if you are led astray off the path you will stumble and fall, but you can still get back up and get back on the path. The word for "carried away" is used in Galatians 2:13 of Barnabas being led astray by the hypocrisy of Peter and others. But Barnabas (and Peter) recovered their footing and continued their successful journey of faith. Peter might also be thinking of Mark, who was his "son" in the faith (1 Pet. 5:13). Mark stumbled badly (Acts 15:37–38) but recovered wonderfully (2 Tim. 4:11). (On Christians stumbling, see also the unit on James 5:19–20, above.)

3:18 *grow in the grace and knowledge of our Lord and Savior Jesus Christ.* With this Peter returns to where he began his epistle. Believers must continue to grow and mature. Peter used this same word for "grow" in 1 Peter 2:2, also speaking about the need for believers to mature in their faith.

Given that in 3:1 Peter calls this the second letter that he has written to them,[3] it may be that "grace" represents a central idea of 1 Peter and "knowledge" a major idea of 2 Peter. "Grace" is used ten times in 1 Peter, including in the important summary of 1 Peter 5:10–11, and only twice in 2 Peter (here and 1:2). "Knowledge" (*gnōsis* + *epignōsis*) is used seven times in 2 Peter and only once in 1 Peter. Since no other epistle in the New Testament ends with "grace and knowledge," this ending might be Peter's way of tying together the two epistles. "Grace" emphasizes God's sovereignty and care over his people as they endure suffering, and "knowledge" represents the truth that God has provided to guide his people safely through until Christ's return.

Theological Insights

New heavens and new earth. One of the contributions of 3:11–18 (also 3:5–10) is to the theology of the new heavens and the new earth. This theme is mentioned explicitly in Isaiah 65:17; 66:22; and Revelation 21:1–5. But the idea is present in Psalm 104:29–30; Matthew 19:28; Acts 3:21; and Romans 8:18–25 and is at least related to the Pauline doctrine of "new creation" (2 Cor. 5:17; Gal. 6:15). What is not clear in all of these texts is whether the new heavens and new earth involve a transformation/renewal (Matt. 19:28; Acts 3:21; Rom. 8:18–25) or a complete destruction/replacement (Matt. 24:35; 1 Cor. 7:31; Rev. 20:11; 21:1–5) of the current heavens and earth. The fact that there is tension between these two positions indicates that there will be an unexpected level of continuity between the current earth and the new earth and an unexpected level of discontinuity. On this spectrum, 2 Peter 3 leans toward the destruction side.

Teaching the Text

How should believers live in light of the return of Christ? As Peter sets out to answer this question, he first reviews the teaching of Christ's return in 3:12–13. When teaching this section, you may need to do that, especially if 3:1–10 was not taught before. The main point of 3:12–13 is the same point as in chapter 2. The wicked, wickedness, and the things associated with this world's systems and values will be destroyed, and the righteous and things associated with righteousness will endure.

From this review, the teacher who is following Peter's argument in the passage has three main issues to cover or choose from: (1) evangelism, (2) spiritual maturity, and (3) true and false teaching. First, with regard to evangelism, Peter covered this extensively in 1 Peter, mentions it again in 3:8–10, and now returns to it here. Because Christ is coming to judge the world, the wicked are in trouble. But since God's patience means salvation, if believers in Jesus would adopt a lifestyle of godliness whereby they would be at peace with God, this would make them different from the wicked around them (that is, holy). This peace with God, along with the distinction in behavior and God's desire to save everyone, will allow God to work in and through believers to bring people to faith.

Second, because the new heavens and new earth will be a place where righteousness dwells, the believer should make every effort to grow in the grace and knowledge of the Lord Jesus Christ. By growing in the qualities listed in 1:5–7, the believer is assured that these labors will not be in vain but rather will be richly rewarded. Other questions about the theme of the new heavens and new earth could be covered here, questions like the following: To what extent is life now going to be like life in the new heavens and new earth? To what extent should Christians continue to pursue the cultural mandate of Genesis 1:28? To what extent should Christians be longing for a new and different world versus trying to redeem and fix this one?

Third, the discussion of Paul's writings as Scripture and the fact that false teachers distort Scripture in 3:16–17 reintroduces the subject of where righteousness and guidance to peace with God are found. Just as Peter reiterates the need for submitting to and obeying the Scriptures, the teacher may need to reiterate that as well. There may be a point to be made here that usually false teachers are distorting scriptural passages rather than just running off and making up their own teachings and ethics out of nowhere.

2 Peter 3:11–18

Illustrating the Text

Faith is a journey, and there is danger of falling under the influence of false teachers.

Literature: *Pilgrim's Progress*, **by John Bunyan.** In this allegorical work, Bunyan tells the story of Christian, a man whose journey represents the faith walk that every Christ-follower must take. Along the way, he encounters the same pitfalls and temptations that we encounter in our life with Christ. In one encounter, Christian is waylaid on his journey to the Celestial City by Flatterer, who is disguised as an angel of light. Flatterer is similar to the false teachers of 2 Peter 2, and the danger is that they entice Christians off the path.

False teachers use Scripture for their own purposes.

Informational: Most seminary students are taught the difference between "exegesis" and "eisegesis." The former is a good thing, seeking to get to the real message of Scripture, allowing the text to speak for itself. The latter is a bad thing, seeking to conform the message of Scripture to preconceived notions, biases, and agendas. As more than one professor has probably noted, true teachers use the Bible like a light, to illuminate the path they are walking. False teachers use the Bible like a drunk man uses a light post, to lean on for support.

Holy living is a means of evangelism.

Testimony: A friend recently shared that he was being sued for a small amount of money by someone for work he had done for them. My friend prayed and discussed what to do. Although he most likely would have won the court case, he decided instead to go over to this person's house and write them a check. He said, "If I am actually at fault, then this money will cover it. If I am not at fault, then consider this a present from Jesus to you because he loves you." This is not how the world would have handled the situation, but because Jesus is returning, that changes everything. By living differently, my friend communicated the truth of a loving and patient God who does not want anyone to perish.

Introduction to Jude

The Letter of Jude is about contending for the Christian faith. Although Jude originally wanted to write a different letter, he became convinced it was necessary to write this letter based on the presence of ungodly unbelievers among the Christian community.

Importance of Jude

Jude sometimes gets lost, tucked away at the back of the New Testament, but this short book contains a powerful and important message. Christians of every age have had to contend with the danger of ungodly unbelievers infiltrating and affecting the Christian community. Jude mixes together reassuring theological affirmations of God's love and power with pointedly poetic attacks on ungodliness and wise practical instructions regarding what believers are to do when they find themselves in such situations.

As a pastor ministering in a context in America that is growing in antagonism toward God and Christianity—a context in which ungodliness is more and more the rule of the day—I find the book of Jude to be incredibly contemporary and desperately needed. I am horrified by the destructive power of ungodliness on the people whom I minister to and have seen its effects on the church I am called to help lead. I feel the urgent desire that Jude felt to see his readers contend for the faith, and I am grateful to God for this book of Scripture. My prayer is that God would give you insight and power as you preach and teach this book.

Author, Setting, and Date

The author of this letter identifies himself as Jude, a servant of Jesus Christ and a brother of James. The most likely candidate is Jesus's half brother Jude, who is also the brother of James the author of the Epistle of James. This Jude was not a member of the twelve apostles, and we have no indication from the rest of Scripture that he was ever considered an apostle. Jude 17 gives the impression that Jude did not consider himself among the apostles, but Jude would have been held in high regard in the early church because of his connection to Jesus.

It is impossible to identify with any precision or accuracy Jude's original audience. Despite our inability to locate Jude's original audience, the book describes a common experience of all genuine Christian communities. The universality of Jude's message is affirmed in verses 17–18, where Jude tells us that Jesus and his apostles prophesied ahead of time of ungodly unbelievers influencing the Christian community. This prophecy was not for a specific community in a specific situation, but all communities. Jude is quite clear as to what kinds of behaviors and attitudes such ungodly unbelievers demonstrate, without having to identify with precision if they were antinomians abusing the Pauline doctrine of grace, an incipient gnostic sect like the Carpocratians, or something else.

Just as we have very little to go on with regard to the original audience, there are no strong indications as to when the epistle was written. A date in the late 50s or early 60s AD seems reasonable, but it could have been later.

Relationship to 2 Peter

Second Peter and Jude are sister letters. This is especially true of 2 Peter 2:1–18 + 3:2–3 and Jude 4–13 + 16–18. But more than just these passages with similar wording, the themes of Christ's return, growing in maturity, and not stumbling are present in both letters. The majority of commentators today hold that 2 Peter used Jude, a view that is impossible to prove but might likely be true. However, with regard to theories of literary dependence, it is important to keep two things in mind. First, unlike the Synoptic Gospels (or even Ephesians and Colossians), there are many common words but little extended word-for-word correspondence. Second, given Peter's position in the church and the fact that he has known Jude for a long time,[1] they may have interacted personally about these issues before either one wrote their letter, so either may have been the source of the ideas and words they have in common. Beyond these two cautions about literary dependence, the most important thing to keep in mind is that the similarities between 2 Peter and Jude must not blind us to the differences. These include the fact that 2 Peter is addressing a situation where there are false teachers, while Jude is talking about the presence of ungodly unbelievers who may or may not be in positions of leadership. In 2 Peter there is a need to correct misunderstandings about Christ's return. In Jude there is a need for spiritually mature people to help rescue those who have fallen into ungodly behavior.

Theological Themes and Suggestions for Teaching

God's sovereignty and human responsibility. The letter begins and ends with God's sovereign actions on behalf of his people. We are called, loved, and kept by God, and by his power we will enter into God's eternal kingdom. Our responsibility is to contend for the faith by remembering what God told us through the apostles, keeping ourselves in God's love and showing mercy to those around us. Balancing these two is central in teaching Jude's epistle.

Ungodly unbelievers. Throughout the commentary on Jude, I refer to "ungodly unbelievers." This is an attempt to combine "ungodly," which is Jude's most frequent way to describe these people, with "those who did not believe" in verse 5. When Jude introduces these people he says they "pervert the grace of our God into a license for immorality" (ungodly) and "deny Jesus Christ" (unbelief) (v. 4). Using a designation like this can help listeners differentiate among the many different kinds of unbelievers that one can find in a church on any given Sunday. Some unbelievers who are there are seekers (e.g., 1 Cor. 14:23–25), some are people who think they are Christians because of their good deeds but aren't (e.g., Matt. 7:21–23), some are people who claim to be Christians but have no good deeds (e.g., James 2:14–26), and some are there because they are wolves dressed in sheep's clothing (e.g., Matt. 7:15–20). Jesus says the way to identify the wolves dressed in sheep's clothing is by their ungodly deeds, hence the term "ungodly unbelievers."

Contending for the Faith

Big Idea

Jude encourages his readers to contend for the faith against ungodly unbelievers on a path toward destruction who have slipped in among them.

Key Themes

- Believers are loved by God.
- The judgment of God is awaiting the ungodly.

Understanding the Text

The Text in Context

With this opening section, Jude introduces the purpose of his writing: contending for the faith. Contending for the faith is necessary because of ungodly unbelievers who have slipped in among those to whom he is writing. To prepare his readers' minds for what he will say about these ungodly people, Jude cites three Old Testament examples of God's judgment on disobedient disbelief: Israel, fallen angels, and Sodom.

This prepares the way for the next section, verses 8–16, where Jude describes the ungodly unbelievers and the judgment that is waiting for them. Jude will return to what he wants his readers to remember in verses 17–23 and draw out the practical implications of how they are supposed to react to what they see going on around them.

Structure

1. Introduction to the letter: God's love for his people (vv. 1–2)
2. Purpose for writing: to contend for the faith because of the presence of ungodly people who are leading some believers astray (vv. 3–4)
3. Israel, angels, and Sodom as examples of God's judgment on those who express their unbelief through disobedience (vv. 5–7)

Interpretive Insights

1 *Jude, a servant of Jesus Christ and a brother of James.* James is most likely the author of the Epistle of James and one of Jesus's half brothers (see the introduction to James, above). This in turn tells us that Jude is most likely one of Jesus's half brothers also. Matthew 13:55 (// Mark 6:3) lists Jesus's four half brothers, with James seemingly the oldest and most prominent in the church and Jude probably the third youngest or the youngest.

called, who are loved in God the father and kept for Jesus Christ. Love is a key idea for Jude. It shows up twice in the introduction (vv. 1–2) and five times in the body of the letter: three times where the NIV has "dear friends" (= "beloved"; vv. 3, 17, 20), once to describe their "love feasts" (v. 12), and once in verse 21, a parallel use to verse 1. "Kept," likewise, is an important word for Jude. In verses 1 and 21 "kept" refers to believers being preserved, and in verses 6 and 13 (NIV: "reserved") it refers to the wicked being kept for judgment. "Kept" speaks of God's power and plans to protect those who believe and punish those who disobey. Believers are kept by God "for" or "in" Jesus, fitting with the doxology in verses 24–25. "Called" comes last in the Greek and represents the practical expression of God's love and power: God called believers to himself to experience his love and protective power.

2 *Mercy, peace and love.* The order in Greek in verses 1–2 is "love," "kept," "called," "mercy," "peace," "love." Such a pattern might suggest an inverted pairing: "mercy" with "called," "peace" with "kept," and "love" with "love." God expressed his mercy by calling us to salvation; we experience peace as we are kept by him; and all this is wrapped up in his love.

3 *eager to write to you about the salvation we share . . . urge you to contend for the faith.* Reminding us that Scripture was written into specific situations, Jude acknowledges that he originally wanted to write a different letter with a different theme. Recognizing the dangerous situation that his readers were in, Jude changed subjects and wrote them this epistle, the theme of which is contending for the faith. "Contend for" was used in classical Greek literature in the context of athletic contests, military battles, and intellectual arguments. It is noteworthy that Jude doesn't just want to contend for their faith himself; he wants his readers to fight for it themselves.

4 *whose condemnation was written about long ago.* The mention of the condemnation of ungodly people being written about long ago is a reference to the Old Testament Scriptures (see vv. 5–7). The word "written" (*prographō*) is also used in Romans 15:4: "For everything that was written in the past was written to teach us, so that through the endurance taught in the Scriptures and the encouragement they provide we might have hope." In the case of Romans, the Old Testament Scriptures taught endurance and provided hope. For Jude, the Scriptures provide warnings about condemnation for disobedience and unbelief (see also 1 Cor. 10:6–11). For both Paul and Jude, the Old Testament Scriptures speak not just to the original readers of these writings but also to their audiences as well.

who pervert the grace of our God into a license for immorality and deny Jesus Christ. This charge is similar to the one offered in 2 Peter 2, where the same words for "deny" (2 Pet. 2:1) and "immorality / depraved conduct" (2 Pet. 2:2) are used. Some among Jude's audience have taken God's kindness and grace and turned them into opportunities to engage in immoral behavior, including sexual immorality. This is a denial of Jesus's right to be obeyed and therefore is a denial of his lordship. These ungodly people are not believers, as is clear from the fact that Jude says that Jesus is *our* Sovereign and Lord, not theirs.

5 *delivered his people out of Egypt, but later destroyed those who did not believe.* This is the first of three examples Jude uses to make the point that God brings destruction on ungodly unbelievers. It is worth noting that 2 Peter 2 and Jude share two of the three examples (Sodom and fallen angels), but this is the one that is different in Jude (Peter has Noah). The story of the exodus generation's failures after Egypt is the story not of one specific failure but of many expressed over a period of time (cf. 1 Cor. 10:1–12). Within those stories there are many examples of Israelites contending for the faith, including the Levites (Exod. 32), Caleb and Joshua (Num. 14), and, of course, Moses. There are also examples of believers, like Moses, showing mercy to those who doubt. Such examples demonstrate what Jude wants to see his readers do, and so the reference to Israel supports his purpose in a way that using Noah as an example wouldn't.

As in 1 Corinthians 10:1–12 and Hebrews 3:7–19, the exodus generation is meant to be a warning to those among Jude's readers who think that they are believers but are not. Simply self-identifying as a Christian or participating in Christian love feasts (Jude 12) does not prove anything. This is why Jude uses the phrase "those who did not believe." Those who through disobedience are expressing a lack of belief in God will experience eternal punishment.

6 *angels who did not keep their positions of authority but abandoned their proper dwelling.* This is a reference to Genesis 6:1–4 and the sin of angelic beings taking on human form and having sex with human women. Although some believe that the "sons of God" in Genesis 6:1–4 refers to humans (those of the line of Seth or children of the aristocracy), at the time of Jude the book of *1 Enoch* espoused the view that these "sons of God" were angelic beings. Given that Jude quotes *1 Enoch* in verses 14–15, he is clearly familiar with this interpretation. It is also clear from the link to the sexual immorality and perversion of Sodom and Gomorrah in verse 7 that Jude means his readers to understand the angels' sins to be sexual. The angels "did not keep their positions of authority," meaning that they abandoned their position of being above humans in the created order (see Ps. 8:4–6) for sex with human women.

7 *Sodom and Gomorrah . . . gave themselves up to sexual immorality and perversion.* Jude is quite clear that the sin of Sodom and Gomorrah in mind here is sexual immorality. The word translated "perversion" could also be translated "went after other flesh." Some would see this as an indication that the people of Sodom wanted to have sex with angels, but in Genesis 19 the townspeople do not know that the men visiting Lot are angels. Sodom is punished for an ongoing pattern of sexual immorality, among other things (on these other things, see the comments on 2 Pet. 2:7–8). So "went after other flesh" refers to engaging in sexual activity with people of the same sex rather than those of the opposite sex as God had designed. Jude's commentary on Sodom also undercuts the modern conjecture that the sin of Sodom was only gang rape. Jude uses a general word for sexual immorality—one that was used in the Greek Old Testament for illicit consensual sexual activity (e.g., Gen. 38:24; Num. 25:1; Deut. 22:21; Hosea 1:2; 2:7). This would indicate that Jude is focused on the sexual aspect and not the rape aspect of what was happening in Sodom.[1]

They serve as an example of those who suffer the punishment of eternal fire. "They" could be referring just to Sodom and surrounding towns, since in the Genesis account fire rains from heaven and Sodom was often used as the example of God's willingness to punish wickedness as a warning to others (e.g., Deut. 29:23; Isa. 13:19; Lam. 4:6; Zeph. 2:9; Luke 17:29; Rom. 9:29). But "they" probably refers to all three examples, with each contributing an aspect of what eternal punishment looks like. Israel experienced destruction; angels, darkness; and Sodom, fire.

"Eternal fire" is used by Jesus of judgment in Matthew 18:8 and 25:41. The adjective "eternal" used here is the one that is used with the phrase "eternal life." Just as eternal life given by God is unending, so too the fire of judgment mentioned here is unending. On eternal punishment, see "Theological Insights."

Theological Insights

Eternal punishment. Jude 5–7 is part of the larger theological theme of the fate of the unrighteous. Daniel 12:1–2; Matthew 18:6–9; 25:31–46; John 5:28–29; Romans 2:1–11; 2 Thessalonians 1:5–10; and Revelation 20:7–15 are among the many passages that refer to the fate of the wicked and the unbelieving. Jude 5–7 contains a confluence of images, many of which are found in other passages. Destruction (v. 5), eternality (v. 7), judgment (v. 6), punishment (v. 7), fire (v. 7), darkness (vv. 6, 13), and imprisonment (v. 6) are all within the mix of images. The problem is that these images do not all fit neatly together (e.g., how can there be fire and darkness at the same time?). Add to this the emotional complexity of the idea of punishment, and it gets all the more confusing. Many of us cannot fathom what eternal life will be like, let alone eternal death. Yet despite these difficulties, the witness of Scripture is that those who reject Christ through unbelief and disobedience will experience the eternal judgment and punishment of God. Jude affirms this without specifying exactly what this will look like.[2]

Teaching the Text

Jude 3 provides helpful instruction for those who would be teachers. Teachers are to teach not simply what they feel like teaching but what their audience needs to hear. For one thing, this means that Jude 3 can provide an opportunity for instructing teachers how to teach. It is a safe assumption that Jude arrived at his conclusion to change topics through following the Spirit (v. 19), praying in the Spirit (v. 20), and observing what was going on in the people whom he was writing to. That Jude has exercised a level of discernment is obvious in that the ungodly have secretly slipped in among his readers, but Jude has not been fooled. These are important principles for any teacher to follow in planning what they are going to say.

When teaching what people need to hear as opposed to what we might want to talk about, we will be forced to address difficult topics, such as judgment and sexual immorality. In this way, teaching Jude 1–7 is like a self-fulfilling prophecy. It can't be appropriately taught without dealing with these difficult subjects.

In the teaching on judgment, I have tried to persistently identify what is being judged as disobedient disbelief. This is an attempt to recognize that according to Jude it is a lack of believing in Jesus as Lord that causes the judgment. That disbelief manifests itself in certain behaviors, like blatant sexual immorality. But sexual immorality itself does not automatically mean the punishment of eternal fire, any more than Moses's disobedience in the wilderness resulted in eternal separation from God. It might be necessary for the teacher to clarify this.

It can also be useful in teaching on eternal judgment to follow the example Jude has left. His point is not to describe the mechanics of how eternal judgment happens. His point is to emphasize that it does happen and is terrible. What happened to the Israelites, the fallen angels, and the people of Sodom is proof that God judges the wicked, and whatever else might be said about how judgment will work, the final judgment is sure and will be worse than all three of these.

Finally, the point from verse 3 that Jude is not just contending for the faith but wants to teach his readers how to contend for the faith for themselves is an important aspect from this text as well. The teacher who has successfully accomplished Jude's purpose is the one whose listeners are better equipped to contend for the faith themselves.

Illustrating the Text

Teachers must convey not only the pleasant truths of the Bible but the difficult ones as well.

Scenario: Imagine a doctor has been reviewing a difficult case. In examining her patient's charts, she realizes this man has a large, cancerous growth in his right leg. The patient can almost certainly be saved, but only if the leg is removed. The case is particularly tragic because the patient is someone who lives a highly active lifestyle—rock climbing, triathlons, and skydiving barely scratch the surface of his preferred to-do list. The doctor realizes that many of these hobbies will be hampered, if not eliminated, by the surgery. For one moment, can you even imagine this doctor deciding to hand out an easy diagnosis—"Just take two of these"—along with a prescription for placebos? Of course not! No physician who truly cares about their patient would do this. Though the news is terrible, the outcome of failing to convey the truth is even worse. True gospel teachers are willing to speak hard truths for the sake of the people they love.

Believers are loved by God.

Human Experience: Did you have a treasured stuffed animal or blanket as a child? Remember holding it? Carrying it everywhere? For some children, this fuzzy talisman is something that can never be left behind. Like a secret service agent who always knows exactly where the president is, a child fiercely guards their "blankie." In the same way, Jude tells us that God *loves* his children and *keeps* them. God has a fierce love for his people and will let no one or nothing snatch them away from him!

God's judgment will come upon the ungodly.

Film: Many adventure movies pit an unlikely hero against impossible odds. Between the hero and the seemingly unstoppable force is usually the fate of all, or much of, humanity. He must diffuse the planet-destroying atomic bomb. She must stop the earth-impacting meteor. He must prevent the train full of children from falling off the collapsed bridge. We love these stories. They remind us that there is always hope. They encourage us to lay down our lives to save others. There are many noble impulses in such stories. One thing that we fail to recognize, however, is that there is a kind of destruction that is inevitable. Those who will not give their lives to the true Hero of the story, Jesus, will face the destruction no other hero can prevent.

The Ungodly

Big Idea

The acts and attitudes of the ungodly are obvious and pernicious, and they will face judgment from Jesus when he returns.

Key Themes

- The ungodly will be judged at Jesus's return.
- The actions and attitudes of the ungodly are obvious.

Understanding the Text

The Text in Context

Having begun in verses 1–7 by affirming God's love, stating the purpose of his letter, and establishing historical examples where God punished disbelieving disobedience, Jude moves to address the current situation among his readers with regard to those who are disobedient and do not believe. After this section on the opponents, Jude will conclude with exhortations to help those believers among them who have been deceived by these opponents.

Structure

1. Initial charges of slander and rebellion (vv. 8–10)
2. Comparative images denouncing their lack of good works (vv. 11–13)
3. Enoch's prophecy about the judgment of the ungodly (vv. 14–15)
4. Final charges (v. 16)

Interpretive Insights

8 *on the strength of their dreams these ungodly people pollute their own bodies.* Deuteronomy 13:1–5 warns of prophets or dreamers who attempt to turn people away from pure devotion to the Lord. Even if the signs they announce come true, God's people are not to follow them, because God has already made clear in his Word what is proper behavior. The presence of such dreamers and false prophets has been allowed by God as a means of testing the devotion of his people. That is the sense here. In contrast to the clear teaching of Scripture, these ungodly unbelievers are choosing to pollute their bodies, perhaps even claiming to have had a supernatural dream or inspiration encouraging them to do so. To "pollute their own bodies" refers to sin in general but probably sexual immorality more particularly. The *Shepherd of Hermas*, a Christian text from the first or second century, connects "polluting bodies" to adultery.[1]

reject authority and heap abuse on celestial beings. Deuteronomy 13 indicates that false prophets and dreamers incite rebellion. Likewise, Jude says they "reject authority" and "heap abuse on celestial beings." These are separate charges from that of polluting their bodies, but the same spirit that emboldened them to disregard the Lord's clear commandments with regard to their sexual behavior emboldens them to reject authority and speak slanderously of celestial beings, that is, angels. (That these are holy angels and not the fallen angels of verse 8, see the comments on 2 Pet. 2:10–11.)

9 *Michael, when he was disputing with the devil . . . said, "The Lord rebuke you!"* The idea of this dispute between Michael and the devil is believed to have come from the *Testament of Moses*, a Jewish work from the early first century AD.[2] It should be noted, though, that we do not have any extant copies of this actual scene and are less certain about where Jude got this than we are the citation from *1 Enoch* in verses 14–15. The language of "the Lord rebuke you" is from Zechariah 3:2. In that courtroom scene, Satan is accusing Joshua the high priest, and the angel of the Lord responds to Satan's accusations with, "The LORD rebuke you."

From these two sources, it is believed that the devil brought some charge against Moses at his death in an attempt to hinder Michael from burying Moses for God in accordance with Deuteronomy 34:6. Michael, who seemingly has every right to denounce and speak degradingly of Satan, chooses not to but instead pronounces the discernment of God that Satan is wrong. This last part is important because Jude's point can't be that Michael doesn't announce that Satan is wrong as in, "Say whatever you want, Satan. I'll leave it up to the Lord to tell you whether you are right or wrong." By saying, "the Lord rebuke you," Michael is expressing that Satan is sinning, but he is leaving the actual enforcement of the penalty for that error up to God. Likewise, Jude is doing the exact same thing in this letter. He is expressing the God-revealed truth that these ungodly unbelievers are in sin, but Jude is leaving the enacting of the punishment up to God.[3]

10 *slander whatever they do not understand . . . things they do understand by instinct . . . will destroy them.* This could be read two ways: (1) the ungodly speak authoritatively about things they know nothing about, but the things of right and wrong that they know instinctively by nature they don't pay any attention to and are destroyed/corrupted as a result; or (2) the ungodly speak authoritatively about things they know nothing about, but then they turn around and act like unreasoning animals in their behavior and are destroyed/corrupted as a result. The word "by nature" (NIV: "by instinct") does not appear anywhere else in the New Testament, but the adjective form of the word shows up in Romans 1:26–27 (which would favor the first reading) and 2 Peter 2:12 (which would favor the second). Both lead to similar conclusions: their behavior is corrupted.

11 *way of Cain . . . Balaam's error . . . Korah's rebellion.* Three negative Old Testament examples are given here. The way of Cain is hatred, murder, and jealousy (Gen. 4; cf. 1 John 3:12). Balaam's error is love of money (Num. 22–24; cf. 2 Pet. 2:15–16). Korah's rebellion is pride, insolence, and insubordination (Num. 16).

12 *blemishes at your love feasts, eating with you without the slightest qualm.* Apparently the ungodly were participating in the Christian communal activities. If the example at Corinth was the norm, Christian communities met together for a meal and then participated in communion / the Lord's Supper afterward. In 1 Corinthians 11 Paul is furious that those who are participating in the meal before communion are doing so out of selfish desire to fill their bellies, rather than concern for the poor among them. He warns them in the strongest possible terms that the Lord's Supper must be taken only by those who have examined themselves. The ungodly in Jude, far from examining themselves, show no hesitation whatsoever about participating in the holiest of community activities.

shepherds who feed only themselves. All three of the images in this verse circle around the same concept. The ungodly provide nothing of value for anyone else and therefore are agents of death. The reference to shepherds who feed only themselves is reminiscent of Ezekiel 34:1–6, where God denounces the leaders of Israel for their utter lack of concern for anyone other than themselves. This imagery may presuppose that some of the ungodly were in positions of leadership within the Christian community. (Note the contrast with shepherds in 1 Pet. 5:1–5; see the commentary on those verses.)

clouds without rain, blown along by the wind. Clouds without rain are like broken cisterns that cannot hold water (e.g., Jer. 2:13). Whereas God is the spring of living water, these ungodly appear to hold the promise of blessing, but no life flows from them. In this way they are worse than no clouds because they lead people astray.

autumn trees, without fruit and uprooted—twice dead. The image of autumn trees without fruit is reminiscent of Jesus cursing the fig tree (Matt. 21:18–19), the parable of the fruitless tree (Luke 13:6–8), and other times Jesus speaks about trees and their fruit (Matt. 7:17–19; 12:33; Luke 6:43–45). Like clouds without rain and selfish shepherds, these trees are agents of death, which is what "twice dead" indicates. The trees themselves are dead (i.e., "uprooted"), and because they have no fruit they offer nothing but death to those who otherwise would be blessed by them.

14 *Enoch, the seventh from Adam, prophesied about them.* What follows is a quote from *1 Enoch* 1.9, a noncanonical Jewish book believed to have been written in the first century BC. While quoting a prophecy from outside the Scriptures is unusual, it is similar to John's quotation of Caiaphas's prophecy in John 11:49–52. John recognized that although Caiaphas was not a believer, what he said about Jesus dying for the nation was a true revelation from God and therefore prophetic. Jude too, recognizing that *1 Enoch* contains a true revelation from God regarding the second coming of Jesus, identifies this as a prophecy. His quote from *1 Enoch* 1.9 does not validate all of *1 Enoch* any more than John's quote of Caiaphas or Paul's quote of Aratus in Acts 17:28 or Epimenides in Titus 1:12 validates the rest of what they wrote or said.

But why did Jude choose to quote *1 Enoch*? The threefold repetition of the word "ungodly" in the Enoch text may be one important connection.[4] Just as Jude used three examples in verses 5–7 and three in verse 11, here "ungodly" is mentioned three times. Another important connection could be between Enoch and Cain. Just as Cain represents the first example of this kind of unbelieving disobedience, Enoch may represent a person from that era to whom the prophesy of judgment is connected. (It is doubtful that Jude thought Enoch wrote *1 Enoch*, but his use of Enoch's name does link the historical figure to the quote.) Hebrews 11:4–5 does mention Cain and Enoch in consecutive verses. Certainly the forcefulness and scope of what Enoch says—God judging *everyone* for *all* the ungodly acts *and all* the defiant words—fits with Jude's purposes in this letter.

15 *to judge everyone, and to convict all of them of all the ungodly acts.* It is possible that Jude is saying that two things will happen when Jesus returns: (1) everyone will be judged, and (2) the ungodly will be judged for their ungodliness. However, there is no indication in the text that Jude has switched referents for the word "everyone" and then switched back to just the ungodly a few words later. Rather, the repeated use of "all/every" (*pas*) throughout the verse ties the whole verse together so that the referent is the same throughout. Therefore, "to judge everyone" refers to the judgment of every ungodly person, not to the judgment of believers. It is true that all Christians will also appear before the judgment seat of Jesus (2 Cor. 5:10), but that is not what is in mind here.

16 *grumblers and faultfinders; they follow their own evil desires.* More sinful characteristics of the ungodly are now added: grumbling (expressing discontent based in coveting) and fault finding (blaming others or circumstances for their problems), as well as a lack of self-control (being unable to say no to evil desires), arrogance (boasting about themselves), and deceitful selfishness (using flattery for selfish gain).

Theological Insights

Christians struggling with sin versus non-Christians reveling in it. Jude 8–16 presents a picture of ungodly unbelievers who are wicked through and through. Jude 22–23 pictures Christians who might at any moment be struggling with one of the sins listed in verses 8–16. This juxtaposition runs throughout the Scriptures. Consider, on the one hand, Cain, Eli's sons, Doeg the Edomite, Ahab, Jezebel, Sanballat, and Judas, and on the other, Adam, Samson, Eli, David, Solomon, Josiah, Hezekiah, and Peter. The former are presented as ungodly unbelievers; the latter as people of God failing mightily at times in their struggle against sin. Likewise, notice the juxtaposition of Galatians 5:19–21 and 6:1; Hebrews 10:26–31 and 12:4–13; and 1 John 1:9–2:2 and 3:8–9. Jude 8–16 is helpful in seeing that when the Bible is talking about ungodly unbelievers, the sins tend to come in bunches lasting over a long period of time with no remorse—immorality, slander, greed, hatred, pride, and so on—while a true believer is usually struggling with just one of these, or multiple ones, but for a shorter time, and always with remorse.

Teaching the Text

Jude's beautiful rhetorical style in this section can cause readers to miss what he is actually accomplishing. Rather than just denouncing the ungodly, Jude is providing tools to identify the ungodly and warnings to believers not to be deceived or follow in their footsteps.

To this end, the teacher can use Jude 8–16 to help listeners recognize the ungodly. Here are some characteristics:

1. The ungodly emphasize dreams, visions, personal feelings, scientific studies, popular opinion, world history, and so on, as determining right and wrong as opposed to or in contradiction to the Word of God (v. 8). The fact that Jude is speaking directly about people who do this in regard to sexual ethics is applicable today.

2. The ungodly lack submission to authority (vv. 8, 11). Usually this shows itself in being unwilling to stop behaviors when asked by those in the church in positions of authority over them, working divisively to undercut current leadership, or boasting that they would be better fit to lead.

3. The ungodly speak slanderously or boast authoritatively about things that function outside the visible realm: the Holy Spirit, angels, spiritual warfare,

prayer, and God's Word (vv. 9–10). Such ungodly people lack reverence for the mysteries of the spiritual realm.

4. The ungodly have destructive interpersonal relationships. Hatred, jealousy, greed, selfishness, covetous complaining, blaming others, and pride will manifest themselves in broken relationships with family, former friends, employers, and so on (vv. 11, 16).

5. The ungodly have a complete lack of fruit in their lives, despite the promise of fruit. The imagery of verse 12—shepherds, clouds, and trees—is all the more damning because of the sense that good things should be coming from them. The ungodly give the appearance of offering a blessed life but do not actually bless anyone they come in contact with.

6. The ungodly are shameless and unrepentant (vv. 12–13, 16). They do not admit that they are wrong, show no remorse, act in shameless and brash ways, and blame others and circumstances for their struggles rather than take responsibility themselves.

7. The ungodly pile up sins on top of each other. The fact that Jude lists so many ungodly characteristics in one passage reveals that with the ungodly, sins come in bunches, stay for a long time, and seem to multiply.

The teacher can also use these seven characteristics to warn believers. Jude's next section will make this point explicitly, and therefore these same characteristics can be used to warn believers. Those who are godly followers of Jesus can still be in danger of struggling with slandering those in authority, believing lies about sexual ethics, pursuing dishonest gain, and the rest.

In teaching this, it may be important to help identify the difference between the godly who struggle with some of these same sins and the ungodly whom this passage is speaking about (see "Theological Insights," above). The fact that the judgment Jude is talking about is only for the ungodly makes it all the more necessary to help people differentiate between whether this passage is speaking about them directly as disobedient disbelievers or speaking to them indirectly as struggling Christians.

Illustrating the Text

The ungodly bring division through pride and lack of genuine submission.

Mythology: Greek mythology tells the tale of Erysichthon, an ancient king. This pride-filled man ordered his servants to cut down a sacred grove devoted to the goddess Demeter. When the servants came to a great oak tree, hung around with wreaths devoted to Demeter, they refused to cut the tree down. Erysichthon took up an axe and did it himself. The goddess, in return, cursed him. Since Erysichthon was so hungry for his own glory, the goddess afflicted Erysichthon with an insatiable hunger for food. In fact, the more he ate, the more hunger he felt. In the end, Erysichthon ate himself. Likewise, pride and rebellion are two attitudes that can never be satisfied and always, in the end, consume themselves.

The ungodly make big promises but do not deliver.

News Story: On December 22, 2008, Bernie Madoff was arrested for operating the biggest Ponzi scheme in history. The former NASDAQ chairman had spent nearly fifty years building his business and his brand, but for much of that time, Madoff had been providing a fake product and promising investors amazing returns. What they didn't realize was that Madoff only delivered these "returns" by getting new clients to invest with him and using their investment dollars to provide the illusion of amazing returns for his longer-term clients. Prosecutors estimated that Madoff defrauded his 4,800 clients of $64.8 billion dollars. The ripple effects of his arrest and freezing of his assets spread throughout the financial world and forced some businesses and philanthropic organizations to shut their doors.[5] In the same way, the ungodly offer amazing promises—freedom, purpose, meaning, and pleasure. In the end, however, all they deliver is spiritual bankruptcy.

The ungodly are content to live with soul-destroying sin.

Nature: Multimillion-dollar homes built on beautiful seaside vistas can be at risk when the weather gets severe. Waves and driving rain can quickly erode a cliff. In worst-case scenarios, whole homes can disappear into the ocean. In some cases, one wonders how wise it was to build in a place so prone to erosion. Living in ungodliness is like throwing a dinner party as the sea tears apart the ground beneath your home. Eventually, a crash will come![6]

To Contend for the Faith

Big Idea

Contend for the faith by remembering the warnings of God, keeping yourself in God's love, and showing mercy to those who are in danger.

Key Themes

- Fear God.
- Those who are led by natural desires are the opposite of those who have the Spirit.
- Pray in the Spirit.
- Wait for Christ's return.
- Keep yourself in God's love.

Understanding the Text

The Text in Context

Jude 17–23 is the heart of the epistle and contains the three main commands: remember, keep, and show mercy. This is what it means to contend for the faith (v. 3) and is necessary because of the presence of ungodly unbelievers among them (v. 4). So, having finished talking about the ungodly unbelievers in verses 8–16, Jude presents these three commands. This section will be followed by the doxology of verses 24–25.

Structure

Jude 17–23 is structured around the three main commands of the epistle: remember, keep, and show mercy. The third command is actually broken down into three commands.

1. Remember that the presence of the ungodly scoffers is a fulfillment of the warnings given by the apostles (vv. 17–19)
2. Keep yourselves in God's love, and do not follow the ways of the ungodly (vv. 20–21)
3. Show mercy to believers, and save unbelievers (vv. 22–23)
   a. Show mercy to believers who are doubting (v. 22)

b. Save unbelievers (v. 23a)

c. Show mercy with fear to believers who have fallen (v. 23b)

Interpretive Insights

17 *But, dear friends, remember.* Jude begins this section with a clear switch in focus from the ungodly to his readers who are believers. "But, dear friends" could be translated even more emphatically, "But you, beloved." On "remember," see the comments on 2 Peter 1:12.

19 *people who divide you, who follow mere natural instincts.* Whether the ungodly intend to be divisive or not, the result of their presence and behavior is always division. On one side are those who are swayed by what they are doing, perhaps even to the point of approving or participating. On the other side are those who reject them. This is exactly what was going on in the church in Corinth. First Corinthians speaks about divisions and factions in the church (1 Cor. 1:10–12; 11:18), some of which may have been because of blatant sexual immorality (1 Cor. 5) and selfishness and drunkenness at their love feasts (1 Cor. 11)—two issues Jude mentions as well. In addressing this ungodliness and the subsequent divisions, Paul speaks of the difference between the natural person without the Spirit and those who have the Spirit (1 Cor. 2:14–15). The word that Paul uses for "without the Spirit" is *psychikos*, and this is the same word Jude uses here, translated in this passage as "follow mere natural instincts." *Psychikos* is also used in James 3:15 to describe worldly, demonic, "unspiritual" wisdom that brings disorder and quarrels.

do not have the Spirit. Jude makes explicit that these disobedient disbelievers are not genuine Christians by saying that they do not have the Spirit. This recalls the Pauline distinction between the acts of the flesh and the fruit of the Spirit (Gal. 5:19–23). What Jude has described in verses 8–16 are the acts of the flesh, and they make it obvious that such people do not have the Spirit.

20–21 "Keep yourselves in God's love" is the primary command of the entire epistle. This imperative is modified by three participles. The first two give the means by which believers keep themselves in God's love, and they are listed in verse 20.

20 *by building yourselves up in your most holy faith.* First, believers keep themselves in God's love "by building [themselves] up in [their] most holy faith." The word for "building up" is also used in 1 Corinthians 3:10–15, continuing the parallels between Jude and 1 Corinthians. In 1 Corinthians 3, the key is to live life with the day of judgment in mind. The qualities, behaviors, and actions that one should pursue are those that will be left standing after Jesus's purging fire. Second Peter 1:5–7 is probably also helpful here, given Jude's strong connection to 2 Peter. There, Peter urges making every effort to grow in the virtues of goodness, knowledge, self-control, perseverance, godliness, mutual affection, and love.

praying in the Holy Spirit. Second, believers keep themselves in God's love by "praying in the Holy Spirit." This phrase "pray in the Spirit" is used in Ephesians 6:18, where it comes in the context of resisting the forces of darkness so that when evil strikes, believers can stand their ground.[1] Since believers are loved "in God" (Jude 1) and are to keep themselves "in God's love" (Jude 21), praying "in the Holy Spirit" means to pray in God's presence, under God's love and protection, with God's power, and led by God's will. It is a relational idea rather than a functional one. To pray in the Holy Spirit is to engage with God through prayer. Since God draws near to his people in prayer (Deut. 4:7) and the Spirit is God's presence with us, to pray in the Spirit is to regularly engage in prayer with the God who loves us.

21 *keep yourselves in God's love.* To "keep yourselves in God's love" is a beautiful way to put it. Those who are believers in Jesus have been brought into God's love. There is no earning of God's love or searching to find God's love. Believers live in the love of God, meaning that it surrounds, envelops, and undergirds us. The responsibility of Jude's readers is to keep themselves there. Of course, this personal responsibility is balanced by the affirmation in verse 1 that believers are "kept" (same word as here: *tēreō*) for Jesus Christ and in verse 24 that God will "keep" (*phylassō*, a synonym of *tēreō*) believers from stumbling. Jude is encouraging his readers to work with God to remain in God's love and not fight against him. While nothing can separate a believer from the love of God (cf. Rom. 8:35–39), the experience of God's love can be either scanty or abundant, depending on sinful choices. Jude is praying that their experience of God's love would be abundant (v. 2).

as you wait for the mercy of our Lord Jesus Christ. This is the third participial phrase attached to "keep yourselves in God's love." While "building yourselves up" and "praying" tell the means by which believers keep themselves in God's love, "waiting for the mercy of our Lord" (ESV) gives the conditions in which this will take place. It is necessary to work to remain in God's love because now is a time of waiting. The full mercy of Jesus that results in eternal life has not yet arrived.

to bring you to eternal life. While "eternal life" can also be viewed as something that believers already have (e.g., John 3:36; 5:24; 6:47), Jude is emphasizing eternal life as a destination, to be contrasted with "eternal fire" in verse 7.

22–23 There are complicated and difficult text-critical issues in these two verses, but the NIV has the most likely reading, which identifies three groups of people.[2]

22 *Be merciful to those who doubt.* First, there are those who doubt. These are believers whose faith has been shaken by the actions of the ungodly, who may be questioning God's justice, or who may be considering following the ungodly in their actions.

23 *save others by snatching them from the fire.* Second, there are those to be snatched from the fire. This is an allusion to Zechariah 3:2 (see below). In Zechariah 3:2, snatching from the fire refers to God's salvation of Joshua. Because Joshua has been saved, his dirty clothes can be removed and he can be forgiven for ongoing sins against God, which Jude will discuss in the next phrase; but here the reference is to that initial salvation that rescues people from the dangers of hellfire. Therefore, snatching others from the fire refers to the ungodly who can still come to faith and be saved. The same word for "save" in verse 23 is translated "delivered" in verse 5 and speaks about Israel's salvation from Egypt. Israel's deliverance from Egypt is typological for our salvation from Satan, sin, and death, which is why the salvation of Israel is contrasted with the destruction of those who did not believe at the end of verse 5. Also, Jude uses the word "fire" in verse 7 to speak of eternal fire in the context of the example of Sodom.

to others show mercy, mixed with fear—hating even the clothing stained by corrupted flesh. Third, there are those who need "mercy, mixed with fear." These are believers who have fallen into the behaviors of the ungodly, meaning that they are Christians who have been led astray and are now engaged in sexual immorality, rebellious slander, or greedy selfishness. The fact that Jude uses "mercy" for both groups 1 and 3 argues for them both being Christians. But here he adds "mixed with fear" and then alludes to Zechariah 3 with the phrase "clothing stained by corrupted flesh." Zechariah 3, which Jude has already used in verse 9, speaks of the sins of Joshua the high priest in terms of filthy clothes that need to be taken off and forgiven by God. The reason that God is glad to forgive Joshua's sins is because he is a "burning stick snatched from the fire" (Zech. 3:2). Because Joshua represents the people of God who stand by faith, God will continue to forgive Joshua's sins. For Jude's readers who have been saved from eternal fire but have fallen into ungodly behavior, their acts of sin are clothes stained with corrupted flesh that need to be taken off and forgiven.

The reason why this third group needs to be shown mercy mixed with fear is that the fear of God is necessary to successfully help those who are enmeshed in ungodly behavior. It is necessary for the person being rescued, because the fear of God is what helps people get out of sin. It is also necessary to protect those who are doing the rescuing from falling into sin—whether the same sin of the person they are trying to rescue or the sins of pride or harshness.

Theological Insights

1. *Trinity*. Jude 20–21 presents the three persons of the Trinity in their activities. God the Father is the source of love. Jesus Christ is the one who accomplishes the work that God's love has planned. And the Holy Spirit is God's empowering presence, who makes that love a reality here and now.

2. *Rescuing the fallen*. On this theological theme, see the unit on James 5:19–20, above.

3. *Doubt*. Jude 22 summarizes in a beautiful way God's attitude to those who doubt. On the one hand, doubt is not what God wants for us, so in Matthew 14:31 Jesus gently rebukes Peter for doubting. On the other hand, there is a recognition by God that it is a struggle to believe, and those who struggle with doubt are not cast aside. Thomas (John 20:24–29) and the demoniac's father who needed help overcoming unbelief (Mark 9:14–29) are both examples of God's willingness to meet where they are those who doubt. In the Scriptures "struggling to believe" is very different from "refusing to believe."

Teaching the Text

This section provides a clear structure for teaching this material, through the three key commands: remember, keep, and show mercy.

With regard to the command to remember, Jude's point is that the presence of scoffers is a fulfillment of prophecy. Having dealt with divisive, ungodly people masquerading as believers, I can attest that seeing the Scriptures predict these things happening can be exceedingly comforting. Too often people who are experiencing what Jude is writing about feel that they are the only ones who have ever gone through this struggle or that their situation is a result of some failure on their part. In such situations it can also be helpful with Jude to affirm that some of the troublemakers are not believers.

With regard to the command to keep oneself in God's love, Jude presents two participles that say how: (1) building yourself up and (2) praying in the Spirit. The one who maintains this will continue while we wait for Jesus to return. Explaining to people how to go about protecting themselves is important given the reality of ungodly unbelievers. Jude's teaching in this section also affirms the importance of the doctrine of the Trinity for remaining in God's love. The teacher should help people to understand how the three persons of the Trinity relate to one another. A useful analogy is God the Father as an architect who designs the house of salvation, Jesus as the builder who does the work, and the Holy Spirit as a realtor who moves believers into the house (see "Illustrating the Text" in the unit on 1 Peter 1:1–2). To keep yourself in God's love is to stay in the house that God has designed, Jesus has built, and the Holy Spirit has moved you into.

Finally, with regard to the command to show mercy, it is important to help listeners identify three distinct situations that people around them might be in: (1) believers struggling with doubt about the way of God, (2) nonbelievers in need of salvation, and (3) believers who have given in to immoral actions and attitudes. As noted in the previous section of the commentary, if people are struggling to believe and not to give in to certain attitudes and actions, this can be a sign that they are in the first group and not the second. Conviction and remorse can be a good indicator of whether someone is in group 2 or 3.

In all cases, mercy is the driving motivation and should govern all actions. Being harsh and judgmental and lacking grace will not rescue anyone from the power of sin. That said, it would be good to explain how the fear of God needs to be part of any rescue effort for Christians who have fallen into sin, both to protect the rescuer and to encourage the fallen.

Illustrating the Text

We keep ourselves in God's love by building up our faith.

Children's Story: Many of us grew up hearing the tale of the three pigs and the big bad wolf. One pig builds his house with straw. One builds his house with twigs. One builds his house with bricks. When the big bad wolf comes, he easily blows down the first two houses. But he can't move the brick house an inch.

In 1 Corinthians 3:12, Paul encourages believers to build their faith home with gold, silver, and precious stones, not wood, hay, and straw. In other words, our faith life should be our first investment! We don't want to skimp on our walk with Christ, but we should invest our greatest gifts in building it.

We keep ourselves in God's love by praying in the Spirit.

Scenario: Would you rather hear your favorite band on a tinny speaker inside an elevator or live in concert? Would you rather speak with your significant other over the phone or see them in person? Would you prefer a reheated frozen pizza or a fresh deep-dish pizza in Chicago? Either our prayer lives can be marked by rote habit and boring repetition, or they can actually be experienced as times of closeness with God. To "pray in the Spirit" means, at the very least, to pray as one who is in fellowship with the Lord. This experience will trump dutiful task management every time.

Judgmentalism cannot rescue others from the power of sin.

Literature: *Les Misérables*, by Victor Hugo. Early in this story, Jean Valjean has had plenty of encounters with "justice" and "judgment." In some ways, he seems to be a man who feels his entire life is under the weight of condemnation.

Eventually, he becomes like an animal, with no regard for life and no respect for himself or others. It is not a word of judgment or condemnation that turns this hardened criminal into a reformed leader and compassionate benefactor. It is one simple act of extravagant love by a village priest. The man embraces Valjean in the midst of a crime, forgives him for an assault, and, with love, unlocks the prison that Valjean has inhabited inside his own skin. As believers, we need to remember the power of love and grace to break a rebel heart.

The Doxology

Big Idea

Praise God the Savior, for he is preeminent in person, power, majesty, and authority, and he will keep believers from stumbling and bring them safely into his presence with great joy.

Key Themes

- God is unique.
- God has the power to save.
- God forgives.
- God is timeless.

Understanding the Text

The Text in Context

Jude closes out his epistle with a doxology. This returns the focus back to God, just as it was in the introduction at verse 1. The doxology affirms God's promise to accomplish for Jude's readers the very thing that they most need in the face of the presence of ungodly unbelievers in their midst: God will bring them safely and joyously into his presence.

Structure

There are four elements that all doxologies have: the object of praise, the element of praise, the indication of time, and the confirmatory response.[1]

1. Object of praise: "To him who is able to keep you from stumbling and to present you before his glorious presence without fault and with great joy—to the only God our Savior" (v. 24)
2. Element of praise: "Be glory, majesty, power and authority" (v. 25a)
3. Indication of time: "Before all ages, now and forevermore" (v. 25b)
4. Confirmatory response: "Amen" (v. 25c)

24 *To him who is able to keep you from stumbling.* The word for "keep" (*phylassō*) is a word that is parallel to the one translated "keep" (*tēreō*) in verses 1 and 21. They are used together in John 17:12 of Jesus's protection of his disciples. But *phylassō* might be the stronger word, implying active protection and guarding. Jude is closing out his epistle with the affirmation that God will guard and protect those who are called by him. Readers are to participate in this activity (v. 21), but ultimately their rescue is dependent on God's power and love. What readers are kept from is "stumbling." The verb form of this word (*ptaiō*) is used in 2 Peter 1:10 and Romans 11:11 as well as in James 2:10 and 3:2. In James it indicates the stumbling in sin that happens to all believers. In 2 Peter and Romans it refers to stumbling beyond recovery, which is the sense here. God is able to keep believers from stumbling beyond the point of recovery.

To say that God "is able" to do these things does not mean that he can do them but might not. Jude has begun his epistle by affirming that his readers are called, loved, and kept (v. 1). Therefore this affirmation that God is able to do these things is really an affirmation that God will do these things.

to present you before his glorious presence. The focus continues to be solely on God's activity. The word for "present" could also be translated "stand," which is the opposite of "stumble." God is not only able to keep believers from stumbling, but he will also stand them in his glorious presence. A parallel idea is in Romans 14:4: "Who are you to judge someone else's servant? To their own master, servants stand or fall. And they will stand, for the Lord is able to make them stand." Although God has given instructions to believers to keep them in his love, the ultimate responsibility for Jude's readers being able to stand in God's presence is God working in and through them.

without fault. "Without fault" means "blameless." It recalls the idea of Zechariah 3 that Jude referenced in verses 9 and 23. The sins of those who

New Testament Doxologies

Doxologies can be found in a number of places in the New Testament: Romans 11:36b; 16:25–27; Galatians 1:5; Ephesians 3:20–21; Philippians 4:20; 1 Timothy 1:17; 6:16; 2 Timothy 4:18; Hebrews 13:21b; 1 Peter 4:11; 5:11; Revelation 1:5b–6; 5:13b; 7:12.[a] In using this doxology to close this letter, Jude means to provide assurance and confidence to his readers who may be shaken by the presence of ungodly unbelievers in the congregation and what Jude has written about them. Even more than a benediction, the doxology turns the focus back to God.

[a] Weima, *Neglected Endings*, 136–40.

believe in Jesus are like filthy clothes. But God in his mercy removes those clothes and provides us with new garments fitting for his house. On the day that Christ returns, believers will stand in God's presence with sparkling new garments and with all thought or memory of our sins burned and gone. This idea of God's gracious forgiveness in Christ is what is alluded to in Jude 2 with "mercy, peace and love." It is what runs under the surface of the commands in verses 22–23 to show mercy and to save. No matter what the sin, the promise of God is that believers will appear before him blameless and without fault. This is what it means for God to be our Savior (v. 25).

with great joy. This phrase continues the positive affirmation that the day in which Christ returns and believers are brought into God's presence will be accompanied with great joy, not with sorrow or regret. Jude does not specify if it is God who is overjoyed or humans, because it is both. The whole scene is suffused with joy.

25 *to the only God our Savior.* Although it is not mentioned explicitly in verses 5–16, the underlying issue behind all that is happening among the ungodly unbelievers is idolatry. The ultimate example of Israel's failure (v. 5) is the golden calf. Balaam's error (v. 11) is the idolatry of money. Shepherds who feed only themselves (v. 12) are those whose god is their stomach (cf. Phil. 3:19). The ungodly boast about themselves (v. 16) because they put themselves in the place of God in their lives. So Jude concludes his letter with the ultimate affirmation that there is only one God (cf. Deut. 6:4). And that God is "our Savior." Usually it is Jesus who is referred to as "our Savior," but sometimes the title of Savior is applied to God the Father, as it is here (e.g., Luke 1:47; 1 Tim. 1:1; Titus 1:3). God's role as Savior is executed "through Jesus Christ our Lord," so it is fitting to speak of God the Father as Savior and of Jesus as Savior.

be glory. Every doxology except two in the New Testament ascribes to God glory (*doxa*), hence the name. But the word "glory" is not just the most common word. It is by far the most important word in the doxology. To ascribe to God glory means to acknowledge that God is the highest being in existence, above everything and everyone. It means that he is preeminent and supreme. When combined with other words, such as "power," "majesty," and "authority," it means that God's power, majesty, and authority are above everyone else's power, majesty, and authority.

majesty, power and authority. Often in doxologies additional elements are added, and Jude has included the most common one, "power/might" (1 Tim. 6:16; 1 Pet. 4:11; 5:11; Rev. 1:5–6; 5:13). Jude adds two other elements not found in any other doxology in the New Testament: "authority" and "majesty." "Authority" connects to verse 4, where Jesus is affirmed as our only Sovereign and Lord, and verse 15, where Jesus will come with the authority to judge all the defiant words ungodly sinners have spoken against him. Just as the rejection of authority by the ungodly (v. 8) and their rebellion (v. 11) do not affect God's authority, neither does their slander, blasphemy, or complaining affect his majesty. "Majesty" indicates God's radiant transcendence, which cannot be marred or diminished by the words and actions of humans.

before all ages, now and forevermore! Jude's indication of time in his benediction is unique in the New Testament. Normally the phraseology simply expresses "forever." Here Jude includes three aspects: past, present, and future. In this way it is like Hebrews 13:8, where the author affirms in a similar situation that Jesus is the same yesterday, today, and forever. For those who are thinking of changing their views on sexual ethics or money or whatever, Jude's affirmation that God is the same yesterday, today, and forever is meant to stop them from doing so. By including past, present, and future in the doxology, Jude also reminds his readers that they are not just looking forward to Christ's coming in the future. The power, majesty, authority, and glory of God are available to them today as they live by and pray in the Spirit.

Theological Insights

Ascribing God praise. Doxologies do not express merely a desire to see God be glorified or have power as if these things haven't happened yet or might not happen. They are ascribing to him these things and declaring that these *are already true* of him. They therefore fit within the broad theological motif of worship. In the Scriptures worship is presented as the response to the revelation of who God is. There are a number of forms that response can take, including confession of sin, ritual acts, service, physical and emotional expressions like bowing down or crying, fear, commitment, and trust, but one of the most common is verbal adoration and praise. It is ascribing to God the praise that he is due (1 Chron. 16:28–29; Job 36:3; Pss. 29:1–2; 96:7–8). The doxologies of the New Testament, and Jude 24–25 in particular, are an important part of this aspect of worship.[2]

Teaching the Text

While verses 24–25 are short enough that they could be combined with verses 17–23, they have a very different focus and goal: to turn the focus back to God and to the assurance that his love and power provide to those who are facing the challenge of ungodly unbelievers. Whereas verses 17–23 provided the opportunity to teach through the three responsibilities that believers in Jesus have, verses 24–25 undergird those responsibilities with the assurance that God is sovereign over all things. The teacher will need to work out how best to assure people of God's plan to bring them safely into his eternal kingdom, without nullifying the importance of obeying the instructions in verses 17–23.

In some ways, teaching a doxology can be difficult because the goal of teaching is so clear that success or failure becomes obvious immediately. If those who are being taught this passage leave thinking, "That's very interesting," then the teacher has failed. If those who are being taught this passage leave praising God because he is so glorious, then the teacher has succeeded. Jude did not write this passage for any other reason than to help people come face-to-face with the glorious nature of God and to give them words to be able to express their praise.

For this reason, Jude 24–25 allows the teacher to emphasize themes that have appeared throughout the epistle but may not have been brought to the surface until now. These themes include the following:

1. God's saving power. God will ensure that his children will not stumble beyond recovery, and he will arrange all things so that we come joyfully into his eternal dwelling. The presence of ungodly unbelievers will not deter God from saving his people.

2. God's forgiveness. No matter what sins we have committed, God's promise is that he is able to make believers blameless by forgiving our sins and remembering them no more.

3. God's holiness. There is only one God. He is unique and preeminent in power, majesty and authority. He alone is qualified to judge. He alone is able to save.

4. God's timelessness. Because God is the same yesterday, today, and forever, his people are not destroyed, and the love, power, and mercy of the future are available today through the Holy Spirit.

Illustrating the Text

God is the highest being in existence.

Science: Show a variety of images reflecting the size of the earth relative to the universe.[3] Cycle through the images, showing the relative size of the earth to the solar system, interstellar neighborhood, Milky Way, local galactic group, Virgo Supercluster, local superclusters, and observable universe. Surrounded by all these stars, we feel very, very small. But that is not all we should feel. Consider for a moment the sentiment of Psalm 147:4—our God has given names to each of these hundred octillion stars. What kind of mind must God have?

God has the power to save and keep his children.

Testimony: Pastor Adam Barr reflects on a vivid childhood experience of his father's power to rescue.

As a child, I grew up spending summer days on the sandy beach in Avon by the Sea, New Jersey. As often as we could, our family walked the three blocks to the ocean, set up our chairs, and spent time building sandcastles and bodysurfing the Atlantic. My parents even gave me my very own body board. One day, while I was waiting for the next wave, I was caught in a pretty severe rip current. As hard as I paddled, I could not move toward shore. An older boy tried to help me, to no avail. Soon, my concern had morphed into stark panic. Just as I was considering whether I would be able to survive a drift across the ocean, I looked up and saw my father running down the beach. I can still remember seeing him strip off his wristwatch and run full tilt into the breakers. He swam out to me and, with ease, brought me back to shore.

God promises to forgive our sins, no matter how high they loom.

Prop: Using an Etch A Sketch, talk about the way that sin leaves a mark on our lives. Every time we rebel, we not only mar our very self; we leave a black mark in God's ledger. Continue making patterns on the device as you speak. Finally, hold up the Etch A Sketch and ask, "How many of you look at your life and see marks all over?" Some Christians live their whole lives convinced that nothing can be done about these marks. They strive in a constant state of self-condemnation. But that's not what God wants! In Christ, all these marks can be erased. Shake the device, producing a new surface. Now our lives can be marked by God's amazing grace. Now they can be used by God to give witness to a life redeemed.

Notes

Introduction to James

1. For the discussion and reasons that support the traditional view that this is James the Just, see Moo, *James*, 9–22.

2. The use of the Greek word *synagōgē* for the church (NIV: "meeting") in James 2:2 rather than the standard *ekklēsia* might suggest that James was written early on, before *ekklēsia* became the technical term for church.

James 1:1–12

1. On the idea of James being written to all Christians and not just Jewish Christians, see further Richardson, *James*, 54–56.

2. I don't believe that James is referring to a blanket request for wisdom in general such as Solomon received from God (1 Kings 3). Rather, the request is for specific guidance, counsel, direction, and understanding needed in particular situations. For more examples of this and a fuller discussion of asking God for wisdom, see Samra, *God Told Me*.

3. For further discussion of this topic, see Samra, *God Told Me*.

James 1:13–18

1. BDAG 217 (s.v. "*deleazō*").

2. Jesus is making a similar point in the Sermon on the Mount when he states that thoughts like lust and anger are themselves sin (Matt. 5:21–30). So while the temptations to lust and to become angry are not sin, the temptations left unchecked will lead to lustful and angry thought patterns, which are sin.

3. Even if the temptations to sin come through genetic predisposition, which is likely in some cases,

this doesn't mean that they come from God. God cannot tempt people to sin (1:13), either actively or by directly encoding temptations into our genetic code. Genetic predispositions toward sin come from the fact that we are born into sin. Therefore we *by nature* crave sin and are deserving of wrath (Eph. 2:1–3).

James 1:19–27

1. Johnson, *Brother of Jesus*, 173–74.

2. Kierkegaard, *For Self-Examination*, 35; quoted in Bauckham, *James*, 6. For more on Kierkegaard's reading of James 1:22–27, see Evans, "Seeing Ourselves," 62–69.

3. For a simple introduction to this way of "living the Bible," see http://biblica.com/livingthe script, or *The Books of the Bible New Testament* (Colorado Springs: Biblica, 2011). For a more in-depth look at this idea, consider Meadors, *Bible to Theology*, especially Kevin Vanhoozer's article, as well as Vanhoozer, *Drama of Doctrine*. For help on thinking through practical ramifications of how to live out narrative sections of the Old Testament, including how to deal with characters who are presented negatively, see Wenham, *Story as Torah*.

4. Charles Spurgeon, *The Treasury of David*, 3 vols. (Peabody, MA: Hendrickson, 1990), 2:92.

James 2:1–13

1. *Epistle to Diognetus*, in Holmes, *Apostolic Fathers*, 549.

2. See the comments on James 2:11 in Moo, *James*.

James 2:14-26

1. For the eight most common explanations, see McCartney, *James*, 158–60.
2. Hort, *James*, 60–61 (cited by McCartney, *James*, 158), suggests this same punctuation, but he makes the phrase "you have faith" into a question, which McCartney shows doesn't work.

James 3:1-12

1. On teachers in the New Testament and James's self-identification as a teacher, see Brosend, *James and Jude*, 93–96.
2. See, e.g., Martin, *James*, 103–7.
3. See also the GNT and the discussion in Loh and Hatton, *Letter from James*.
4. Westminster Shorter Catechism (1674), Q & A 1.
5. Akoshia Yoba, "She's Always Watching: The Impact of Fathers on Daughters' Self Esteem," September 14, 2011, *Huffington Post*, http://www.huffing tonpost.com/akoshia-yoba/daddy-i-see-you-daddy -i-h_b_954304.html.

James 3:13-18

1. BDAG 381 (s.v. "*epistēmōn*").
2. It is well worth reading what the seventeenth-century author William Gurnall has to say about spiritual pride in the church (*Christian in Complete Armor*, 1:191–99). Interestingly, the two main passages he references are 1 Cor. 1–4 and James 4.

James 4:1-10

1. For further discussion, see Johnson, *James*, 280–82.
2. For more on the world, the flesh, and the devil and their interrelations, see Arnold, *Spiritual Warfare*, 20–26.
3. "Flip Benham," *Wikipedia*, last modified August 26, 2015, https://en.wikipedia.org/wiki/Flip _Benham.

James 4:11-12

1. Some of these Old Testament citations are from Adamson, *James*, 177.
2. Karl Barth, *Church Dogmatics* IV/1, 529.
3. Mitch Albom, "Bears Player, Lions Fan Prove Cyber Insanity," *Detroit Free Press*, November 16, 2014, http://www.freep.com/story/sports/columni sts/mitch-albom/2014/11/16/lions-fan-bear-player -twitter-fight/19126991/.

James 4:13-17

1. Richardson, *James*, 201. For more on business as mission, see Stevens, *Doing God's Business*.
2. Claire Suddath, "Top Ten Failed Predictions," *Time*, October 21, 2011, http://content.time.com

/time/specials/packages/article/0,28804,2097462_20 97456_2097489,00.html.

James 5:1-6

1. For the view that these are not Christians, see Moo, *James*.
2. France, *Gospel of Mark*, 402.
3. *Sabaōth* is the Greek transliteration of the Hebrew word *tsᵉba'ot*, which means "armies." The title is used some 285 times in the Old Testament as a name for God, but the Greek term is used only here and in Rom. 9:29 in the New Testament. See *TWOT* 2:750–51.
4. See Ralph Keyes, *The Quote Verifier: Who Said What, Where, and When* (New York: St. Martin's Griffin, 2006), 20.
5. Pliny to Valerianus, letter 15, in *The Letters of Pliny the Younger*, trans. William Melmoth (London: George Bell and Sons, 1905), 61.

James 5:7-12

1. Keener, *IVP Bible Background Commentary*, 702.
2. Ladd, *Presence of the Future*, 123. See also "Theological Insights" in the unit on 1 Pet. 1:3–12.

James 5:13-18

1. For more on the connection between Satan and illness, see Gaiser, *Healing in the Bible*, esp. chap. 11.
2. On divine power and authority flowing from God through the elders, see, for example, 1 Tim. 4:10, where God's gift to Timothy comes through the elders, laying on of hands; Acts 15, where they are ruling alongside the apostles; and Acts 11:30, where Paul delivers his financial gift to the elders for them to administer.
3. On spiritual warfare, see Arnold, *Spiritual Warfare*.
4. For more on healing and the local church, see Samra, *Gift of Church*, esp. chap. 5.
5. Charles H. Spurgeon, *Spurgeon's Sermons on Prayer* (Peabody, MA: Hendrickson, 2007), 86–87.

James 5:19-20

1. Bauckham, *James*, 12.
2. Johnson, *James*, 337.

Introduction to 1 Peter

1. See Bockmuehl, *Simon Peter*, 170.
2. This is recorded, for example, in the early fourth century AD by Eusebius in his *Church History*, 2.25. See Maier, *Church History*, 84–86. On the traditions surrounding Peter's martyrdom, see Helyer, *Life and Witness*, chap. 15.

1 Peter 1:1-2

1. On Peter in Matt. 16:18, see further France, *Matthew*, 620–23.

2. Karen Jobes presents an interesting hypothesis that 1 Peter is addressing believers whom Peter knew from Rome, who had been relocated by imperial mandate to these five provinces (Jobes, *1 Peter*, 28–41).

3. See Fee, *God's Empowering Presence*.

4. Keener, *John*, 1:479n466.

1 Peter 1:3-12

1. See further Michaels, *1 Peter*, 48.

2. Although angels don't "need" salvation, one would imagine that the inestimable wonder and the eternal blessing of God becoming a human and humans being united to God through Jesus and being conformed to Christ's image would be a prize beyond value for angels.

3. See Bock and Fanning, *Interpreting the New Testament Text*, 23–27.

1 Peter 1:13-25

1. Tacitus (*Histories* 5.5) speaks of gentiles who have no use for the religion of their fathers, demonstrating that religion handed down from ancestors can apply to gentiles as well as Jews (cited by Achtemeier, *1 Peter*, 127).

2. The phrase "with minds fully alert and sober" can be translated "girding up the loins of your mind," which recalls the preparedness with which Israel was to eat the Passover in Exod. 12:11; see Marshall, *1 Peter*, 50–51.

3. Peter's emphasis on the "preached" word that brought salvation indicates that he is referring to the gospel, whereas James's emphasis in 1:23 on believers obeying the Word indicates that he is referring to the Bible.

4. Sometimes this theological phenomenon is entitled the "indicative and imperative," after the two Greek verbal moods used to show what is and what ought to be, respectively.

1 Peter 2:1-3

1. In other words, it is the lexical aspect (*Aktionsart*) of the verb "crave," and not the grammatical aspect of the aorist tense, that indicates the ongoing nature of these two linked commands.

2. E.g., Schreiner, *1, 2 Peter, Jude*, 100.

3. For more on Paul's idea of how believers mature, see Samra, *Being Conformed*.

4. See, e.g., Williard, *Spirit of the Disciplines*.

1 Peter 2:4-10

1. See Samra, *Gift of Church*, chap. 1 ("God in Concert").

2. Minear, *Images of the Church*. In addition to "People of God," Minear uses these three headings to organize all the different images of the church in the New Testament.

3. See for example Martin Luther's treatise "On Keeping Children in School," reprinted and discussed in Willimon, *Pastor*, 11–21.

1 Peter 2:11-17

1. For more on this, see Chaplin, "Government," 415–17; Reed, "Government," 337–40.

2. Cited by Schrage, *Ethics*, 273.

1 Peter 2:18-25

1. See Samra, "Biblical View of Discipleship."

2. "Christian Persecution," OpenDoorsUSA .org, accessed January 8, 2016, https://www.open doorsusa.org/christian-persecution/.

3. For more information, see the Open Doors International website (https://www.opendoors.org), or Nik Ripken with Gregg Lewis, *The Insanity of God: A True Story of Faith Resurrected* (Nashville: B&H, 2013).

1 Peter 3:1-7

1. Bartman, "Hair and the Artifice," 1, 5.

1 Peter 3:8-22

1. Cf. Davids, *First Epistle of Peter*, 138–43.

2. Sue Thoms, "God Told Me to Give You One of My Kidneys—A Transplant Story," *MLive*, January 16, 2014, http://www.mlive.com/news/grand -rapids/index.ssf/2014/01/god_told_me_to_give _you_one_of.html.

1 Peter 4:1-6

1. On this verse, see further Watson, "First Peter," 99.

1 Peter 4:7-11

1. On hospitality, see Pohl, *Making Room*.

2. Goppelt (*1 Peter*, 304) says, "Human speech can and will become, even according to Jesus' promise [i.e., Luke 10:16], like his own words, speech that comes from God for those who listen, if it is actually determined by the gospel that seeks out each person in his or her situation."

1 Peter 4:12-19

1. Cf. Hainz, "*Koinōnia*," 2:305.

2. See Hengel and Schwemer, *Paul*, 225–30.

3. See, e.g., Exod. 31:3; Num. 11:25; 24:2; Judg. 3:10; 6:34; 11:29; 14:6; 1 Sam. 16:13; 19:20–23; Ezek. 2:2; 3:24; Matt. 3:16; Luke 1:41, 67; Acts 2:4; 4:8, 31; 13:9.

4. Jeff Robinson, "Romanian Josef Tson Recounts God's Grace amid Suffering," *Baptist Press*, July 19, 2004, http://www.bpnews.net/18713/roman ian-josef-tson-recounts-gods-grace-amid-suffering.

1 Peter 5:1-9

1. For more on the Biblical theme of shepherds see Laniak, *Shepherds after My Own Heart*.
2. For more on elders, see Strauch, *Biblical Eldership*.

1 Peter 5:10-14

1. See Macaskill, *Union with Christ*, 159–62, 271–83.
2. See Michaels, *1 Peter*, 306–7.
3. This is recorded, for example, in the early fourth century AD by Eusebius (*Church History* 2.25). See Maier, *Church History*, 84–86. On the traditions surrounding Peter's martyrdom, see Helyer, *Life and Witness*, chap. 15.
4. For more on this, see Bauckham, *Jesus and the Eyewitnesses*, chap. 7.
5. Ryken, Wilhoit, and Longman, "Babylon," 69.
6. For example, Elliott, *1 Peter*, 137.

Introduction to 2 Peter

1. Those interested in the evidence should consult the introductions in Green, *2 Peter and Jude*; Schreiner, *1, 2 Peter, Jude*.

2 Peter 1:1-11

1. See Wallace, *Greek Grammar*, 276–77.
2. Irenaeus, *Against Heresies*, preface to book 5, 164.
3. Käsemann, commenting on 2 Pet. 1:4, says, "Only then [as a person moves from the corruptible to the incorruptible] does he become what he is meant to be—not merely man, but a partaker of the divine *physis*" ("Apologia," 180).

2 Peter 1:12-21

1. Merrill, "Remembering," 27–36.

2 Peter 2:1-9

1. Peter's only use of the word "teacher" (*didaskalos*) in his two epistles or in his speeches in Acts is embedded in the word for "false teachers" in 2:1, whereas Peter views prophet much more formally like an office (see 1 Pet. 1:10–12; 2 Pet. 2:16; 3:2; cf. Acts 2:16; 3:18–25; 10:43). For Peter, prophets were the authors of Scripture, and Jesus fulfills the role of Prophet (Acts 3:22), both of which give more weight to the designation "prophet." Outside of Peter, the more formal and foundational role of prophet can be seen in passages like Eph. 2:20, where prophets stand alongside of the apostles as foundational to the church.

2. Many point to parallels in language with masters purchasing slaves (e.g., Green, *Jude & 2 Peter*, 240–41) to indicate that these teachers at one time belonged to Christ. But this metaphor does not imply that they accepted Jesus as their Lord any more than Onesimus accepted Philemon as his master before he became a Christian.
3. See Bock, *Luke 9:51–24:53*, 1431, for examples.

2 Peter 2:10-22

1. If the slightly more likely textual reading "before the Lord" is correct, this would support the point even more—the reason angels do not slander false teachers is because they are conscious that God is watching.
2. For this interpretation of Luke 17:11–19 and 11:26 see Bock, *Luke 9:51–24:53*, 1093, 1405–6.
3. It may also be noteworthy that Peter uses a different preposition in 1:3 than he does in 2:20. In 1:3 believers access the great and precious promises "*through* our knowledge of him," while here these false teachers escaped the corruption of the world "*by* the knowledge" of Jesus. In the first case, believers' knowledge of Jesus is the means through which we take hold of the promises of God. In this case the false teachers see that there is a way to escape the corruption of this world in the knowledge of Jesus, but they do not access God's promises through this knowledge. The preposition *en* is also used in 1:2 for believers receiving grace and peace, but this confirms the same point. The grace and peace is accessible to them in the knowledge of Jesus, but they have not yet taken hold of the grace and peace Peter is referring to them in 1:2, which is why he wishes it for them in the optative mood.
4. See Bateman, *Warning Passages*, 438–40.

2 Peter 3:1-10

1. On modern-day expressions of this kind of "scoffing," see Keller, *Reason for God*, esp. chaps. 2 and 5.

2 Peter 3:11-18

1. *Dei* + infinitive in Greek can act like an imperatival infinitive (Blass, Debrunner, and Funk, *Greek Grammar*, section 389), giving the phrase the force of an imperative, i.e., "You ought to live holy and godly lives," as the NIV has translated it.
2. Cf. Davids, *2 Peter and Jude*, 290–91.
3. On this second letter being 1 Peter, see Schreiner's comments on 2 Pet. 3:1 (*1, 2 Peter, Jude*).

Introduction to Jude

1. Because Jude appears to be Jesus's third youngest or youngest half brother and we do not know how much of a gap there was in age between Jesus and Jude, it is possible that Jude was still a young man when Peter first met him.

Jude 1-7

1. The most common Hebrew word for "rape" in the Old Testament belongs more readily in the semantic domain of power than of sexual intercourse (see *TDOT* 11:237). Likewise, Deut. 22:25–27 connects rape to the violent crime of murder and differentiates it from presumed consensual sex in 22:23–24.

2. For discussion about eternal punishment in the Scriptures, see Chan and Sprinkle, *Erasing Hell.*

Jude 8-16

1. Shepherd of Hermas, *Mandates* 4.1.9.

2. See further, Bauckham, *Jude, 2 Peter*, 65–76.

3. For more on the difference between announcing something is wrong and enacting punishment in the language that Jude uses, see the helpful discussion in Green, *Jude & 2 Peter*, 82–84.

4. On which version of *1 Enoch* that Jude may have been using, see ibid., 94–96.

5. Stephanie Yang, "5 Years Ago Bernie Madoff Was Sentenced to 150 Years in Prison—Here's How His Scheme Worked," *Business Insider*, July 1, 2014, http://www.businessinsider.com/how-bernie-madoffs-ponzi-scheme-worked-2014-7.

6. "Excessive Erosion Sweeps Hawaii Homes Out to Sea," *Huffington Post*, December 30, 2013, http://www.huffingtonpost.com/2013/12/30/erosion-hawaii-homes_n_4520959.html.

Jude 17-23

1. On praying in the Spirit in Ephesians, see Fee, *God's Empowering Presence*, 729–32.

2. For an opposing point of view that supports the two-clause reading, see Green, *Jude & 2 Peter*, 124–29.

Jude 24-25

1. Weima, *Neglected Endings*, 136–40.

2. For an excellent study of the biblical theology of worship, see Ross, *Recalling the Hope of Glory.*

3. One example of a progression of images can be found at http://en.wikipedia.org/wiki/File:Earth%27s_Location_in_the_Universe_SMALLER_(JPEG).jpg.

Bibliography

Recommended Resources

Bauckham, Richard. *Jude, 2 Peter*. Word Biblical Commentary. Nashville: Nelson, 1996.

Green, Gene. *Jude & 2 Peter*. Baker Exegetical Commentary on the New Testament. Grand Rapids: Baker Academic, 2008.

Grudem, Wayne. *1 Peter*. Tyndale New Testament Commentaries. Downers Grove, IL: InterVarsity, 1988.

Johnson, Luke Timothy. *James*. Anchor Bible Commentary. New York: Doubleday, 1995.

McCartney, Dan G. *James*. Baker Exegetical Commentary on the New Testament. Grand Rapids: Baker Academic, 2009.

Michaels, J. Ramsey. *1 Peter*. Word Biblical Commentary. Nashville: Nelson, 1988.

Moo, Douglas. *James*. Pillar New Testament Commentary. Grand Rapids: Eerdmans, 2000.

Richardson, Kurt. *James*. New American Commentary. Nashville: Broadman & Holman, 1997.

Schreiner, Thomas. *1, 2 Peter, Jude*. New American Commentary. Nashville: Broadman & Holman, 2003.

Select Bibliography

Achtemeier, Paul. *1 Peter*. Hermeneia. Minneapolis: Fortress, 1996.

Adamson, James. *James*. New International Commentary on the New Testament. Grand Rapids: Eerdmans, 1976.

Arnold, Clinton. *Spiritual Warfare: What Does the Bible Really Teach?* London: Marshall Pickering, 1999.

Austin, J. L. *How to Do Things with Words*. 2nd ed. Cambridge, MA: Harvard University Press, 1975.

Bartchy, S. Scott. "Slavery (Greco-Roman)." In *Anchor Bible Dictionary*, edited by David Noel Freedman, 6:66. 6 vols. New York: Doubleday, 1992.

Barth, Karl. *Church Dogmatics*. Vol IV/1, *The Doctrine of Reconciliation*, translated by G. W. Bromiley. London: T&T Clark, 2004.

Bartman, Elizabeth. "Hair and the Artifice of Roman Female Adornment." *American Journal of Archaeology* 105 (Jan. 2001): 1–25.

Bateman IV, Herb, ed. *Four Views on the Warning Passages in Hebrews*. Grand Rapids: Kregel, 2007.

Bauckham, Richard. *James*. New Testament Readings. London: Routledge, 1999.

———. *Jesus and the Eyewitnesses*. Grand Rapids: Eerdmans, 2006.

Blass, F., and A. Debrunner, *A Greek Grammar of the New Testament and Other Early Christian Literature*. Edited and translated by Robert W. Funk. Chicago: University of Chicago Press, 1961.

Bock, Darrell. *Luke 9:51–24:53*. Baker Exegetical Commentary on the New Testament. Grand Rapids: Baker Academic, 1996.

Bock, Darrell, and Buist Fanning. *Interpreting the New Testament Text*. Wheaton: Crossway, 2006.

Bockmuehl, Markus. *Simon Peter in Scripture and Memory*. Grand Rapids: Baker Academic, 2012.

Bradley, Keith. *Slavery and Society at Rome*. Key Themes in Ancient History. Cambridge: Cambridge University Press, 1994.

Brosend, William. *James and Jude*. New Cambridge Bible Commentary. Cambridge: Cambridge University Press, 2004.

Chan, Francis, and Preston Sprinkle. *Erasing Hell: What God Said about Eternity, and the Things We've Made Up*. Colorado Springs: David C. Cook, 2011.

Chaplin, J. P. "Government." In *New Dictionary of Christian Ethics and Pastoral Theology*, edited by D. J. Atkinson, D. F. Field, A. F. Holmes, and O. O'Donovan, 415–17. Downers Grove, IL: InterVarsity, 1995.

Curtis, Edward M. *Ecclesiastes and Song of Songs*. Teach the Text Commentary Series. Grand Rapids: Baker Books, 2013.

Davids, Peter. *The First Epistle of Peter*. New International Commentary on the New Testament. Grand Rapids: Eerdmans, 1990.

———. *The Letters of 2 Peter and Jude*. Pillar New Testament Commentary. Grand Rapids: Eerdmans, 2006.

Elliott, John H. *1 Peter*. Anchor Bible. New York: Doubleday, 2000.

Evans, C. Stephen. "Seeing Ourselves in the Mirror of the Word." *Christian Reflection*, May 2012 (*The Letter of James*), 62–69.

Fee, Gordon D. *God's Empowering Presence: The Holy Spirit in the Letters of Paul*. Peabody, MA: Hendrickson, 1994.

France, R. T. *The Gospel of Mark*. New International Greek Testament Commentary. Grand Rapids: Eerdmans, 2002.

———. *Matthew*. New International Commentary on the New Testament. Grand Rapids: Eerdmans, 2007.

Gaiser, Frederick. *Healing in the Bible*. Grand Rapids: Baker Academic, 2010.

Goppelt, Leonhard. *A Commentary on 1 Peter*. Grand Rapids: Eerdmans, 1993.

Green, Michael. *2 Peter and Jude*. Rev. ed. Tyndale New Testament Commentaries. Grand Rapids: Eerdmans, 1987.

Gurnall, William. *The Christian in Complete Armor*. 2 vols. in 1. Peabody, MA: Hendrickson, 2010.

Hainz, J. "*Koinōnia*." In *Exegetical Dictionary of the New Testament*, edited by H. Balz and G. Schneider, 2:303–5. Grand Rapids: Eerdmans, 1991.

Helyer, Larry. *The Life and Witness of Peter*. Downers Grove, IL: IVP Academic, 2012.

Hengel, Martin, and Anna Maria Schwemer. *Paul between Damascus and Antioch: The Unknown Years*. Louisville: Westminster John Knox, 1997.

Holmes, Michael W., ed. and trans. *The Apostolic Fathers: Greek Texts and English Translations*. 2nd ed. After the earlier work of J. B. Lightfoot and J. R. Harmer. Grand Rapids: Baker, 1992.

Hopkins, Keith. *Conquerors and Slaves*. Sociological Studies in Roman History 1. Cambridge: Cambridge University Press, 1981.

Hort, F. J. A. *The Epistle of St. James*. London: Macmillian, 1909.

Irenaeus. *Against Heresies*. In *Irenaeus of Lyon*, translated by Robert M. Grant, Early Church Fathers, 55–186. New York: Routledge, 1997.

Jobes, Karen. *1 Peter*. Baker Exegetical Commentary on the Bible. Grand Rapids: Baker Academic, 2005.

Johnson, Luke Timothy. *Brother of Jesus, Friend of God*. Grand Rapids: Eerdmans, 2004.

Käsemann, Ernst. "An Apologia for Primitive Christian Eschatology." In *Essays on New Testament Themes*, 169–95. London: SCM Press, 1964.

Keener, Craig S. *Gospel of John*. Vol. 1. Peabody, MA: Hendrickson, 2003.

———. *The IVP Bible Background Commentary: New Testament*. Downers Grove, IL: InterVarsity, 1993.

———. *Paul, Women, and Wives: Marriage and Women's Ministry in the Letters of Paul*. Grand Rapids: Baker Academic, 2004.

Keller, Tim. *The Reason for God*. New York: Dutton, 2008.

Kierkegaard, Søren. *For Self-Examination*. In *For Self-Examination; Judge for Yourself*, edited and translated by Howard V. and Edna H. Hong, Kierkegaard's Writings 21, 1–87. Princeton: Princeton University Press, 1990.

Ladd, George. *The Presence of the Future*. Rev. ed. Grand Rapids: Eerdmans, 1974.

Laniak, Timothy S. *Shepherds after My Own Heart: Pastoral Transitions and Leadership in the Bible*. New Studies in Biblical Theology. Downers Grove, IL: InterVarsity, 2006.

Loh, I., and H. Hatton. *A Handbook on the Letter from James*. United Bible Societies Handbook Series 110. New York: United Bible Societies, 1997.

Macaskill, Grant. *Union with Christ in the New Testament*. Oxford: Oxford University Press, 2013.

Maier, Paul L. *The Church History: A New Translation with Commentary.* Grand Rapids: Kregel, 1999.

Marshall, I. Howard. *1 Peter.* IVP New Testament Commentary Series. Downers Grove, IL: InterVarsity, 1991.

Martin, Ralph. *James.* Word Biblical Commentary. Nashville: Nelson, 1988.

Meadors, Gary, ed. *Four Views on Moving beyond the Bible to Theology.* Grand Rapids: Zondervan, 2009.

Merrill, Eugene. "Remembering: A Central Theme in Biblical Worship." *Journal of the Evangelical Theological Society* 43 (2000): 27–36.

Minear, Paul. *Images of the Church in the New Testament.* Louisville: Westminster John Knox, 1960.

Pohl, Christine. *Making Room: Recovering Hospitality as a Christian Tradition.* Grand Rapids: Eerdmans, 1999.

Reed, Esther D. "Government." In *Dictionary of Scripture and Ethics,* edited by Joel Green, 337–40. Grand Rapids: Baker Academic, 2011.

Ross, Allen. *Recalling the Hope of Glory.* Grand Rapids: Kregel, 2006.

Ryken, Leland, James C. Wilhoit, and Tremper Longman III, eds. "Babylon." In *Dictionary of Biblical Imagery,* 68–69. Downers Grove, IL: InterVarsity, 1998.

Samra, J. *Being Conformed to Christ in Community.* Edinburgh: T&T Clark, 2006.

———. "A Biblical View of Discipleship." *Bibliotheca Sacra* 160 (2003): 219–34.

———. *The Gift of Church.* Grand Rapids: Zondervan, 2010.

———. *God Told Me.* Grand Rapids: Baker Books, 2012.

Schrage, Wolfgang. *Ethics of the New Testament.* Philadelphia: Fortress, 1988.

Stevens, R. Paul. *Doing God's Business.* Grand Rapids: Eerdmans, 2006.

Strauch, Alexander. *Biblical Eldership: An Urgent Call to Restore Biblical Church Leadership.* Colorado Springs: Lewis and Roth, 1995.

Treier, Daniel J. *Proverbs and Ecclesiastes.* Brazos Theological Commentary on the Bible. Grand Rapids: Baker Academic, 2011.

Vanhoozer, Kevin J. *The Drama of Doctrine: A Canonical Linguistic Approach to Christian Doctrine.* Louisville: Westminster John Knox, 2005.

Wallace, Daniel B. *Greek Grammar beyond the Basics.* Grand Rapids: Zondervan, 1996.

Watson, Duane F. "First Peter." In Duane F. Watson and Terrance Callan, *First and Second Peter,* Paideia, 1–127. Grand Rapids: Baker Academic, 2012.

Webb, William. *Slaves, Women and Homosexuals.* Downers Grove, IL: InterVarsity, 2001.

Weima, Jeffrey A. D. *Neglected Endings: The Significance of the Pauline Letter Closings.* Sheffield: Sheffield Academic Press, 1994.

Wenham, Gordon J. *Story as Torah: Reading Old Testament Narrative Ethically.* Grand Rapids: Baker Academic, 2000.

Williard, Dallas. *The Spirit of the Disciplines: Understanding How God Changes Lives.* Grand Rapids: Zondervan, 1990.

Willimon, William H. *Pastor: A Reader for Ordained Ministry.* Nashville: Abingdon, 2002.

Wright, Christopher J. H. *The Mission of God: Unlocking the Bible's Grand Narrative.* Downers Grove, IL: IVP Academic, 2006.

Contributors

General Editors
Mark. L. Strauss
John H. Walton

Associate Editors, Illustrating the Text
Kevin and Sherry Harney

Contributing Author, Illustrating the Text
Adam Barr

Series Development
Jack Kuhatschek
Brian Vos

Project Editor
James Korsmo

Interior Design
Brian Brunsting
William Overbeeke

Cover Direction
Paula Gibson
Michael Cook

Index

fear of God, 64, 116–17, 118, 119–21, 139, 151, 158, 161, 198, 261
fig tree, 40–41, 253
filled with the Spirit, 178
final judgment, 218
fire, 71, 176, 261
1 Enoch, 254
firstfruits, 16
1 Peter, introduction to, 97–100
fishing terminology, 13
flood, 160, 217, 230
following Jesus, 143
food sacrificed to idols, 216
foreigners, 118, 137, 176
foreknowledge, 104
forgetting, 229–30
freedom, 138–39, 140–41
free will and determinism, 131
friendship with the world, 19, 46, 51, 52
fruitless tree, parable of, 253
fruit of the Spirit, 259
future plans, 63–74

Galatia, 103–4
gentle and quiet spirit, 152, 154
gentleness, 44–48, 152
glorifying God, 172
"glorious exchange," 144
glory, 111, 183, 190
God
  authority of, 267–68
  care for poor and oppressed, 73
  compassion of, 78, 94
  delay in coming, 232
  does not show favoritism, 30, 51
  does not tempt to sin, 12
  forgiveness of, 269
  generosity of, 7
  glory of, 98, 267
  goodness of, 14, 17
  holiness of, 269
  jealousy of, 52
  keeps believers from stumbling, 260, 266
  love of, 260, 262
  majesty of, 267–68
  nearness of, 80–81
  as only Lawgiver and Judge, 59–60
  opposes the proud, 70, 72
  patience of, 230, 231, 232
  permanence of, 14–15
  power of, 191, 267–68
  presence of, 76, 89
  sovereignty of, 63, 67, 98, 107, 109, 190, 191, 243, 268–69
  swears an oath, 79
  timelessness of, 268, 269

godliness, 136, 140, 152, 197, 203, 205, 236
gold, 70
good fruit, 46–47
goodness, 203
good works, 7, 22, 45, 205
governing authorities, 138–39
grace, 93, 172, 189–90, 238
grapevine, 40
grass and flowers, 8
Greco-Roman slavery, 145
greed, 222–23, 225, 256
growing in grace, 125, 238
grumblers, grumbling, 76–77, 78, 80, 254–55
Gurnall, William, 272

hairstyles, 151
Hannah, 23
healing, 85–86
healing prayer, 88
heaping abuse, 165
Heidelberg Catechism, 62
hell, 14
hellfire, 261
heresies, 208, 216
holiness, 116–18, 120, 198, 236
holy priesthood, 130
Holy Spirit, 112
  hovering over creation, 230
  inner witness of, 205
  no explicit reference in James, 2
  and prayer, 260
  presence in suffering, 178–79
  and prophecy, 211, 213
  resting on believers, 176–77, 178
  sanctifying work of, 104, 107
holy women, 152
homosexuality, 218
honor, 111
honoring the emperor, 138–39
hope, 116–17, 120, 122
hospitality, 99, 170–71, 173
human anger, 20
human development, 13, 15
human life, fragility of, 8
humility, 8, 45, 48, 52, 185
husbands, 149–53
hypocrisy, 124

idolatry, 165
imitating others, 144
immaturity, 93
immorality, 197, 243. See also sexual immorality
imperatives, 6, 116
imperishable, 119
imprisoned spirits, 165–66
inaugurated eschatology, 79

new covenant, 211
new-covenant law, 28–29, 58
new creation, 80, 238
new heavens and new earth, 238–39
Noah, 159–60, 161, 217, 219, 230
non-Christians, among believers, 225
non-retaliation, 164

oaths, 79, 80, 81
obedience, 7, 66, 67, 91, 107, 116
  to the Holy Spirit, 104
obedient children, 104, 117, 118
oil, 83
Old Testament, 198, 246–47
  prophecies of suffering of Christ, 112, 113,
  114
oppression, 27, 73
orgies, 165
orphans, 1, 3
outward appearance, 26, 151
overseer, 144

parenting, 127
participating in sufferings of Christ, 176
participating in the divine nature, 197, 203,
  204–5, 206, 211, 225
partying, 173
Passover, 118
patience, 76–77, 79, 80, 81
patriarchal culture, 153
Paul
  in prison, 180
  rebuke of Peter, 237
  writings as Scripture, 237, 239
peace, 46, 48, 192, 246
peacemakers, 47, 53
Pentecost, 176, 177
perfect law, 21
performatives, 42, 43
"performing the Scriptures," 23
persecution, 99–100, 111
perseverance, 6, 111, 114–15, 203, 204, 205
personal experience, and Scripture, 212–13
perversion, 248
Peter
  as author of 2 Peter, 198
  complements Paul, 98
  denial of Jesus, 216–17
  as fellow elder, 183
  as foundational to the church, 97, 102, 106
  humility of, 237
  martyrdom of, 192, 209
  as servant, 202
Peter (name), 101–2, 106
Pilgrim's Progress, 240
pleasures of sin, 167

pledge of a clear conscience toward God, 160
Pontus, 103
poor, oppression of, 1, 3, 27, 29, 73, 93
poverty, as asset, 8
praise, 109, 111, 268
praising God, and cursing others, 40
prayer, 76, 82, 125, 170
  in faith, 8, 9
  in "Jesus's name," 65
  power of, 85–88
  and restoring Christians, 91
  for the sick, 1, 3, 83–85
  in the Spirit, 260, 262, 263
  unanswered, 54
preaching, 180–81
presence of God, 76
pride, 8, 47, 51–53, 54, 57, 58, 62, 65–66, 185,
  212, 222–23, 225, 229
priesthood of all believers, 132–33
proclamation, 160
prodigal son, parable of, 56
prophecy, 211–12, 274
prophetic continuity, 201
prophetic diatribe, 70
Proverbs, 1
psychikos, 259
punishment, 218
purification, 191, 194
"putting off," 124

quarrels, 47–48, 51–53, 54

rain, 77–78
rape, 248, 275
rebuke, 226
rejoicing, 176. See also joy
relational knowledge, 202, 206, 211
religion, 22
remembering/reminding, 209, 228, 229, 258
repaying evil with blessing, 158
repentance, 54–55, 231, 236
  of the rich, 69–74
resisting the devil, 52–53, 55
respect for everyone, 139
restoring believers, 90, 92–93, 190–91
rich, 69–71
  in faith, 30
rich fool, parable of, 64
rich man and Lazarus, parable of, 74
ridding oneself of evil practice, 123–24
righteous, rescue of, 219, 220
righteous anger, 22
righteousness, 20, 34, 47, 92
  and hurrying the coming of Christ, 236
robbing workers, 69–75
Robinson, Marilynne, 107

Rome, as Babylon, 98, 192–93
royal law, 27, 28, 59
royal priesthood, 131–32
rudder, 39
Ruth, 152

salvation, 21
   present and future aspects of, 110, 113, 116
salvation history, 134
sanctification, 126–27, 130, 199
Sarah, 150, 152
Satan
   deception of, 14, 17, 185–86
   and suffering, 187
saving grace, 189–90
scattered, 103
Schelkle, Karl, 141
scoffers, 229, 232, 262
Scripture, 237
   authority of, 237
   as completely reliable, 210
   human authors and divine Author, 22
   interpretation of, 113
   and prophecy, 198
2 Peter, introduction to, 197–99
self-control, 203
self-indulgence, 72
selfish ambition, 46, 51–53, 54
selfishness, 57, 155, 256
self-restraint, 165
Sermon on the Mount, 51, 271
servant, Peter as, 202
serving, 172
sexual immorality, 16, 165, 216, 217–18, 222,
   247–48, 249
Shadrach, Meshach, and Abednego, 180
shepherd, 144
Shepherd of Hermas, 252
shepherds, as selfish, 253–54
shepherds of God's flock, 183–84, 187
sick, prayer for, 1, 3, 83–85
signs and wonders, 179
Silas, 191
silver, 70
Simon, 106
sin
   covering of, 92
   enslaving power of, 225, 226–27
   gives birth to death, 18
   and sickness, 85–86
   struggle with, 255
sinful desires, 137, 140
singing, and prayer, 83
slander, 57–62, 93, 124, 226, 252–53, 255–56
slaves, 142–43, 145–46
slow to speak, 20

snake that poisons, 39
snatching others from the fire, 261
sobriety, 170–71
Sodom and Gomorrah, 217, 222, 247–48
Son, 1–7
sons of God, 247
sow, wallowing in the mud, 224
speaking, 172
Spirit baptism, 60, 161, 164
spiritual gifts, 172, 173
spiritual growth, 125, 126–28, 197, 205–6
spiritual house, church as, 129–33
spiritual sacrifices, 131
spiritual warfare, 1, 53–54, 167
spring, 40
sprinkled, 105
Spurgeon, Charles, 23–24, 87
steadfast, 191
stealing, 71–72
strangers, 176, 192
stumbling, 39, 266
submission
   to authority, 138, 140, 150, 255
   to God, 52, 54, 61, 66
substitutionary atonement, 144
suffering, 9, 77, 99, 106, 111, 175, 177–78, 204
   and choosing to live for God's will, 163
   and Christian community, 99–100
   enduring, 143, 182, 185, 186
   leads to glory, 99, 112, 159, 164, 190
   maturity through, 5–6, 9, 10
   necessary in light of judgment day, 163
   of righteous, 157–62
   and salvation, 110, 194
Suffering Servant, 144
sustaining grace, 189–90
swearing, 76–77, 78–79, 80, 81
swift destruction, 217

tabernacle, 131
tasting that the Lord is good, 125–26
teachers, 39, 249–50, 274
temple, 131
temple of living stones, 129
temptation, 5, 12–17
tenants, parable of, 131
Ten Commandments, 51, 71
Testament of Moses, 252
testing of faith, 6, 17, 111
theosis, 204
Thomas Aquinas, 30
thousand years, 230–31
tomorrow, 66
tongue, control of, 19, 22, 38–43
tongues of fire, 176
transfiguration, 209–10, 212–13

trees without fruit, 253–54
trials, 5, 6, 9–10, 17, 83, 100, 111
Trinity, 104–5, 107–8, 112, 262
trouble, 83
true and false teaching, 239
true prophecy, 208–12
"twelve tribes scattered among the nations," 2, 6, 7, 91

unanswered prayer, 54
unbelief, 243, 249
understanding, 45
unfading beauty, 151–52, 154
ungodliness, 127, 241
ungodly unbelievers, 241, 243, 252, 254, 255–56
union with Christ, 98–99, 107, 112–13, 190
universal church, 130
unjust suffering, 99, 142, 143

virtue, 203

walking away from the faith, 89
walking by the Spirit, 119
wandering from the truth, 90–92, 93
water baptism, 160, 161, 164
wealth, 65, 69, 70–71
weeds and wheat, parable of, 225

weeping, 70
wicked, judgment of, 219, 220
widow and two mites, 30
widows, 1, 3
will of God, 66–67, 167
will of the world, 167
wisdom, 7, 45, 46, 94
Wisdom literature, 1
wisdom of the world, 46
"without fault," 266–67
wives, of non-Christians, 99
wives and husbands, 149–53
women, as "weaker partners," 153, 154
Word of God, 60, 119, 172
word of truth, 3, 15
words
    bring life or death, 41
    as performatives, 42
    as sign of maturity, 38
work, 146–47
world, the flesh, and the devil, 46, 57
worry, about tomorrow, 66

younger people, submission to older people, 184

zeal, 203

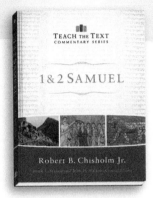
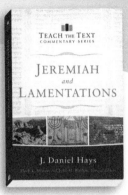

Printed and bound by CPI Group (UK) Ltd, Croydon, CR0 4YY

13/04/2025

14656460-0003